"This book presents the architect, scholar, and teacher, Marco Frascari's offering to architecture. It achieves a rare unity of theory with design exploration and project design in both text and image. Beginning students will receive a comprehensive view of what design entails and advanced architects will enjoy following the paths traced out by his winged compass, the golden instrument of Frascari's mobile and erudite imagination."
– *Paul Emmons, Washington-Alexandria Architecture Center, Virginia Tech, USA*

MARCO FRASCARI'S DREAM HOUSE

This previously unpublished work is essential reading for anyone who has followed Marco Frascari's scholarship and teachings over the last three decades. It also provides the perfect introduction for anyone new to his writings. As ever, Frascari does not offer prescriptive tools and frameworks to enact his theories of drawing and imagination; instead, he teaches how to build one's own through individual practice. An illuminating introduction places the text in a wider context, providing the reader with a fascinating and important context and understanding to this posthumous work. Frascari's sketchbooks are reproduced faithfully in full color to provide the reader with a remarkable insight into the design process of this influential mind.

Marco Frascari (1945–2013) was a dedicated teacher of architecture, an extraordinary storyteller, and an eminent thinker and theorist of architecture. He was the Director of the Azrieli School of Architecture and Urbanism at Carleton University, Ottawa, Canada, since 2005. From 1997 to 2005 he held the chair of G. T. Ward Professor at the Washington-Alexandria Architecture Center at Virginia Tech, USA. Previously, he spent seventeen years as professor at the Architecture School at the University of Pennsylvania, USA, with an interruption of two years that he spent teaching at The Georgia Institute of Technology, Atlanta, USA, where he wrote *Monsters of Architecture* (1991). He earned his *Dottore in Architettura* (1969) at the IUAV (*Istituto Universitario di Architettura di Venezia*). He moved to the United States in 1975 and received the Master of Science in Architecture at the University of Cincinnati, USA (1978). In 1981, he completed a PhD at the University of Pennsylvania. His work has been widely disseminated in journals, books, and magazines. His scholarly activity included academic conferences, lectures, and teaching periods in Europe, Australia, and New Zealand. His well-read article, "The Tell-Tale Detail", a seminal essay translated in Spanish, Japanese, and Chinese, continues to stimulate discussion as one of the most influential pieces of its kind since its publication in 1981. His last book *Eleven Exercises in Architectural Drawing: Slow Food for the Architect's Imagination* was published by Routledge (2011).

Federica Goffi is Associate Professor (2007–present) and Associate Director, Graduate Programs, at the Azrieli School of Architecture and Urbanism at Carleton University, Ottawa, Canada. She is currently teaching architectural drawing, studio, and a PhD colloquium. She was Assistant Professor at the Interior Architecture Department of the Rhode Island School of Design, USA (2005–2007). She holds a PhD from the Washington-Alexandria Architectural Center at Virginia Tech, USA. She has published book chapters and journal articles on the threefold nature of time–weather–tempo, as it informs notions of "built conservation" (*AD*, *ARQ*, *In.Form*, *Interstices*, *Int.AR*). Her book *Time Matter[s]: Invention and Re-imagination in Built Conservation: The Unfinished Drawing and Building of St. Peter's in the Vatican* was published in 2013. She holds a *Dottore in Architettura* from the University of Genoa, Italy. She is a licensed architect in her native country, Italy.

MARCO FRASCARI'S DREAM HOUSE

A Theory of Imagination

Marco Frascari

Edited by Federica Goffi

LONDON AND NEW YORK

First published 2017
by Routledge
2 Park Square, Milton Park, Abingdon, Oxon OX14 4RN

and by Routledge
711 Third Avenue, New York, NY 10017

*Routledge is an imprint of the Taylor & Francis Group,
an informa business*

© 2017 Marco Frascari and Federica Goffi

The right of Marco Frascari and Federica Goffi to be identified as authors of this work has been asserted by them in accordance with sections 77 and 78 of the Copyright, Designs and Patents Act 1988.

All rights reserved. No part of this book may be reprinted or reproduced or utilised in any form or by any electronic, mechanical, or other means, now known or hereafter invented, including photocopying and recording, or in any information storage or retrieval system, without permission in writing from the publishers.

Trademark notice: Product or corporate names may be trademarks or registered trademarks, and are used only for identification and explanation without intent to infringe.

British Library Cataloguing in Publication Data
A catalogue record for this book is available from the British Library

Library of Congress Cataloging in Publication Data
Names: Frascari, Marco, author. | Goffi, Federica, editor.
Title: Marco Frascari's Dream House : A Theory of Imagination / Marco Frascari ; Edited by Federica Goffi.
Description: New York : Routledge, 2017. | Includes bibliographical references and index.
Identifiers: LCCN 2016036331| ISBN 9781138189645 (hb : alk. paper) | ISBN 9781138189652 (pb : alk. paper) | ISBN 9781315641485 (ebook)
Subjects: LCSH: Architectural drawing. | Creative ability. | Frascari, Marco--Notebooks, sketchbooks, etc.
Classification: LCC NA2705 .F73 2017 | DDC 720.28/4--dc23
LC record available at https://lccn.loc.gov/2016036331

ISBN: 978-1-138-18964-5 (hbk)
ISBN: 978-1-138-18965-2 (pbk)
ISBN: 978-1-315-64148-5 (ebk)

Typeset in Sabon
by Saxon Graphics Ltd, Derby

This book was conceived in February, begun in March, and ended in late January. This book is dedicated to my wife, Paola.

Many are the influential thinkers who have been fundamental in setting my mind on this work. I would like to recognize four of them in particular. The first one is an odd Neapolitan philosopher, Giambattista Vico, who believed in the power of imagination and understood the ontological dimension of stench and saw in that the origin of humanity. The second is Gaston Bachelard, an unusual yet influential epistemologist concerned with the perception of "elements" (earth, water, air, and fire) as "stuff" and the history of this "stuff" as imagined. The third is Carlo Lodoli, a bad-smelling Franciscan friar, who knew that to rebuild, it is necessary to destroy. Last but not least is Teofilo Folengo, who loved *"fojade"* (home-made pasta in the Mantuan dialect) as I do, and with his magic *"Baldus"* has shown the convenient way to a proper cosmology of Chaos. The approach to theory taken by these four authors has decisively shaped both my design and my writing.

Marco Frascari

CONTENTS

List of figures — xi
Notes on contributors — xix
Acknowledgements — xxiii
List of abbreviations — xxv

Introduction — 1
FEDERICA GOFFI

Panta rhei: *in the drawn and written lines of the "Dream House"* 1
Reading drawings: *"A science without a name"* 10
Notes 20

1 **A congenial inauguration** — 25
MARCO FRASCARI

The magic meal 26
The ingredients 29
Notes 35

2 **Telling and casting** — 38
MARCO FRASCARI

The requirements of the play 41
The incubation 45
Notes 49

3 **The importance of dreaming in architecture** — 52
MARCO FRASCARI

The magic threshold 53

CONTENTS

A mantic view 57
The magic of translation 64
The trade 67
Notes 71

4 **The origin and beginning of the Dream House**   73
MARCO FRASCARI

The practice of dreaming 76
Description of the design of the house-tower 79
Notes 81

5 **The present architecture smells bad**   83
MARCO FRASCARI

Vita Beata 84
The happiness of bathroom imagination 86
Notes 92

6 **The analogical monster**   95
MARCO FRASCARI

The drawings of the house-tower 97
The recto and the verso 98
Notes 99

Conclusion   101
MARCO FRASCARI

Dream long and hard enough 101
Notes 102

Portfolio: Drawings, model, and sketchbooks for the house-tower   103

Postscript: Interview with Claudio Sgarbi   182
FEDERICA GOFFI AND CLAUDIO SGARBI

Oneiric recollections of a design 182

Bibliography   189
Index   204

FIGURES

F.1 Marco Frascari in Piazza San Marco, Venice, ca. 1963–1964. xvii
0.1 Design brief by Marco Frascari for *The Architect's Dream Exhibition Catalogue*. 4
0.2 Poster. *Construction Drawings* by Marco Frascari. 1994 Exhibition, Upper Gallery, Meyerson Hall, Philadelphia. 5
0.3 *Construction Drawings* by Marco Frascari. 1994 Exhibition, Upper Gallery, Meyerson Hall, Philadelphia, PA. 6
0.4 Book cover. *Una Pillola per Sognare… una Casa* by Marco Frascari. 7
0.5 *The Science Without a Name* by Marco Frascari, 2006–2007. 11
0.6 *Different Theory Lines. Drawing Theory and Theory of Drawing* by Marco Frascari, ca. 2006–2007. 12
0.7 *Fight Design* by Marco Frascari, ca. 2006. 13
0.8 *The Facture of Architecture and its Lines*, 2006. 15
0.9 *Templum* by Marco Frascari, ca. 2008. 17
0.10 *Microhistory* by Marco Frascari. Hybrid drawing. 18
1 *A Dream House for the Next Millennium*. Preliminary design by Marco Frascari. Perspective of the house-tower. 104
2 *A Dream House for the Next Millennium*. Preliminary design by Marco Frascari. Plan of the ground floor of the house-tower. 105
3 *A Dream House for the Next Millennium*. Preliminary design by Marco Frascari. Partial section of the house-tower under construction. 106
4 *A Dream House for the Next Millennium*. Preliminary design by Marco Frascari. Section of the house-tower. 107
5 *A Dream House for the Next Millennium*. Preliminary design by Marco Frascari, 1993. Detailed design of the bathroom. 108
6 *A Dream House for the Next Millennium*. Weathervane detail by Marco Frascari. 109
7 *A Dream House for the Next Millennium*. Hand-drafted ground floor plan of the house-tower by Marco Frascari and Alice Min Soo Chun. 110

FIGURES

8	*A Dream House for the Next Millennium*. Hand-drafted ground floor plan of the house-tower by Claudio Sgarbi.	111
9	*A Dream House for the Next Millennium*. Hand-drafted plans of the intermediate levels of the house-tower by Marco Frascari and Alice Min Soo Chun.	112
10	*A Dream House for the Next Millennium*. Hand-drafted plans of the intermediate levels of the house-tower by Claudio Sgarbi.	113
11	*A Dream House for the Next Millennium*. Hand-drafted plans of the loggia, the cantina and the roof top of the house-tower by Marco Frascari and Alice Min Soo Chun.	114
12	*A Dream House for the Next Millennium*. Hand-drafted plans of the loggia, the cantina and the roof top of the house-tower by Marco Frascari and Alice Min Soo Chun.	115
13	*A Dream House for the Next Millennium*. Hand-drafted section of the house-tower by Marco Frascari and Alice Min Soo Chun.	116
14	*A Dream House for the Next Millennium*. Hand-drafted section of the house-tower by Claudio Sgarbi.	117
15	*A Dream House for the Next Millennium*. Hand-drafted, partial section of the house-tower by Marco Frascari and Alice Min Soo Chun.	118
16	*A Dream House for the Next Millennium*. Hand-drafted, partial section of the house-tower by Claudio Sgarbi.	119
17	*A Dream House for the Next Millennium*. Hand-drafted construction details of the bathroom by Marco Frascari and Alice Min Soo Chun.	120
18	*A Dream House for the Next Millennium*. Hand-drafted construction details of the bathroom by Marco Frascari and Alice Min Soo Chun.	121
19	*A Dream House for the Next Millennium*. Wooden model of the house-tower by Marco Frascari and Alice Min Soo Chun.	122
20	*A Dream House for the Next Millennium*. Wooden model of the house-tower by Marco Frascari and Alice Min Soo Chun. South-east view.	123
21	*A Dream House for the Next Millennium*. Wooden model of the house-tower by Marco Frascari and Alice Min Soo Chun. South-west view.	123
22	*A Dream House for the Next Millennium*. Wooden model of the house-tower by Marco Frascari and Alice Min Soo Chun. North-west view.	123
23	*A Dream House for the Next Millennium*. Wooden model of the house-tower by Marco Frascari and Alice Min Soo Chun. North-east view.	123

FIGURES

24 Sketchbook 161, back and front cover. August 1993. *The Architect's Dream, House for the Next Millennium* by Marco Frascari. 124
25 Sketchbook 161, f.1v/2r. August 1993. *The Architect's Dream, House for the Next Millennium* by Marco Frascari. First study of the site. 125
26 Sketchbook 161, f.2v/3r. August 1993. *The Architect's Dream, House for the Next Millennium* by Marco Frascari. Notes about the sketchbooks and the nature of the project. 126
27 Sketchbook 161, f.3v/4r. August 1993. *The Architect's Dream, House for the Next Millennium* by Marco Frascari. Study for the layout of the drawings and notes. 127
28 Sketchbook 161, f.4v/5r. August 1993. *The Architect's Dream, House for the Next Millennium* by Marco Frascari. Study for the layout of the drawings. 128
29 Sketchbook 161, f.5v/6r. August 1993. *The Architect's Dream, House for the Next Millennium* by Marco Frascari. Study for the ground floor plan. A "ponderous column" determines the layout and orientation of the plan. 129
30 Sketchbook 161, f.6v/7r. August 1993. *The Architect's Dream, House for the Next Millennium* by Marco Frascari. Sketches for the model and notes ("I think therefore I dream ..."). 130
31 Sketchbook 161, f.7v/8r. August 1993. *The Architect's Dream, House for the Next Millennium* by Marco Frascari. Design sketches. 131
32 Sketchbook 161, f.8v/9r. August 1993. *The Architect's Dream, House for the Next Millennium* by Marco Frascari. New layout of drawings evocation and sketch for the section of the house-tower. 132
33 Sketchbook 161, f.9v/10r. August 1993. *The Architect's Dream, House for the Next Millennium* by Marco Frascari. Notes on the materials of the tower. 133
34 Sketchbook 161, f.10v/11r. August 1993. *The Architect's Dream, House for the Next Millennium* by Marco Frascari. Preparatory sketches for fireplace details. 134
35 Sketchbook 161, f.11v/12r. August 1993. *The Architect's Dream, House for the Next Millennium* by Marco Frascari. Weathervane sketches. 135
36 Sketchbook 161, f.12v/13r. August 1993. *The Architect's Dream, House for the Next Millennium* by Marco Frascari. Sketches of the roof. 136

FIGURES

37 Sketchbook 161, f.13v/14r. August 1993. *The Architect's Dream, House for the Next Millennium* by Marco Frascari. Detail of the waterwheel and sketches for the layout of the exhibition of the drawings. 137

38 Sketchbook 161, f.14v/15r. August 1993. *The Architect's Dream, House for the Next Millennium* by Marco Frascari. Weathervane sketches and list of the drawings to be drafted. 138

39 Sketchbook 161, f.15v/16r. 30 August 1993. *The Architect's Dream, House for the Next Millennium* by Marco Frascari. Notes about the presentation layout of the drawings. Plan and section studies for a bathroom. 139

40 Sketchbook 161, f.16v/17r. August 1993. *The Architect's Dream, House for the Next Millennium* by Marco Frascari. Plan studies for a bathroom. 140

41 Sketchbook 161, f.17v/18r. August 1993. *The Architect's Dream, House for the Next Millennium* by Marco Frascari. Elevation and section studies for a bathroom. 141

42 Sketchbook 161, f.18v/19r. August 1993. *The Architect's Dream, House for the Next Millennium* by Marco Frascari. Transfers and studies for the column. 142

43 Sketchbook 161, f.19v/20r. August 1993. *The Architect's Dream, House for the Next Millennium* by Marco Frascari. Notes on Carlo Mollino's 1940 drawings for the Architect's House. 143

44 Sketchbook 161, f.20v/21r. August 1993. *The Architect's Dream, House for the Next Millennium* by Marco Frascari. The compass of divination and notes on a dream of the author. 144

45 Sketchbook 161, f.21v/22r. August 1993. *The Architect's Dream, House for the Next Millennium* by Marco Frascari. Two angels holding the model of the house-tower. 145

46 Sketchbook 160, back and front cover. August–September 9, 1993. *The Architect's Dream, House for the Next Millennium* by Marco Frascari. 146

47 Sketchbook 160, f.1v/2r. August–September 9, 1993. *The Architect's Dream, House for the Next Millennium* by Marco Frascari. "I think therefore I dream ..." Hand-written text and transfer from *Little Nemo*. 147

48 Sketchbook 160, f.2v/3r. August–September 9, 1993. *The Architect's Dream, House for the Next Millennium* by Marco Frascari. Notes and sketches for the first detail for the house-tower: a column with a soul in the entrance area. 148

FIGURES

49	Sketchbook 160, f.3v/4r. August–September 9, 1993. *The Architect's Dream, House for the Next Millennium* by Marco Frascari. "This is a building where Poe's Angel of Bizarre dwells." Section and elevation for a column and other sketches for the roof of the tower-house.	149
50	Sketchbook 160, f.4v/5r. August–September 9, 1993. *The Architect's Dream, House for the Next Millennium* by Marco Frascari. Loom. The Origin of Architecture.	150
51	Sketchbook 160, f.5v/6r. August–September 9, 1993. *The Architect's Dream, House for the Next Millennium* by Marco Frascari. Notes on the materials of the tower and the importance of *Little Nemo*. Plan sketch for a numinous bathroom with a gold poché.	151
52	Sketchbook 160, f.6v/7r. August–September 9, 1993. *The Architect's Dream, House for the Next Millennium* by Marco Frascari. The divination of architecture is a reading and a translation.	152
53	Sketchbook 160, f.7v/8r. August–September 9, 1993. *The Architect's Dream, House for the Next Millennium* by Marco Frascari. A compass and a winged triangle. Notes about dreaming.	153
54	Sketchbook 160, f.8v/9r. August–September 9, 1993. *The Architect's Dream, House for the Next Millennium* by Marco Frascari. Studies for a model box that has not been realized.	154
55	Sketchbook 160, f.9v/10r. August–September 9, 1993. *The Architect's Dream, House for the Next Millennium* by Marco Frascari. Model sketches.	155
56	Sketchbook 160, f.10v/11r. August–September 9, 1993. *The Architect's Dream, House for the Next Millennium* by Marco Frascari. Sketches for the model that was made after but was conceived before.	156
57	Sketchbook 160, f.11v/12r. August–September 9, 1993. *The Architect's Dream, House for the Next Millennium* by Marco Frascari. The dimensioning cherubim and the module of 11 centimeters. Mantic Paradigm.	157
58	Sketchbook 160, f.12v/13r. August–September 9, 1993. *The Architect's Dream, House for the Next Millennium* by Marco Frascari. Notes and sketch inspired by Scarpa's window design based on the first Euclidean proposition.	158
59	Sketchbook 160, f.13v/14r. August–September 9, 1993. *The Architect's Dream, House for the Next Millennium* by Marco Frascari. Studies for the fireplaces and the kitchen table with a dark mirror.	159

FIGURES

60 Sketchbook 160, f.14v/15r. August–September 9, 1993. *The Architect's Dream, House for the Next Millennium* by Marco Frascari. Studies for the room of Morpheus and the room of Metis. — 160

61 Sketchbook 160, f.15v/16r. August–September 9, 1993. *The Architect's Dream, House for the Next Millennium* by Marco Frascari. Studies for the drafting table of the dream house. — 161

62 Sketchbook 160, f.16v/17r. August–September 9, 1993. *The Architect's Dream, House for the Next Millennium* by Marco Frascari. The reflection. Notes from Millhauser's novel, "The Princess, the Dwarf, and the Dungeon." — 162

63 Sketchbook 160, f.17v/18r. August–September 9, 1993. *The Architect's Dream, House for the Next Millennium* by Marco Frascari. "This design is related to Mollino's house of the architect." The compass of divination. — 163

64 Sketchbook 160, f.18/19r. August–September 9, 1993. *The Architect's Dream, House for the Next Millennium* by Marco Frascari. Sketch of the dream house on site. The compass of divination and some notes about dreaming as a "game of imagination." — 164

65 Sketchbook 160, f.19v/20r. August–September 9, 1993. *The Architect's Dream, House for the Next Millennium* by Marco Frascari. Sketch of a winged compass and notes on dreaming. — 165

66 Sketchbook 160, f.20v/21r. August–September 9, 1993. *The Architect's Dream, House for the Next Millennium* by Marco Frascari. The architect's dream: hand-colored transfers of Mollino's two drawings for the architect's house. — 166

67 Sketchbook 160, f.21v/22r. August–September 9, 1993. *The Architect's Dream, House for the Next Millennium* by Marco Frascari. The dream of the angel. Series of winged compasses. — 167

68 Sketchbook 159, back and front cover. May 1994. *Il Terzo Libro dei sogni d'architettura* by Marco Frascari. With a postcard of the 1932 Lonely Metropolitan. — 168

69 Sketchbook 159, f.1v/2r. May 1994. *Il Terzo Libro dei sogni d'architettura* by Marco Frascari. Transfers of cumulous clouds, Frascari's *ex libris* and other sketches. — 169

70 Sketchbook 159, f.2v/3r. May 1994. *Il Terzo Libro dei sogni d'architettura* by Marco Frascari. Gunzo's dream and other sketches. — 170

71 Sketchbook 159, f.3v/4r. May 1994. *Il Terzo Libro dei sogni d'architettura* by Marco Frascari. Saint Aubert's third dream and other sketches. — 171

FIGURES

72	Sketchbook 159, f.4v/5r. May 1994. *Il Terzo Libro dei sogni d'architettura* by Marco Frascari. Magazine clipping of a tattooed hand and clipping of Thomas Cole's 1840 painting "The Architect's Dream."	172
73	Sketchbook 159, f.5v/6r. May 1994. *Il Terzo Libro dei sogni d'architettura* by Marco Frascari. Transfers of Thomas Cole's 1840 painting "The Architect's Dream."	173
74	Sketchbook 159, f.6v/7r. May 1994. *Il Terzo Libro dei sogni d'architettura* by Marco Frascari. House plans transfers with a citation from Shakespeare's *The Tempest*.	174
75	Sketchbook 159, f.7v/8r. May 1994. *Il Terzo Libro dei sogni d'architettura* by Marco Frascari. Hand-colored transfers of photographs of the model of the dream house.	175
76	Sketchbook 159, f.8v/9r. May 1994. *Il Terzo Libro dei sogni d'architettura* by Marco Frascari. Transfer of a photograph of the model of the dream house.	176
77	Sketchbook 159, f.9v/10r. May 1994. *Il Terzo Libro dei sogni d'architettura* by Marco Frascari. Transfers of a bed frame, floating mattresses and feathers.	177
78	Sketchbook 159, f.10v/11r. May 1994. *Il Terzo Libro dei sogni d'architettura* by Marco Frascari. Transfers of floor patterns and photo of the model of the dream house.	178
79	Sketchbook 159, f.11v/12r. May 1994. *Il Terzo Libro dei sogni d'architettura* by Marco Frascari. Hand-colored transfers of patterns.	179
80	Sketchbook 159, f.12v/13r. May 1994. *Il Terzo Libro dei sogni d'architettura* by Marco Frascari. Geomater. Sketch of a pregnant woman and floor patterns by Carlo Scarpa for the main entrance to Palazzo Steri, Palermo.	180
81	Sketchbook 159, f.13v/14r. May 1994. *Il Terzo Libro dei sogni d'architettura* by Marco Frascari. Transfer of Carl Jung's Bollingen Tower.	181
P1	*Above and Below*. Ink and watercolors on paper by Claudio Sgarbi.	188

CONTRIBUTORS

Figure F.1 Marco Frascari in Piazza San Marco, Venice, ca. 1963–1964.
Source: © Courtesy of Marco Frascari Estate.

CONTRIBUTORS

Marco Frascari was a dedicated teacher of architecture, an extraordinary storyteller, and an eminent thinker and theorist of architecture. Frascari was born on March 29, 1945, in Mantova, the city of Alberti's Basilica of Sant'Andrea, for which he later became an advisor to the committee in charge of conservation. He died in Ottawa, Canada, on June 2, 2013. Frascari obtained his diploma at the *Accademia di Belle Arti* in Venice with the title of *Professore di Disegno*. He studied at the Liceo Artistico Cignaroli in Verona (1958–1962), and at the end of the four-year period he took his diploma exam in Venice.

Upon earning his *Dottore in Architettura* (1969) at the IUAV (*Istituto Universitario di Architettura di Venezia*), Marco moved to Verona where he had been hired to work in Arrigo Rudi's office (1969–1971). He also traveled periodically to Venice and worked as Rudi's assistant in the teaching group led by Scarpa.

Arrigo Rudi (1929–2007), whose firm was based in Verona, collaborated with Carlo Scarpa on the Castelvecchio project from 1958–1964. Frascari's father knew Arrigo Rudi, and knowing that his son wanted to pursue his studies in architecture, introduced them to each other. During the preliminary survey of Castelvecchio, Marco was allowed to work with the firm's team as an unpaid apprentice.

During the period 1969–1975, Frascari was exposed to the cultural milieu fostered by the Venetian school of thought gathered around Carlo Scarpa, which included Sergio Los, Arrigo Rudi, Valeriano Pastor, Umberto Tubini, Franca Semi, and Domenico Sandri among others. Having obtained his license in architecture in 1970, he secured professional registration in Verona and started his own practice in collaboration with architect Adriano Mason (1971–1972) and later with architect Caterina Boschini (1972–1975). He maintained a small practice throughout his teaching career.

In 1975, he moved to the United States and received the Master of Science in Architecture at the University of Cincinnati (1978). In 1981, he completed a PhD at the University of Pennsylvania under the mentorship of Dean Holmes Perkins. Upon graduation, Frascari joined the faculty in the same school, and spent seventeen years of his career in this academic setting, with a short interruption of two years that he spent teaching at the Georgia Institute of Technology in Atlanta, where he wrote *Monsters of Architecture* (1991). From 1992–1995, he was the Associate Chair to the PhD Program at the University of Pennsylvania and from 1995–1997, he was the Acting Chair in the same university.

From 1997 to 2005, he held the chair of G. T. Ward Professor at the Washington-Alexandria Architecture Center at Virginia Tech, where he established a PhD program focused on architectural representation and education. In 2005, he took on the Directorship of the Azrieli School of Architecture and Urbanism at Carleton University in Ottawa, Canada, where he founded, in collaboration with his colleagues, a new doctoral program in architecture hinged on the culture of practice. Uniquely this program fosters new architectural knowledge through both textual and physical probing.

Frascari taught and lectured at other leading architectural institutions worldwide, including the Architectural Association, Columbia University, Harvard University, Penn State University, Rensselaer Polytechnic Institute, Nottingham University, the School of Art and Design at Auckland University, and many others.

Frascari's lectures inspired students, academics and practitioners through his engaging storytelling style, his critical yet playful drawings and his profound understanding of architecture. A truly eclectic scholar and prolific writer, he has written much on the topics of architectural representation and tectonics published in *AA Files*, *RES*, *Terrazzo*, *JAE*, *Nexus Network Journal*, *Assemblage*, *Nordic Journal of Architectural Research*, and many other scholarly journals and magazines.

Marco Frascari's *Monsters of Architecture* (1991) is well read in contemporary architectural theory. Frascari's work gained prominence in the North American context and the wider English-speaking academic and professional world of architecture, and he extended his readership and academic presence through conferences, lectures, and teaching periods in Europe, Australia, and New Zealand. His well-read Tell-Tale Detail article, a seminal essay translated into Spanish, Japanese, and Chinese, continues to stimulate discussion as one of the most influential pieces of its kind since its publication in 1981. The Japanese version was published in 1999 in *10+1*, n. 16. The article has been republished in Kate Nesbit's *Theorizing a New Agenda for Architecture: An Anthology of Architectural Theory, 1965–1995* (Princeton Architectural Press, 1996). To this day, it remains a critical source in the theory and role of details in architectural design.

His academic and professional work have been the subject of scholarly research. Two symposia in Australia in 2004 were inspired by his research. In this context he delivered three guest lectures: "Macaronic architecture," at the Adelaide Bank Festival of Arts: The Architecture Symposium (Adelaide); "A Short Storytelling Regarding the Nature of Architectural Drawings," the Dean's Lecture, Faculty of Building and Planning, Melbourne University; and "Curiosity Kills Cats not Architects," Louis Laybourne Smith School of Architecture & Design, University of South Australia.

The Pleasure of a Demonstration, a recent book authored by Dr. Sam Ridgway, an Australian architect and scholar, delves into Frascari's professional built works (Ashgate 2015). Two symposia have been organized to honor Frascari's legacy. The first symposium, *Towards a Critical Phenomenology*, was held in February 2013 at Carleton University, Ottawa, Canada, while the second, *Confabulations, Storytelling in Architecture*, was held at WAAC, Virginia Tech in 2014. A third symposium is in preparation at WAAC, Virginia Tech.

CONTRIBUTORS

Federica Goffi is Associate Professor (2007–present) and Associate Director, Graduate Programs, at the Azrieli School of Architecture and Urbanism at Carleton University, Ottawa, Canada. She is currently teaching architectural drawing, studio, and a PhD colloquium. She was Assistant Professor at the Interior Architecture Department of the Rhode Island School of Design, USA (2005–2007). She holds a PhD from the Washington-Alexandria Architectural Center at Virginia Tech, USA. She has published book chapters (Routledge, Ashgate) and journal articles on the threefold nature of time–weather–tempo, as it informs notions of 'built conservation' (*AD*, *ARQ*, *In.Form*, *Interstices*, *Int.AR*). Her book *Time Matter[s]: Invention and Re-imagination in Built Conservation: The Unfinished Drawing and Building of St. Peter's in the Vatican* was published by Ashgate in 2013. She holds a *Dottore in Architettura* from the University of Genoa, Italy. She is a licensed architect in her native country, Italy.

Claudio Sgarbi is a practicing architect in Italy, and has been Adjunct Research Professor at the Azrieli School of Architecture and Urbanism, Carleton University, Ottawa, Canada, since 2011. He coordinated the Bologna Directed Studies Abroad (2011–2013). He has lectured in Canada, Europe, and the United States. He graduated in 1982 from the IUAV in Venice, Italy. His PhD dissertation at the University of Pennsylvania, USA (1993), concerned the discovery of a Renaissance Vitruvian manuscript from Ferrara. He has published several articles and book chapters, and a book, *Vitruvio Ferrarese. "De Architectura": la Prima Versione Illustrata* (Franco Cosimo Panini Editore, 2004).

ACKNOWLEDGEMENTS

It is with heartfelt gratitude that I thank, first and foremost, Ms. Paola Frascari for the encouragement offered throughout every stage of the work. Her collaboration has been essential on many levels, from bringing together the materials needed for this publication and making them available to me, to contributing ideas and suggestions. Her fulsome attention to my questions and the time she has devoted in support of this publication cannot be understated, and deserves earnest acknowledgement. This work would not have been the same without her unwavering support.

I am deeply grateful to Fran Ford, Senior Editor for Architecture at Routledge. She welcomed the prospect of this publication with enthusiasm. Her reception for Frascari's work has been unparalleled. I am indebted for the inclusion of a substantial body of drawings by Frascari and his collaborators. Fran Ford suggested the title for this book, which accurately captures the spirit of the work and draws attention to the fundamental ideas expressed within it. I would like to acknowledge also her colleagues at Routledge who supported this book with the utmost professionalism.

I relished the generous support of William Whitaker, Curator and Collection Manager at the Architectural Archives at the University of Pennsylvania. He made this publication possible on many levels. I am indebted for the assistance received during my visit to the archives. It was a pleasure learning from him that the drawings are often shown to students to discuss ideas pertaining to *recto/verso* drawings. The courtesy and care taken in coordinating the photographic reproduction of the design drawings in support of this book were exceptional, and I am most grateful.

Dr. Paul Emmons provided exquisite and poignant advice on the overall editing at a critical time of development, when the final version of the text was being prepared for the publisher's review. Francie Hankins, a doctoral student at WAAC, kindly verified some of the original bibliographical references in the Marco Frascari Library Collection at WAAC.

Dr. Daniel Freedman corresponded with me and offered significant insight on the planning stages of *The Architect's Dream: Houses for the Next Millennium* exhibition at the Contemporary Arts Center in Cincinnati

ACKNOWLEDGEMENTS

in 1993, for which he served in the role of guest curator at the time. I thank also Dr. Claudio Sgarbi for allowing me to interview him and contributing a postscript for this book. Alice Min Soon Chun offered clarifications about her role in the preparation of Frascari's drawings and the model for the tower-house.

I acknowledge with gratitude Claudia Zambonini, a long-time friend of Paola and Marco Frascari, who read the draft of Frascari's text with me in the early stages of editing and selflessly devoted time and effort in support of this work. Dr. Donald Kunze, Dr. Elizabeth English, and Dr. Qi Zhu offered incisive and pointed advice on specific elements in the text while seeking clarification on a few bibliographical sources. Dr. Sam Ridgway offered encouragement and discussed with me his research on the Dream House, which has been published in his insightful book, entitled *Architectural Projects of Marco Frascari: The Pleasure of a Demonstration,* published by Ashgate in 2015. I sincerely appreciated the helpful information offered by architect Caterina Boschini on the early professional career of Marco Frascari, when they were partners in Verona.

I wholeheartedly acknowledge architect Sergio Los and his wife and partner architect Natasha Pulitzer, for welcoming me into their studio and talking to me about the period when Marco was a student and later an assistant at the IUAV in Venice. This insight was very helpful to me to understand the intellectual and cultural context in which Marco's works developed during his early formation.

I also acknowledge, with the fondest memory, Dr. Marco Frascari for the remarkable opportunity to work on the final editing of this book. Frascari shared with all of us—his students—throughout his teaching career, the lessons of the school of Venice.

Last but not least, I thank in advance the future readers for dedicating their leisure time to this book.

ABBREVIATIONS

AAUP Architectural Archives of the University of Pennsylvania, Harvey and Irwin Kroiz Gallery, Philadelphia, PA, USA
CAC Contemporary Arts Center, Lois & Richard Rosenthal Center for Contemporary Art, Cincinnati, OH, USA
IUAV Istituto Universitario di Architettura di Venezia, Università degli Studi di Venezia, Venice, Italy
MFLC The Marco Frascari Library Collection, Washington-Alexandria Architecture Center, Virginia Polytechnic Institute and State University, Alexandria Old Town, VA, USA
WAAC Washington-Alexandria Architecture Center, Virginia Polytechnic Institute and State University, Alexandria Old Town, VA, USA

INTRODUCTION

Federica Goffi

Panta rhei: in the drawn and written lines of the "Dream House"

The "Dream House" is an open work that can be entered from many directions and constitutes an original point of departure to orient the contemporary theory and practice of architecture.[1] This work not only encompasses a theory of imagination through key scholarly claims, including the fundamental abductive hypothesis that dreams are the primary mode of imagining,[2] drawing and thinking, but it also opens the doors for everyone to construe and construct architecture beyond dreams (see Figures 30, 47 in the Portfolio).[3] Offering a generous cosmology, Marco Frascari affirms an imagination contrary to that which many believe cannot be taught; a thinking that he has put into practice over his teaching career.[4] On opening this book the reader enters a written and drawn daydream, which is informed by ideas that are not so much explained as enacted.

This book is a must-read for anyone who has followed the work of eminent architectural theorist and author Marco Frascari. He tackled architecture through multiple indirect lenses, rather than through a singular and direct sight. Alongside a central interest in architectural imagination and representation, Frascari addressed relevant questions that pertain to the contemporary condition of professional practice, including: the play of details versus the tolerance of precision; the role of the body and the tradition of architectural anthropomorphism; the influence of alchemy, magic, semiotics, synesthesia, and, most recently, he expanded his research by delving into the relationship between neurology and architecture.[5]

This work also introduces Marco Frascari's thoughts for anyone who is new to his writings. Several critical concepts found in his previously published texts are in dialogue here with ideas centered on the notion of dreams, revealing Frascari's own cosmopoiesis in architecture. The Dream House is also a *first read* to unlock instrumental notions in his architectural theory and practice.[6] It furthers Frascari's theories of imagination by developing the idea of drawings as forms of dreams, and constitutes an addition to his latest book, *Eleven Exercises in the Art of Architectural Drawing: Slow Food for the Architect's Imagination* (2011), which embodies his legacy as an architectural theorist.[7] The theoretical links between drawing and building are examined herein, delving into the nature of architectural imagination in the context of present practice.

Frascari's scholarly writings span three decades and demonstrate the knowledge of an architect dealing with curiosity in architectural tradition and history.[8] The body of his written, drawn, built and lectured work delves into the depths of the architect's own first-hand making through the medium of drawing. His speculations contribute to illuminating a shared present condition and the theoretical discourse on architectural representation, which he developed alongside and in dialogue with the works of contemporary theorists such as Robin Evans (1944–1993), Joseph Rykwert, Dalibor Vesely (1934–2015), Alberto Pérez-Gómez and Paul Emmons.[9] Profoundly and better defined as a maker who shaped architecture through a chiasmus of material and intellectual constructs, he made of the study of architectural imagination a life-long project.

The Dream House has been in the making for over two decades, starting in 1992. This work began when guest curator Daniel Friedman[10] invited Frascari to join *The Architect's Dream: Houses for the Next Millennium* exhibition that was to be held from November 19, 1993, to January 23, 1994 at the Contemporary Arts Center in Cincinnati, Ohio. Friedman reached out to invited participants, including Frascari, in the late Fall of 1992, shortly before announcing the competition publicly.[11] However, the inception of this work can be traced back, in Frascari's own writing, to the early years that he spent as a student and apprentice of Carlo Scarpa at the IUAV (Istituto Universitario di Architettura di Venezia) in Venice (1962–1975).

Frascari's theoretical work was born in sketches and drawings, before the written word. A set of three complete sketchbooks,[12] preliminary design drawings, a series of *recto/verso* drawings on Mylar and a model included in this publication are the pre-texts for the textual probing. The sketchbooks include collages, transfers, prints, hand drawings, and textual annotations. They are vital documents to help understand his process of conceiving the theoretical position made in the Dream House. These three sketchbooks constitute the drawn inception of the work. Frascari's working process in fact entailed sketching ideas in drawn form first and later annotating them to lay the foundations for his theoretical work.[13]

During the period of the original conception of the Dream House, Frascari was teaching at the University of Pennsylvania, and some of his colleagues included influential thinkers, such as Joseph Rykwert and Ivan Illich (1926–2002). He worked alongside well-known architectural theorists and practitioners, such as David Leatherbarrow, Moshen Mostafavi, Homa Farjadi, and Amedeo Petrilli (1945–2005) among others. Frascari invited Claudio Sgarbi, a Visiting Assistant Professor of Architecture and a recent

INTRODUCTION

graduate of the doctoral program in architecture at the University of Pennsylvania, to collaborate in the project of the house-tower, which lasted a few months (Figure 0.1; see Figure 32 in the Portfolio).[14] The design dialogue resulted in four *recto/verso* drawings on Mylar that were to be placed back to back and mounted under Plexiglas panels for viewing on both sides during the exhibition. The *recto* sheets were authored by Frascari and the *verso* sheets by Sgarbi (Figures 7–8, 9–10, 13–14, 15–16 in the Portfolio).[15]

Claudio Sgarbi answered some questions I posed about the development of the project in an interview that is documented in the postscript to this book. In my exchanges with Daniel Friedman, he recalled Frascari and Sgarbi's project as well as Merrill Elam's project as the most oneiric among those exhibited.[16] Alice Min Soo Chun, a Master of Architecture student at the University of Pennsylvania at the time, who had shown extraordinary drawing and modeling skills, was invited by Frascari to participate in the original act of drawing the *recto* design. In my conversations with her, Chun recalled closely following Frascari's preliminary drawings in her execution of the *recto* design drawings on Mylar and the model of the house-tower (see Figures 19–23 in the Portfolio).[17] The drawings and models were shown again together with other works by Frascari in 1994 at the *Construction Drawings* exhibition, held at the University of Pennsylvania, Upper Gallery, Meyerson Hall, Philadelphia (Figures 0.2, 0.3).

A central source of reflection for the house-tower design comes from Turinese architect, designer and photographer Carlo Mollino (1905–1973) and his "Architect's House" project, of which two drawings survive, dating from 1940 (Figures 43, 63 in the Portfolio).[18] These perspective line drawings were transferred by Frascari into one of his sketchbooks. They were subsequently drawn over,[19] colored and subtitled "*il sogno dell'architetto*" (the architect's dream) (see Figure 66 in the Portfolio). Frascari enters Mollino's own dream through a vivid double dreaming condition: a drawing-within-another-drawing. Mollino's "tower-house" becomes the mirrored substratum for the imaginative reflection of Frascari's "house-tower".[20] Frascari and Mollino share a large window opening into the imaginal world (*mundus imaginalis*),[21] through a *recto/verso* condition. Their gazes meet through a viewpoint/counter-viewpoint condition to meet the imagination of the Other. Frascari inhabits the *intermondo* of Mollino's imaginal drawing. He draws over a transfer of Mollino's perspective a series of elements, such as a gold column that runs the full height of the tower approximately in the center of the south façade, a water wheel on the West side and an angelic compass on the roof summit. Frascari's gold column is a "ponderous" architectural element marking the center from which the winged "compass of divination," a Feng Shui compass, orients the house-tower (Figures 63, 64 in the Portfolio).[22] Lastly, the façade-threshold of Frascari's house-tower is Mollino's own gate into the imaginal dimension: a

3

MARCO FRASCARI & CLAUDIO SGARBI

The chronicles of this design were initiated in Venice. As appointed chair of the committee administering the registration exam, Professor Carlo Scarpa, albeit not a registered architect, authored the design problem.

Thinking that to test the design ethics of a future architect, a designer should be forced into a condition of pure afflatus originated by an ontological reflection, Scarpa composed a program for a tower-house to be inhabited by an architect on a site located near Asolo (Treviso). The undeclared client was Scarpa himself. Through this program, he was asking for a projection, a graphic evocation of the magic that must lie in a thaumaturgic, therapeutic, and consequently critical design. He was postulating a *numinous* building. When invited to design a dream house, I remembered this event, realizing I was expecting an opportunity to design a numinous building.[1]

I convinced Claudio Sgarbi, a friend and a pupil, to follow my dream and we designed a tower-house in Intercourse, Pennsylvania. Alice Chun and I did the *recto*-design. Claudio did four drawings for the *verso*-design. Both designs are mantic.

I. The Recto: Little Nemo is a friend of Dionysus.
Marco Frascari and Alice Chun

Water powers the house, lifts up weights, and turns the wheel. Two cellars (one for wine, the other for the salami and other foods) ground the building. The top floor, a terrace with a double crane, is crowned by a compassed weathervane. The bathrooms are carefully designed and the kitchen is the most important room. Other spaces exemplify or suggest rather than determine or impose.

II. The Verso: Plan of flight for a vague house.
Claudio Sgarbi

This house will last forever. It will never be completed, always quasi-built. A corner of the dwelling sits on a *mundus* next to a fig-tree and an apple-tree. The tower is approximately 21x21 and 72 feet high. The *mundus* is 21x21 and 63 feet deep. High-tech furnishes for house. High-tech feeds the *mundus*. The house is self-sufficient. Sleeping, cooking, love-making, sitting, chatting, bathing, peeing, eating…are everywhere in the tower. The underground floor is a room filled with water and steam. On the ground floor, the walls are dedicated to the revolving sun. On the first floor things lose their names and bolognas hang everywhere. On the top floor, under the ark—a water tank—an Eolic organ plays.[2]

1. Rudolf Otto, a German scholar of religions, coined the term *numinous*. He derived this term from the Latin *numen*. The word *numen* is connected with the word *sacer* (holy), indicating the holy dimension of magic.

2. For any missing written information, see "The Recto," designed by Marco Frascari, or write to Claudio Sgarbi, Via C.U. Barberi 155, 41100 Modena, Italy.

Figure 0.1 Design brief by Marco Frascari for *The Architect's Dream Exhibition Catalogue* (Friedman 1993: 20–21).

Source: © Courtesy of the Center for Contemporary Art, Cincinnati.

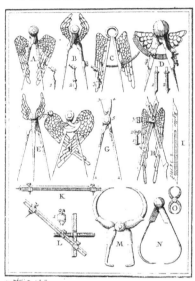

Figure 0.2 Poster. *Construction Drawings* by Marco Frascari. 1994 Exhibit, Upper Gallery, Meyerson Hall, University of Pennsylvania, Philadelphia, PA.

Source: © Courtesy of Marco Frascari Estate.

Figure 0.3 Construction Drawings by Marco Frascari. Upper Gallery, Meyerson Hall, University of Pennsylvania, Philadelphia, PA, 1994.
Source: © Courtesy of Marco Frascari Estate.

window in front of, and analogous to, the architect's vertical drafting table. In the first preparatory drawing Frascari once again redraws Mollino's perspective and this time he brings within the space of the dream/drawing his own drafting tools, a copy of *Little Nemo in Slumberland*, other books and enough food for a feast. He then lays them all out on the tables located on the left and right side of his drafting board (see Figure 1 in the Portfolio). A bolt of white lightning strikes the Tarot-like perspective drawing of the house-tower. Frascari writes herein that "a dream is a foil for epistemological inquiries into the nature of perception. In the dream we seek clarification of the ontological dimension of our human construction." In the "evocative thread" (story), on the unfolded left side of the drawing, he stated that "the dream is the genesis of imagination, its absolute origin." Below this well-laid-out architect's drafting table, the author signs it "Marco in a dream."[23]

Likewise, Claudio Sgarbi's *verso* drawings inhabit Frascari's *recto* daydream condition: a dream within a dream within another dream, exist one within the Other through a process of *mise en abyme*.[24] Frascari and Sgarbi worked for the most part distantly and on two separate sheets of Mylar.[25] Their respective designs are concurrent rather than coincident architectural representations; they are a project within another project. They shared ideas, architectural elements and the rules of a game which implies the construction of a dream within the dream of another. Misalignments create the spaces where the *idios kosmos* (personal world) enters a *koinos kosmos*

INTRODUCTION

(shared world).²⁶ Frascari's exterior stone and brick walls' pochés are solid, rectilinear and filled with gold; Sgarbi's rammed earth walls have thick jagged golden edges and transversal cuts that allow the light in at unique angles. Frascari followed the rules in Mollino's game; likewise, Sgarbi followed the rules in Frascari's own dream. Working together they shared an "arché of archi-tecture," that is, a genetic idea of "the tower," which has the power to fore-cast and back-cast at the same time *ad infinitum*, rejoining a present condition with a mythical beginning of architecture.²⁷

Soon after the Cincinnati exhibition, Frascari began writing on the topic of dreams and architectural representation and in 1995 he published a poignantly succinct Italian work entitled "*Una Pillola per Sognare ... una Casa*," literally "A Pill to Dream a House." This is a short text that offered the inception for a new way of thinking about design (Figure 0.4).²⁸ Frascari's writing style is like a Gordian knot: tight, to the point, enigmatic and brief, like the novels of American poet Edgar Allan Poe, and imaginative like those of Italo Calvino, one of his favorite authors. Poe suggested that a self-imposed limit is desirable, as regards to length, in works of literature to achieve a "unity of impression."²⁹ Frascari's text is ambiguous but not vague. The efficacy, rather than the efficiency of the story relies on the fact that both text and drawings can be

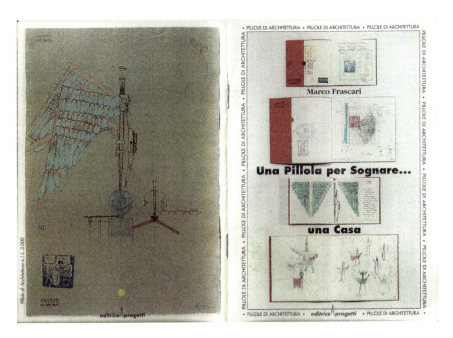

Figure 0.4 Book cover. *Una Pillola per Sognare... una Casa* by Marco Frascari. Milan: Editrice Progetti, 1995 (16 × 23 cm).

Source: © Courtesy of Marco Frascari Estate.

taken in at one sitting, in one brief, uninterrupted reading event, that promises to change one's thinking through the medium of drawings.

Throughout his academic career as an architectural theorist, Frascari's countless articles are, each in their own right, "dream pills" that offer condensed reflections sifted through a deeply contemporary and imaginative gaze.[30] Frascari conceived his books,[31] including the ones that are unpublished to date, as a collection of essays to be savored through short reading episodes.[32] In 1997, an English version of *Una Pillola per Sognare* was announced to be forthcoming even though he never actually prepared a book proposal.[33] The Dream House was incarnated in a few prospective titles:

Una Pillola per Sognare (1995)
Voglia d'Architettura: A Musing Storytelling for Architects of the Next Millennium (1997)
The Dream House. A Magic Storytelling for Architects (1997)
The Materia Prima of Architecture: An Alchemic Tale for Architects (2000)

Short sections of the Dream House, intended to come together in a book, were published separately over a period of time.[34] In 2000, Frascari moved to other projects and yet periodically revisited the Dream House and continued to draw inspiration from it.[35] The complete text remained unpublished like an image in the ground of the representation. It is surfacing only now and it allows us to envision an invisible scope, tracing the inception of his theory of imagination. As to the reason why the work is coming to press only now, after a few decades of consideration, it could be said that Frascari never really started and finished an article or a book as a self-contained piece, rather, the process of conceiving was a continuous stream linking all his published and unpublished writings and drawings. The Dream House became a 'place' to return to and to draw from. It constitutes the threshold into Frascari's own *mundus imaginalis*. It was a fertile ground in-the-making for over two decades. Parts of it were disseminated through seminal writings, drawings and teachings over the period of 1993–2011.

Since 1997, this has been a self-contained and open text offering Frascari's own intellectual biography, presenting his central ideas on a theory of imagination based on dreams, while also situating the scope of the work.[36] He returned to this unfinished text in 2012 when he began to reorganize, with some assistance, his body of work for future archival purposes. The work was unfortunately interrupted by his death and has been continued since by the editor of this book.[37] While the original text by Frascari has been preserved in its conceptual integrity, some changes have been made to complete the English editing and the footnotes. In order to distinguish the original footnotes by the author from those added by the editor, the latter have been placed in square parentheses.

The theory presented herein is best described as an unfinished, yet complete work, which represents a mature stage in Frascari's thinking, but not the latest one *per se*. In the last period in fact, and before his illness, Frascari paid close attention to the ground-breaking developments in the field of cognitive science and neuroscience in relation to vision and emotion, and was engaged in the writing of a book draft provisionally entitled *The Happiness and Misery of Architecture: A Few Indications Regarding the Architectural Métier*.[38] This work was meant to orient architectural theory in its relations to the new discoveries in brain neuroscience and possibly also divert it from potential misreadings.

The work presented here does not offer prescriptive tools and frameworks to enact Frascari's theories of drawing and imagination. On the contrary, the author suggests building one's own within a given realm of dreams, daydreams and wakeful consciousness. Neither does he advocate exploiting dream and daydream states towards a productive use of the unconscious and conscious embodied mind—like the daunting fictional future envisioned in the movie, directed by Christopher Nolan, *Inception* (2010).[39] Conversely, Frascari advocated considering the fact that dreams are real experiences that shape everyday reality, and further affirmed that they are the best suited tool to grasp the nature of architectural representation. According to Frascari, this is essential to a proper conception of architectural drawings towards the attainment of a *Vita Beata*.

Coming to the point, contemporary neuroscience is producing a new hypothesis about the nature and the reasons why we dream. Some neuroscientists and psychologists argue that to understand consciousness, we must understand the nature of dreams.[40] Contemporary Finnish cognitive neuroscientist Antti Revonsuo explained that the relation between dreams and unconscious is of such a kind that it could be said that

> We are dreaming all of the time, it is just that during wakefulness our dreams are shaped by stimulus information that is coming through our senses, whereas during dreaming the same consciousness within our brain is not shaped by any external information, but it is generated internally ... life is a dream which is guided by the senses.[41]

The theory of imagination expounded in this book, explored by Frascari since 1993, is outstanding for its visionary character and may foster future inquiries into the field of architectural drawings as forms of daydreams generated through a fully embodied condition of sensory perception. This theory is all the more relevant at a time when the debate on architectural representation focuses predominantly on the tools employed, with the risk of reducing scholarly discussion to the perceived analogue versus digital polarities. Instead, Frascari reminds contemporary architects of the importance of questioning the 'how' of the thinking/dreaming through the act of drawing, which is the *"materia prima"* of architecture.[42]

Reading drawings: "A science without a name"

Marco Frascari's research into the workings of architectural imagination is the key to his life's work, and is a continuous thread unraveling the active "facture" of architectural making.[43] In the Spring of 2000, Frascari was writing *A Grimoire of Architecture*, a work that stemmed from the *Dream House*, and later became the *Eleven Exercises in the Art of Architectural Imagination*.[44] At this time he delivered a doctoral seminar at the Washington-Alexandria Architecture Center of Virginia Tech (WAAC),[45] entitled "Exercises in Architectural Imagination." He lamented the fact that architectural theory borrows from several other disciplines despite the fact that it has its own deeply historical tradition, and he argued that the discipline of architectural imagination needs to be placed at the center of the inquiry into architectural theory. He explained that architectural imagination is not taught in architectural schools even though it is practiced in studios, and described this absence as a *lacuna* in the education of future architects.[46]

Between 1998 and 2005, he held a series of lectures and PhD seminars at WAAC. During a 2004 lecture entitled "How to read a drawing," he suggested that the necessity of re-reading architectural drawings was inspired by a desire for a revision of how architecture is taught by placing drawings at the core of what we teach and how we learn, through and beyond architectural studios.[47] The search for the proper way to read drawings was essential to his critique of the linearity of the one-eyed views of the Western scientific worldview, which results in the production of strict methodological paths, which order existence to produce known outcomes. Frascari searched for pluralistic tactics, layering multiple research paths with and against each other to account for the complexity of a "maze of interactions" weaving thoughts about the making and reading of drawings through storytelling.[48]

Frascari's architectural "cosmopoiesis," "an act of world making,"[49] becomes visible in a 2006–2007 series of four hand-drawn "cosmopoietic maps" that are based on the four elements (air, water, earth and fire). The material conception of the cosmopoietic maps was inspired by the writings of French philosopher Gaston Bachelard (1884–1962) and his concept of "material imagination," which states that "to dream profoundly one must dream with substances."[50] These material imagination maps are more than diagrammatic illustrations of a concept; they make visible a drawn material, spatial, cultural and timely embodied cosmopoiesis.[51] These maps reveal yet another image in the ground of the representation in Frascari's own body of work.

Borrowing from Aby Warburg, Frascari subtitled one of the maps, which is based on the element of air: "science without a name" (Figure 0.5). Not unlike Warburg's own field of research, a "science without a name", which was later acknowledged as the emerging field of iconology,[52] Frascari's life's work should be acknowledged as an emerging new approach to a theory of

INTRODUCTION

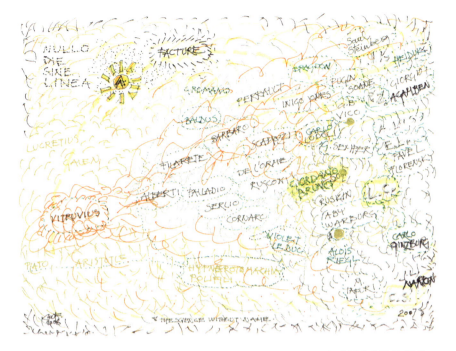

Figure 0.5 The Science Without a Name by Marco Frascari, 2006–2007. Yellow highlighter, black and color pens on paper (23 × 30.5 cm).
Source: © Courtesy of Marco Frascari Estate.

imagination in architecture. A constellation of influences point to potentialities resulting from cross-disciplinary intersections reciprocally affecting and affected by architecture. These intersections take place between the works of thinkers such as Giambattista Vico, Giordano Bruno, and Aby Warburg, drawn as fixed stars marked by circular golden symbols. Vitruvius appears on the left side above Plato and Aristotle. An Eastern wind propels a constellation of authors and architects, such as Alberti, Filarete, Barbaro, but also Palladio, Serlio and Cornaro, Delorme and Rusconi, Perrault, Inigo Jones, Pugin, Soane, and Carlo Lodoli.[53] The right-hand side of this atmospheric diagram shows thinkers and architects soaring together, from the bottom up CS, Carlo Ginzburg, LC, Pavel Florensky, EL, Adolph Loos, Giorgio Agamben, Hejduk, and others.

These authors are combined in Frascari's cosmopoiesis through scholarly investigations into the notion of facture.[54] Triangular light rays, expediently traced with a yellow highlighter, emanate from an imaginative sun symbolizing architecture and illuminating the map of a sketched-in "science without a name." The associative nature of this synaptic diagram constitutes a dynamic map with multiple centers informed by a Kublerian shape of time, where a seemingly continuous fabric of events linearly organized in historical

11

time is replaced with a disjointed series of time-events connected through conceptual narrative threads, which occasionally resurface as in a dream.

Frascari approached research through interdisciplinary openings to allow for emergent new readings. As evidenced by his library collection, his interests spanned from art and architecture to literature, fiction, history, philosophy, semiotics, neurology, cognitive science, the history of magic, astrology as well as science, linguistics, and anthropology, embracing a wide range of fields and scholarship.[55] Frascari stated that we do not grasp what "the discipline of architectural imagination" actually is,[56] and urged the emergence of a "science of imagination," achieved through interdisciplinary readings in architecture as well as in other fields of knowledge. When reading Frascari's work one gains an appreciation of the fact that the science of imagination is perhaps an unfinished and much-needed opera, yet evidently one well begun in his drawings and writings.[57]

The search for a key narrative thread is evidenced in a second cosmopoietic map based on the element of water, which is entitled: "Different Theory Lines. Drawing Theory and Theory of Drawing" (Figure 0.6). In this Heraclitean river, four currents of theory cross paths. These textual-lines-of-

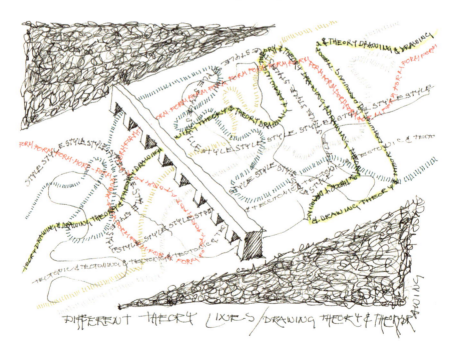

Figure 0.6 Different Theory Lines. Drawing Theory and Theory of Drawing by Marco Frascari, ca. 2006–2007. Yellow highlighter, pencil, black and color pens on paper (23 × 30.5 cm).

Source: © Courtesy of Marco Frascari Estate.

INTRODUCTION

thinking are based on: form, style, tectonic, theory of drawing and drawing theory. The latter is highlighted to draw attention to a chosen undercurrent, his predominant mode of thinking within architectural theory. Frascari traced our ability to read drawings back to the well-known motto "Verum Ipsum Factum" (the real is what is made) by the seventeenth-century Italian philosopher Giambattista Vico (1668–1744).[58] The word "facture" introduced by Frascari in reference to the drafting of drawings is imbued by Vico's philosophy to entail that a drawing is something humanly made and therefore knowable.

In the third cosmopoietic map, based on the element of earth and entitled "Fight Design" (Figure 0.7), a Hollywood-type sign is under siege from diverse kinds of weaponry under the flags of "*disegno*," "*lineamenta*," "*fantasia*," "drawing," "*grafia*" and "*progetto*." This Saul Steinberg-like ironic scenario hints that the corrupted meaning of the Italian word *disegno* is at the root of the word "design," and yet the word "design" no longer expresses the essence of that from which it received its inception.[59] This condition is one of the triggers behind Frascari's search for new etymological keys to renew architectural thinking. This is essential to move the discipline

Figure 0.7 *Fight Design* by Marco Frascari, ca. 2006. Black and gold pens on paper (23 × 30.5 cm).

Source: © Marco Frascari Collection, The Architectural Archives, University of Pennsylvania (aaup.104_15.22).

away from a limited notion of drawing as artistic production,[60] towards the writing and reading of "factures."[61]

Frascari observed that the viewpoint of the architectural theorist is one addressing the 'how' and the 'why' of the thinking through drawing within a culturally specific place and time, offering a reading of drawings, which reveals through contextual re-readings of the traces of factures, an inherent significance, not just for the past but also in regard to contemporary time.[62] The possibility of reading drawings and of inferring an embedded theory rests on the fact that there is always a relationship between image, support and the technique of representation within a given historical time, place, and cultural milieu. Documented paradigm shifts demonstrate how new tools and mediums of representation generate different conceptions of architecture.[63]

Frascari's multiple readings were revealed through his unmistakable storytelling style, aimed at seeding questions for a future generation of architects. A first story would lead into a next, from one *storytelling* to another, bringing to the fore that which lies in the ground of the imagination; new readings gradually opened up drawings, and related texts allowing one to enter architectural theory through a process of activation by reading factures. Frascari's unique contribution rests in looking at drawings as particularities, as details, revealing a unique tale through sensorial and cultural readings.[64]

Drawings are the records of their own having been made; they are particularities resulting from unique factures.[65] Relying on the ambiguity of the word "facture," the author hinted at the process of making but also at the magic of drawing, with its ability to act on the imagination of a gazer,[66] who enters and is entered by the drawing through contemplation, suggesting a mutual relationship between writing and reading. We write drawings and drawings read us. To imagine in architecture is to offer a construction of the thinking through making by means of memory-drawings, which carry the readable signs of their dream inception and occurrence.[67]

David Summers' reading of the factures of works of art, much like Frascari's reading of architectural drawing factures, are informed by Charles Sanders Peirce's notion of indexical inference. David Summers explained that "every artifact – considered indexically – is a record of its own having been made."[68] Frascari advocated for architectural drawings what Summers advocated for artwork: that a close reading of the process of making and materiality informs the reading itself.[69] Drawing factures instruct on both how to think through drawing and how to construct edifices. From this viewpoint, the drawing sequence elucidates the intention while illuminating the temporal dimension of the on-site assembling performance.[70]

In the last cosmopoietic map, which is based on the element of fire and is entitled "The Facture of Architecture and its Lines," the recto/verso condition of architecture is explored (Figure 0.8). Architecture is drawn as a free-hand straight line, which divides an unfolded recto from a folded verso condition, forming an illuminated surface reflecting and merging threads,

INTRODUCTION

Figure 0.8 The Facture of Architecture and its Lines, 2006. Yellow highlighter, black and color pencils and pens on paper (23 × 30.5 cm).

Source: © Courtesy of Marco Frascari Estate.

moving within and without the mirror of architecture, revealing unique relationships between *disegno* and *lineamenta*,[71] *ideai* (*ichnographia, orthographia, scaenographia*)[72] and *fantasia*, icon and *graphia, modello* and *prun*,[73] *merz*, and *paradigma*.[74] The threads of ideas are clues to the workings of architectural imagination that need to be followed to read into meandering lines of thought. The theory of architecture becomes apparent in Frascari's writings through time cross-sections re-uniting disjointed periods and events, while dealing with cross-narratives that are woven together through a dialogue among authors and buildings separated by chronology and yet united by the specificity of discourse.

The re-reading of architectural education through the re-reading of drawings is essential to distance oneself from a present condition of over-codification, which flattens the architect's role.[75] Drawings work within and without professional conventions. Being affected by the cultural, economic, artistic milieu of a period, drawings have the potential to reveal a comprehensive account. The 'how' of the reading is crucial. Cognitive scientist David Olson has argued that new ways of reading change the ways of writing. He claimed that Early Modern science narrowed the act of reading to a univocal interpretation, advocating for a singular reading that can be duplicated by any person, unambiguously.[76] Under these rules any kind of reading between the lines, deviating from a literal one, was considered an imaginative and unreliable activity that should best be avoided.[77]

Frascari argued that the reading of drawings dating from the Middle Ages to the Renaissance period should be based on a system of interpretation, abducted from the four ways of reading described by the early Christian theologian Origen (c.184–c.254).[78] This would entail reading based on four different levels, moving from a literal, to an allegorical, moral and anagogical level.[79] Frascari operated a Peircian abduction,[80] based on the hypothesis which is inferred from effects that the traditional way of reading the Bible would apply to reading in other fields, such as the reading of images, for example, in the same period.[81]

An enigmatic visual metaphor for the different levels of reading is provided in a hand drawing by Frascari entitled *Templum* (Figure 0.9). The *templum* formed by the intersection of the *cardus* and the *decumanus* is traced in three *loci*: below ground, at ground level and in the sky above. That which appears at ground level could be interpreted as the face value of the *templum*, or the literal reading that can be physically apprehended, perceived, and surveyed by someone perusing the site. That which lies underground relates to a deeper history grounding the story, the structure, and reflecting the moral value of the reading. The *templum* in the sky offers a reading of the metaphorical significance. The fourth level of reading, the anagogical, can be achieved through an awareness and understanding of the other three.

By interpreting the process of tracing drawings, it is possible to perform a literal reading diving into the thinking, which informed and is informed by making.[82] This condition of performance entails that reading is a making sequence, asking which is the first line traced, and what has followed, thus it is possible to reveal ideas about the original facture. Phenomenological reduction comes into play to inform the material, historical, and sensorial reading of drawn lines,[83] by defining the horizon of the drafting table, the tools, the techniques, and the boundaries which define its context. A phenomenological reading of the drawing further unravels by defining the cultural, geographic, epistemic, temporal (beginning and origin),[84] spatial, and geometrical boundaries, and it is completed through a sensorial reading of material lines, which are traced, scored, incised or cut in a medium. The reading between the lines is a reading of the lines.[85]

According to Frascari, a close-up construing of drawings, as material records of theory, may work out the full spectrum of the tale of architectural imagination towards a microhistorical account of the design process. Carlo Ginzburg's microhistorical research method coupled with Frascari's "tell-the-tale" approach to architectural design entails observing details in the making, which in turn have the potential to illuminate larger tales, reading from everyday, seemingly un-noticeable elements (Figure 0.10). A history of

Figure 0.9 Templum by Marco Frascari, ca. 2008.
Source: © Courtesy of Marco Frascari Estate.

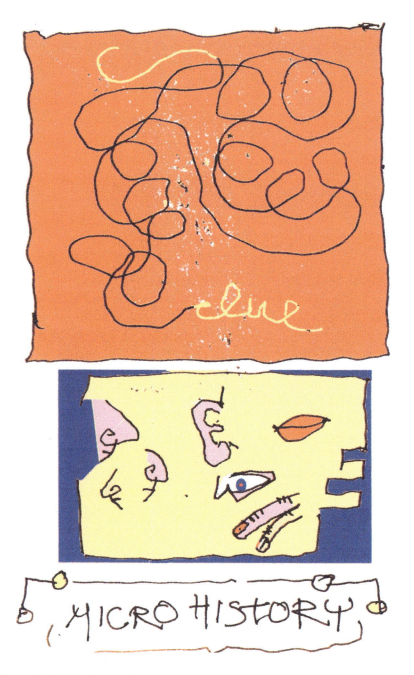

Figure 0.10 Microhistory by Marco Frascari. Hybrid drawing. Line drawing in brown pen on white paper. Colors added digitally.

Source: © Courtesy of Marco Frascari Estate.

INTRODUCTION

the reading of drawings must become itself inseparable from the reading. Frascari's approach offers significant value for present-day research and teaching through the reading of drawing factures.[86] The reading of drawings as types of dreams further raises the issue of the accuracy of readings that arise from a merely literal viewpoint, looking at drawings as didactic illustrations rather than as a result of material thinking.

Frascari further suggested initiating a proper literal reading of drawings through the Aristotelian theory of causality,[87] identifying the final, formal, material, and efficient cause in a drawing process. As part of an anti-Cartesian phenomenological interpretation of the drawing process,[88] Aristotle's fifth cause, the accidents, are considered opportunities to be read into. Unforeseen drawing events become part of a game of reading and writing, which has to remain adaptable to circumstances in the process of construction and beyond. Drawings can also be read in terms of primary (measurable) and secondary (sensorial) qualities, as defined by Aristotle.[89]

The historical and theoretical studies of architecture need to penetrate beyond a reading of the built surfaces of architecture and move into discussions about the factures of making in order to open up new readings, both in the drawing and in the building. In-depth re-readings of buildings and drawings require the experience of a personal encounter, beyond a mediated reading through the medium of digital or printed reproductions, which flattens the impression to a retinal experience. Drawing embodies memory by weaving the fabric of culture in time. In order to activate a reading in the lines, it is necessary to introduce a new way of reading drawings through a pluralistic approach, moving beyond a descriptive reading of a literal appearance on the support paper, towards a deeper reading into the sensorial corporeality of factual lines, support material, and their interaction, observing and interpreting their materiality, geometry, and cultural dimensions.

With the intent of opening up a new field of possibilities, Frascari looked for an adequate theoretical approach to the reading of drawings. This led him to suggest that dreams are the provisional metaphor best suited to understand the working of the architect's imagination through embodied acts of representation. Re-reading drawings also entails new ways of weaving thoughts through drawing. Frascari stated the momentous necessity to re-think our teaching methods through an in-depth piece of research into drawing as a mirror of a twinned theory in the flesh of architecture.[90]

Frascari's multi-focal viewpoint is relevant to the current North American educational context where emphasis is placed on professional accreditation criteria, but also because of the enslaving production of photorealistic and farmed images of buildings. The attention given to the construction of architectural details and drawing-thinking is disappearing from the academic curriculum. Frascari's prolific writings, drawings, and teachings, which deserve each in their own right, and in relation to each other, in-depth re-

readings, offer to contemporary architectural theory and practice a powerful compass, constructed through a personal cosmology inscribed into a deep architectural tradition to sow relevant questions for the next generation of academics, students of architecture and practitioners.

Notes

1 Eco (1989b: 1–23).
2 Peirce (1931–1958: CP 5.171: 105–106) introduced the notion of "abductive hypothesis" as a form of explanatory inference based on a hypothesis that produces deductions tested through inductions (Frascari 2011: 54; Burks 1946: 301–306).
3 Frascari (1981); Hedges (2012).
4 Frascari's teaching tactics have yet to be analyzed. He crafted "imagination exercises" to enact a process, which in turn taught students how to think, to draw and to dream, putting his theory of imagination into his practice of teaching. The syllabi of his academic seminars, lectures and studio courses can be found in his digital archives. The digital archives are in the process of being organized and have been donated by Paola Frascari to the Architectural Archives of the University of Pennsylvania (AAUP). A collection of sketches, drawings and writings was donated in 2013 to the AAUP by Paola Frascari. This body of work joined an earlier donation of architectural drawings (over 300) in the same archive.
5 See the bibliographical section on Frascari in this book. See also 'Thoughts on Neuro-Architecture' presented by Frascari at the OAA Meeting (May 19–20, 2011) in Toronto. Available at: www.scribd.com/doc/57072291/Frascari-NeuroArchitecture) (accessed May 16, 2016).
6 Ridgway (2015: 75–85).
7 Frascari (2011).
8 Braham and Frascari (1995: 307–310); Zuss (2012).
9 Rykwert (1982; 1984; 1998a; 1998b); Pérez-Gómez (1983; 1992); Evans (1995; 1997); Pérez-Gómez and Pelletier (1997); Rykwert (1998b); Vesely (2004); Emmons (2005); Emmons and Frascari (2006).
10 Friedman inherited the role of guest curator, developed the theme, gave a title to and oversaw the competition and exhibition. Funds for the exhibition came from a National Endowment for the Arts grant and the AIA, Cincinnati, OH. The selection process for the exhibition was twofold. Architects were either invited based on a review of their portfolio, or selected based on a juried national competition. Frascari was an invited participant. The jury included, among others, Charles Gwathmey and Michael Rotondi. The first prize competition winners were Kevin Kennon (KPF, New York) and Peter Moore (Friedman 1993: 2–9, 20–21).
11 Frascari (1997: 176, fn 5).
12 Sketchbook 161 was completed on August 31, 1993 (25 cm x 25 cm); sketchbook 159 dates from May 1994 (25 cm x 25 cm); sketchbook 160 was prepared during August 1993 and was completed on September 9, 1993 (18 cm x 18 cm). The *Dream-House* sketchbooks will be donated to the AAUP by Paola Frascari.
13 This process holds true for the writing of other works. There are about two hundred notebooks and sketchbooks in Frascari's archive in the AAUP.
14 Maurena Lodi, Stefano Lodi and Antonello Bellucci collaborated with Sgarbi in his verso design. Sgarbi completed his doctoral dissertation "Between Words and Drawings. Dissertation on a Newly Found Illustrated Version of 'De architectura'" in 1993. Marco Frascari was one of his committee advisors (Friedman 1993: 66).
15 The format of the final presentation, the number and the type of drawings were decided on August 30, 1993 (see Figure 39 in the Portfolio).
16 Merrill Elam's project is available at: http://msmearch.com/type/residential/house-above-the-bug-line (accessed May 21, 2016).
17 Alice Min Soo Chun is an architect and co-founder of Solight Design and a non-profit organization called Focus on Art Architecture Research and Making (FAARM). She was an

INTRODUCTION

Assistant Professor of Design and Material Culture at Parsons The New School for Design, in New York.
18 Mollino's original drawings can be seen in (Brino 1987: 79).
19 Mollino's drawing is a "brouillon," a drawing intended to be recopied (Frascari 2011: 87–91).
20 Frascari refers in one of his sketchbooks to Mollino's project as the "tower-house" (see Figure 43 in the Portfolio), while in the Dream House text he refers to his design as a "house-tower" or just the "tower."
21 Corbin (1976: 9–11).
22 Frascari owned a few old and contemporary Feng Shui compasses, which are now at the AAUP. Feng Shui is an ancient Chinese form of geomantic divination by means of a compass used to explain everyday occurrences (Bruun 2011).
23 This preparatory drawing by Frascari is akin to the condition portrayed in Michael Gandy's 1818 watercolour entitled *Selection of public and private buildings' parts according to Sir John Soane's projects* [...], where the architect is depicted at his working table surrounded by his projects, englobed in an imaginal dimension of architectural design.
24 Dällenbach (1989: 169–174). This is not unlike the condition set in Brunelleschi's mirror tablet experiment discussed by Frascari in the text of the Dream House.
25 Frascari was in Philadelphia, while Sgarbi was in Modena. Sgarbi's sketchbooks entitled "The Verso" (17.5 x 17.5 cm) can be found at the AAUP.
26 Heraclitus (1987: 55).
27 Frascari (2011: 87); Minkowski (1983: 8–89).
28 The pamphlet was part of an initiative by Editrice Progetti to publish pocket books on architecture called 'pills' (Italian *pillola*). Frascari wrote the first book in this series. It is a pamphlet of 48 pages (11 x 16 cm). This publication contained a few of the preliminary drawings by Frascari and the design drawings by both Frascari and Sgarbi (Frascari 1995: 37–46, 48). This book was used as a model to prepare the final version of the Dream House book. I had an opportunity to discuss this concept with Frascari when we first entertained the idea of bringing the Dream House to press.
29 The title chosen "The Tell-The-Tale Detail" (Frascari 1981) is inspired by two sources: Edgar Allan Poe's "The Tell-Tale Heart" (1843) and a book on semiotics entitled *The Tell-Tale Sign*, edited by Thomas Sebeok (1975).
30 Agamben (2009: 39–54).
31 Frascari (1991; 1995; 2011).
32 Other unfinished works in Frascari's archive include a draft for a book entitled *The Mirror of Architecture: Bodies and Machines in the Architecture of Carlo Scarpa, Venetian Architect*, dated April 5, 1987. The structure for the book was conceived in 1984 as can be gathered from notes in a printed copy dating from 1987. See Frascari (1987; 1990; 1991). Frascari prepared in collaboration with David Leatherbarrow a translation provisionally entitled *Alvise Cornaro's Treatise on Architecture*. They worked on it for a period of time, before Frascari joined Virginia Tech in 1997. A book proposal co-authored with Paul Emmons and entitled *Air-Borne Architecture: Looking Backwards toward a Future Sensible Sustainable Architecture*, is dated to July 2005. Another book proposal (2008) was completed for a book entitled *The Facture of Architecture: A Gentle Manifesto Based on a Blend of Macaronic and Alchemic Meditations on the Anti-Cartesian Nature of Architectural Imagination*. A co-authored book proposal entitled *Geomater of Architecture: The Tracing of Elegant Lines*, was written with William Braham (February 1994).
33 Frascari (1997: 176, note 1). This chapter was an extract from the Dream House.
34 Longer and shorter sections of the Dream House were published in Frascari (1997: 162–180; 1998: 67–91; 2004: 191–203; 2011).
35 The titles of two of the Dream House digital files in the archive, dating from 2000, seem to hint that Frascari abandoned the idea of publishing the work. These are called "The Dream House *Demolita*" (demolished) and "Dream da *Saccheggiare*" (to be looted). Additional works by Frascari draw ideas from the Dream House (Frascari 2004: 191–203; 2011).
36 There are numerous versions of the Dream House in the archive dating from 1995, 1997, 1999, 2000, 2001, 2002, 2006, 2007, 2008, 2009, and 2010. A complete draft was prepared in 1997.

37 In the last 15 months of his life, Frascari could not speak or write because of a debilitating stroke, yet he was able to communicate, read and work. While in the process of organizing his archive, he decided to return to this unpublished piece. After the stroke, Frascari and the editor of this book developed a system of communication. By hearing his text read out loud while following it on the computer screen, the author was able to identify things to be modified and choose from among suggested alternatives. It was an exercise in putting his seal of approval on the work (*Canadian Architect*, June 25, 2013, www.canadianarchitect.com/news/marco-frascari-director-of-the-azrieli-school-of-architecture-and-urbanism-1945-2013/1002418766/?&er=NA). The editor of this book continued to review the text and compared key versions of the Dream House in the digital archive (1997, 2008 and 2010), while also reviewing published excerpts of the Dream House in both English and Italian (Frascari 1995; 1997; 1998; 2011). An homonymous website, "Dreamhouse Architecture: Marco Frascari," is devoted to his legacy and was created in December 2013: www.marcofrascaridreamhouse.com/.

38 The latest book draft, of which an Introduction, sample chapters, index and cover exist in the digital archive, is written following key concepts explored in the Dream House, and was announced as forthcoming at the Ontario Architectural Association Annual Conference, in Toronto, in May 2011. The provisional title of Frascari's book ties into the book by British neuroscientist, Semir Zeki, *Splendors and Miseries of the Human Brain: Love, Creativity and the Quest for Human Happiness* (Chichester: Wiley-Blackwell, 2009).

39 Recent cognitive neuroscience research has modeled dynamic brain activity in the occipitotemporal visual cortex and decoded this to reconstruct cortical representations. A claim has been made that this type of research might lead to the ability to decode dreams and hallucinations and produce images of them (Nishimoto *et al.* 2011: 1641–1646). Clearly, the literal harvesting of dream images is not advocated in Frascari's work. Frascari acknowledges a state of "wakeful slumber," which is an imaginative dimension of drawing and thinking (Frascari 1997: 164). Ridgway (2015: 75–76) noted this aspect of Frascari's design work and described this condition as a "self-induced state of creative imaging."

40 *Why Do We Dream?* (BBC Horizon, February 10, 2009).

41 From a documentary film about the threat-simulation theory entitled *Why Do We Dream?* (BBC Horizon, February 10, 2009: 49:45–50:23). See also Revonsuo (2009: 76–77). Revonsuo has been conducting research on dreams since 1995. He rejects the embodied cognition theory (Revonsuo 2009: XVII); conversely Frascari, an anti-Cartesian thinker, is a supporter of the embodied mind theory (Frascari 1997; 2003).

42 See Treib (2008); Belardi (2014); Scheer (2014); Welton (2015). Spiller (2013: 14–19) argues that the lessons reside in comparing the analogue and digital condition.

43 Frascari (2011: 10–16, 30–38, 45–56, 70–73, 90–91, 122–125).

44 The first draft of *A Grimoire of Architecture* was completed in November 2001. It stemmed from the Dream House project (Digital archive, file name: First Draft Grimoire 2001-11-23). The *Grimoire* draft was completed in 2004. Frascari continued working on this text, which later became the *Eleven Exercises in the Art of Architectural Drawings* (Frascari 2011).

45 Between 1998 and 2005, Frascari held the G. T. Ward Professorship and founded the PhD in Design and Research, at the Washington-Alexandria Architecture Center of Virginia Tech, hinged on questions of architectural representation.

46 This lecture, entitled "The Primacy of Tectonic Imagination: Sight, Site, Cite," was held at WAAC on January 20, 2000. The syllabus had been prepared in 1998. Audio recordings of this course made by Matthew Mindrup, a doctoral student at the time, exist in the digital archive.

47 He suggested, for example, using drawings, ranging from sketches to construction drawings, as the key tools to learn and teach architectural history and theory. See also Frascari (2011: 93–94, 133).

48 Feberayend (1993: 9–21).

49 Frascari (2011: 93–108).

50 These material imagination 'cosmopoietic maps' were drawn shortly after Frascari joined Carleton University in 2005. At this time, he began thinking and planning for a new doctoral program. Admissions to this program began in September 2011 (Bachelard 1983: 22; 1994: XIII, 23, 102).

51 Ingold (2007a: 1–16); Frascari (2011: 103).

INTRODUCTION

52 Pattuelli (2011: 4).
53 Frascari's dissertation at the University of Pennsylvania (1981) entitled "Sortes Architectii in the Eighteenth-Century Veneto" is an inquiry into architectural origins in the "Verum Ipsum Factum," of Venetian tradition, inspired by the works of Giambattista Vico and Carlo Lodoli.
54 Kubler (2008: 15).
55 A preliminary list of Frascari's book collection (MFLC) was compiled by Adriana Ross with the assistance of students of the Azrieli School of Architecture and Urbanism at Carleton University.
56 Frascari (2011: 93).
57 Frascari (2011). The study of Frascari's own syllabi and "imagination exercises" awaits scholarly study to reveal the tacit knowledge implicit in the workings of architectural imagination, of which the scholar had an understanding.
58 According to Vico's philosophy for a New Science (1984), humans have knowledge of what they make. Scientific knowledge is acquired through a process of anatomical dissection. The word *science* comes from the Latin *scire*, which means "to cut" (Vico 1988: 49).
59 The Italian equivalent of the verb "to design" is *progettare*.
60 Frascari (2011: 38).
61 Frascari (2011: 10–16, 30–43, 70–73, 90–91, 122–125); Quek (2007: 43–63).
62 This was evident in his lectures but also in his writings, where an historical excursus always brings the reader back to the present condition (Frascari 1999; 2001). See also Agamben (2009: 39–54); Kubler (2008).
63 Emmons (2007: 31–39); Frascari (2011); Evans (1997: 153–193).
64 Frascari (2011: 10–11).
65 Frascari (2011: 10–16, 31–32).
66 Illich (1998).
67 Frascari (2011: 170–172) discusses the presence of both intentional and unintentional elements in drawings.
68 According to Summers (2004), this type of reading is something very different from a traditional analysis of works of art through a symbolic reading.
69 Frascari was interested in the correlation between indexical inference and symbolic interpretation, being further inclusive of the brain's own response to visual stimuli, increasing the complexity of the reading of architectural drawings through a pluralistic approach (Zeki 1999; Gombrich 2000; Michaud 2004; Onians 2008).
70 The process of architectural drafting is a demonstration of the inner workings of buildings analogous to the anatomical lecture where through careful dissecting one demonstrates the assembly of the body through disassembly (Frascari 1988b).
71 Lang (1965); Alberti (1966a: 19–20; 1997: 7); Frascari (2011: 96–102); Hendrix (2011).
72 Vitruvio (1997: I.2.1: 26–27).
73 Tupitsyn (1999: 12–14).
74 Burns Gamard (2000: 14, 40).
75 Frascari (2007b: 22–33).
76 Olson (1994: 118) argued that both the scientific method and Protestant theology converged towards literal readings and generated new forms of writings for a strictly literal interpretation.
77 Olson (1994: 163) concluded that the new deterministic way of reading generated new ways of writing in the Early Modern period.
78 Frascari (2007b: 26–29).
79 Vandevelde (2005: 111–126).
80 Frascari (*Elegant Curiosity* 24/07/2007: 17–18) explains "abductive reasoning" in the work of Charles Peirce, as

[a] reasoning in which explanatory hypotheses are formed and evaluated. Abduction is sometimes creative; hypotheses may be revolutionary, completeness is elusive, and simplicity is seen as complex. Abductive reasoning may be visual and non-sentential, but above all is based on an elegant sorting of clues and evidences, a conjectural reasoning that infers by an elegant selection the presence of absent invisible entities from their perceptible traces.

(Frascari 2008b: 69–79)

81 Frascari explained that the literal interpretation is operated by reading the very lines of the drawing in their factuality (materiality and geometry). The moral reading is expressed in the method of construction; the structural elements express the morality of the building. The allegoric reading tells us how the drawing is going to move us, expressing emotions. The anagogic reading is the secret meaning, revealing a future plan. Frascari also explained that design drawing allows for four kinds of reading. Understood in this way the literal reading of construction drawings becomes reductive of the power of design drawings when taken separately, or when understood as the predominant way of reading, in contrast with a reading articulated through the four levels. From Federica Goffi's notes from a 2004 lecture by Frascari entitled "How to Read a Drawing" (WAAC).
82 Bachelard (1994: XIII, 23, 102).
83 Husserl (1989); Merleau-Ponty (2012).
84 Said (1975).
85 Frascari (2011: 43).
86 Ingold (2007b); Frascari (2011: 124).
87 Aristotle (2003: 76–79).
88 Frascari (2003).
89 Frascari sees in this dichotomous structure the work of the architect and the engineer. The architect makes design decisions based on an appreciation of secondary qualities, based on the senses, while the engineer bases his work primarily on empirically measurable phenomena. The analogy between food and architecture, which is pervasive in Frascari's work, relates to this dichotomy.
90 Merleau-Ponty (2012).

1

A CONGENIAL INAUGURATION

Marco Frascari

We are such a stuffe
As dreams are made on, and our little life
Is rounded with a sleepe.
          William Shakespeare[1]

I'm Lost, Lost! Mama! I'M LOST! OH! I AM LOST!
You are not lost, NEMO. Go to sleep and Behave! Hear?
              Winsor McCay[2]

Our life is not a dream—but it shall,
and maybe will, become one.
                Novalis[3]

This is an ambiguous book, not intended for a linear reading, but is not indigestible; nor is it merely the story and description of a design using fine and ornate words. It is constructed to follow the rhizomatic path from which relevant architectural design can be contrived. It is an edifice that includes vistas and secret gardens. It is an assembly of open and closed rooms that house verbal and visual icons for architectural edification. Being a dwelling in wonder within the dreamland of design, this text should be grasped as architectural drawings are scanned; by injecting yourself in them and wandering from room to room, from detail to detail, from plan to section, from section to elevation. This work consists of, in the order in which they were made, first, dreamed images, second, drawings, and, finally, words. The drawings were done following the dreamed images, and then the narrative was written to emulate the drawings.

My suggestion for the reader is to wait until after dinner to interpret the riddle I offer in this book. Having drafted most of this book and drawn the majority of its images before dinner, I was forced by my longing to be concise. Readers may delight and even indulge in this verbal and visual medley, by using their *post-prandium*,[4] active imagination, that is, by taking advantage of mental images elaborated during lull moments of reverie. The drawings and the companion text, proffered here, are neither about simulation nor dissimulation in architecture, but about assimilation. Assimilation is an act of proper cognitive musing. Cognitive assimilation is a form of incorporation, whereby we ingest the outside world into ourselves. Simulation and dissimulation predominate amid both academic likings and professional kitsch. The idea of assimilation is proposed as a novel and venerable approach to counteract the current degraded state of theoretic sentimentality and visual vulgarity that dominate the ostentatious and pretentious architecture of today. Cognitive assimilation is an illumination. It is a productive inference based on instinct, just as oral tasting during childhood is an instinctive part of cognitive appropriation.

Behind the words, behind the lines and colors composing this text, there is the same experiential knowledge that can be found beneath the architecture of well-conceived *haute cuisine* plates, properly paired with a correct selection of wines: a perfect way to begin a daydream.[5] As Novalis (Georg Friedrich Philipp von Hardenberg, 1772–1801) suggested in his *Allgemeine Brouillon*, dreams instruct on the facility of our spirit to penetrate every object and to transform itself into every object.[6] In his *Scientific-Natural Studies of Freiberg* (1799), Novalis indicated that the peristaltic movement of the brain originates dreams and, furthermore, he defined daydreaming as a beatific circumstance.[7]

An inner light generated by gourmet activity illuminates our dreams. An active member of the Neoplatonic School of Chartres and a follower of the sensible dietetic principles of the School of Salerno,[8] William of Conches, a Norman scholar, born toward the end of the eleventh century, gives us a great description of the metabolic nature of the light of imagination. Conches took from Galen the conception that food transforms from matter into light through a sequence of transformations. The first transformation occurs in the liver where digested matter becomes natural virtue, which then trickles through the heart and is transmuted into spiritual virtue and, finally, it is exuded in the brain where it is changed into a luminous wind.[9] This wind is a pneumatic light; it is the imagination that edifies our minds and provides visions of past, present and future edifices. It works through the dual act of constructing images and construing meanings within a tectonic environment.

The magic meal

Dreaming architecture is like a gourmet craft that, when carefully translated into constructed artifacts, promotes a beatific life. The analogy between food and architecture is an old one. Isidore of Seville (560–636), in his etymological and truly macaronic studies, postulated the origin of architecture in the dining hall, rather than in the primal hut.[10] One of the most powerful concepts developed by Leon Battista Alberti (1404–1472) in his architectural theory is the application of the Latin concept of *concinnitas* to the production of a harmonious architecture.[11] The ontological origin of the concept of *concinnitas* records the figurative transposition of the harmony of taste present in a well-cooked dish, where the dosing of the components is properly calibrated.[12] In the *De Re Aedificatoria* (1443–1452), Alberti states that *concinnitas* is "*vim et quasi succum*" (energy and almost a sauce).[13]

The analogy between gastronomy and architecture is not solely Isidore's fanciful etymological interpretation, it has been invoked many times. Ben Jonson (1572–1637), an English playwright who disliked architects, used the analogy to craftily criticize Inigo Jones' belief in the cultural predominance of architects in one of his Masques. In the Masque entitled "Neptune's Triumph for the Return of Albion" (1624), Jonson described the master-builder as a preposterous master-cook.[14] Nevertheless, to be a master-cook is not a contrary circumstance for an architect, nor is to be an architect a negative condition for a great chef of cuisine. The first, and, in many ways, the most important of all French chefs, was Marie-Antonin Carême (1784–1833), who was called the "architect of French cuisine."[15] This label is a metaphor used to point out Carême's dominant role in the rise of French gastronomy. It also indicates his interest in architecture and his search for the common ground between the two disciplines. Architecture was one of Carême's main interests. He carefully studied the architectural monuments of the past and he designed elaborate table decorations called *pièces montées* (mounted pieces) as an outlet for his architectural passion. Those pieces were rotundas, temples, columns, and arches, constructed with sugar, icing, and pastry dough. Each of these was carefully designed with the eye of an architect, for Carême considered confectionery to be the main branch of architecture.

To further the discussion and to keep it within this edifying edible analogy, I should forewarn the reader that the structure and theories presented in this book are products of a gourmet manner of thinking that, in its critical form, is called a macaronic art.[16] Macaronic thinking is a monstrous way of thinking[17] that I am using to fashion a constructive dream to demonstrate that the architectural discipline is, and will always be, sustainable, flexible and fertile.[18] As already mentioned, this macaronic achievement was conceived before my meals—my favorite dinner being *maccheroni al sugo*—and the thoughtful reader should sample it with their after-dinner macaroon.

Macaronic undertakings are autobiographical in nature and display the other as self. Non-macaronic theories are like *maccheroni senza sugo* (macaroni *without* sauce), they lack taste and *concinnitas*. As I recently came to realize, I am a macaronic thinker. As the progenitor of all the macaronics, Merlinus Cocaius,[19] and like all other macaronic persons, I am not a revolutionary. My point of view is incompatible with any great program for the reordering of the world. I consider critical thinking beyond politics, religion, or morals: it is a critique of the imaginal foundation of our comprehension and representation of the world. The aim of a truly macaronic person is not revolution but demonstration: a permanent presentation of monstrous evidences. The macaronic art is a special way to investigate the non-empirical, by making analogies resonate in the mind and on the tongue.

Macaronic persons know the power of edible expressions that, instead of being simulated or dissimulated, can be assimilated by an audience. To digest these resonating and analogical utterances, the audience is compelled to carry out phenomenological readings. The importance of a phenomenological reading lies in the enlightenment of a person's awareness, wonderstruck by the possibility of associations built through images.

We live in a civilization and culture where scientific thinking is extending its control over the production of images. Contrary to tradition, images no longer reveal culture. They mostly result from acritical production. It is commonplace to speak of a civilization of the image, nevertheless, this commonplace conceals a radical misunderstanding. Our Macs and PCs are controlled by the use of icons, but we no longer know what an "icon" really is beyond its functional or logistic reference. Images are reduced to the level of primary, rational, sensory perception. The result is a complete degradation of the images that are supposed to feed our thinking processes. The cognitive power of images is lost to the power of pretentious expectations or fictional fulfilling. Architectural images suffer unfortunately the same fate. Architectural drawings and buildings no longer yield to cognitive power, they have become mere instruments of the building industry, real estate investments, and not-so-commodious habitations.

Dreams are the way in which myths are created.[20] The macaronic art is employed as a playful technique to access daydreaming to ascertain the power of architectural images. Oneiric images show the possibility of translation: a conversion that makes visible the invisible. A dream is a mode of production whereby images can be manipulated through dimensional combinations, scale changes, and analogical relationships that result in the creation of new forms and new understandings.

In dreams, visual images are dominant and a monstrous semiosis takes place. While dreaming, everybody learns the subtle art of representation, because a dream is always a representation of either being awake or asleep. Dreams are not irrational instruments; they are efficacious visual tools for penetrating the rigor of reason; they enlighten the imaginal aspects of human thinking. Through dreaming, a person can enter any building. Dreams are a non-verbal structure. They are a way of thinking by using images (see Figures 30, 47 in the Portfolio).[21]

Daydreaming is the only proper way to read drawings of architecture. No other procedure allows the transmutation of the composition of lines describing a future building into an assembly of meaningful rooms and details. Architectural practice (the art of construction) and architectural theory (the art of drawing) have been separated from each other. These two arts are no longer mutually correspondent. They are no longer alchemic twins.[22] Predictive drawings are a parched basis for construction, and construction is no longer a mold for drawings. Drawings have lost the power to embody dreams of possible constructed worlds. Dreaming is the critical procedure to draw and to understand architecture towards the attainment of a *vita beata*.

The *vita beata*, herein, is not the beatific life that a few may achieve in the presence of their god, but more broadly a human beatific life. The *vita beata* results from an architecture that has been designed for a "happy existence." This *vita beata* is described in poetic manner by Angelo Beolco (1502–1542), alias Ruzzante, in a comic play entitled *I beati*.[23] Ruzzante points out that a beatific existence, a *vita beata*, is a way of life without impairment caused by disquieting psychic activity. Ruzzante's *vita beata* is what the Greek philosophers called *eudaimonia* (εὐδαιμονία).[24] The attainment of a *vita beata*, a good spirit, was the *telos* of human existence, an *arete* (virtue). *Vita beata* is virtuous happiness.[25] The only architect who addressed the topic of virtuous happiness in an explicit manner was Antonio Averulino (1400–1469). He was so conscious of the ethical importance of an architect to implement a *vita beata* through his constructed work that he carefully chose Filarete (Φιλαρετε, meaning "lover of virtue") as his professional name. According to Filarete, architecture provokes a beatific life when an edifice increases the potential to foster the psychic ability of the inhabitant.[26] A dream house is a place where one may achieve virtuous happiness by leading a *vita beata*.

The ingredients

By dream, daydreaming, reverie, slumber, *sogno*, *somnium*, *sopor*, and any other dream-related word used in this text, I refer to specific moments of dreaming. First, there is the hypnagogic dream, which is the dream that ushers us to sleep; second, the hypnopompic dream, which is the dream that takes place as we awaken; third, the dreaming that occurs during the day, viz., daydreaming or awake dreaming. All dreams that happen at other times and are specific to Freudian and Jungian analysis do not pertain to the scope of this book. Although I do mention some intuitions of Sigmund Freud and Carl Jung, they are merely to make comments related to the discussion of how architects conceive buildings. This work is concerned with the design-driving force of the architect in relationship to the Other and not with the infinite problems of analysis of the Self. I use the word 'dream' and its derivatives in a loose way from a psychological point of view to avoid a mental cloaking. The aim of this vague use of language is to avoid hiding behind a psychological screen the notion that dreams imply disciplined work. Herein, I propose the following as an irreducible principle of any good work of architecture:

> The education and the working of imagination are a discipline just as important as the discipline necessary for the education and the working of a rational mind.

A disciplined imagination is essential to any constructed work because, as the pragmatist Charles Sanders Peirce (1839–1914) pointed out: "The whole business of ratiocination and all that makes us intellectual beings, is performed in imagination."[27]

Peirce also stated:

> Many persons, perhaps most persons, have the idea that every observation about the human mind is a psychological observation. They might as well regard the sight or sound of an apple dropping from a tree as an astronomical observation ...[28]

The discussion on imagination is not a peripheral issue, but a central one for making a powerful architecture. To articulate the realm of architecture by identifying it with dreaming is the best way to unravel the role of this undisciplined discipline in figuring out the constructed world.

Freud, Jung, and their followers have interpreted dreams, but the dream in itself has been largely neglected because dreaming is a foil for an epistemological inquiry into the nature of perception. In the dream, we can seek clarification about the ontological dimension because the dream is not a modality of the imagination, but its first possibility. In the dream, we see the light. This light is the *phos* (Greek φως) that is at the root of *Phantasy*, which the Romans called *Imaginatio*.

This book is about the light of dreaming, as Synesius of Cyrene,[29] Charles Sanders Peirce,[30] and Pavel Florensky[31] have musingly theorized. Their theories are presented here as the delightfully indispensable, but philistinely superfluous ingredients for tossing this macaronic salad of architectural musement. The combination of this trinity of authors: a chameleonic, Hellenistic, Pagan and later Christian thinker; an American pragmatist philosopher; a mathematician, mystic, heretic, and Russian revolutionary, in a work devoted to the discipline of architecture, might seem peculiar. The thought of these figures tossed together may generate—at first glance—a very unusual salad. Nevertheless, these three thinkers have dealt with the power and nature of the imaginal through the path of dreams. The tossing together of their ideas can make the salad quite balanced although intensely tangy. Being the means to an imaginal sapience, this salad can serve as an appetizer that may lead to a particular understanding of cognitive imagination that is useful to architectural designers.

Throughout his book on dreams (*De imsomniis*), Synesius argues that everyone, regardless of status and education, can interpret his or her dreams.[32] This is a significant change, since, in antiquity, imagination belonged only to people with a certain status. Only kings, high priests or mystics could have the gift of meaningful dreams or the talent to interpret them. Whoever was born outside these privileged groups was not allowed to have or to use imagination. Nowadays, in architectural schools and in the profession, the status is not one of class, however, there is still a search for the individuals who are 'gifted' with the talent of imagination. Evidence of this not-so-hidden belief is manifested at the time of admissions in the reviews of the portfolios submitted by students. The reason for this incorrect assumption is that architectural imagination is not a discipline and cannot be taught. Furthermore, this would suggest that a proper imagination is an imprint and not something that can be built. As a consequence of this apodictic assumption, no course in the architectural curriculum deals directly with the discipline of imagination as an intermediary to proper design.

To imagine is a crucial activity in architecture. It takes imagination to inhabit a building as well as to design it. Nevertheless, the bias against the discipline of imagination has made us dismissive of it as a fancy and immoral tramp-like capacity that must be repressed or, if it happens, it is merely a trick, a cunning solution, not used to be decorously taught. Consequently, imagination does not have a theoretical or practical standing in architectural design. Architectural dreams fall within the same extravagant cauldron of vaguely and vagrantly imaginative habits. Following the tradition set by Artemidorus, Synesius classifies dreams under two headings, sorted into theorematic and allegorical dreams.[33] Gerolamo Cardano (1501–1576), in his commentary on Synesius, uses two convincing images to explain the difference between these two types of dreams. The theorematic dream is like the imprint left by a seal, whereas the allegorical dream is constructed piece by piece, just as mosaic workers compose their images, *tessera* by *tessera*.[34] The theorematic dream is a stroke marking a presence without mediation, whereas the allegorical dream is always a mediating constructive activity. In the allegoric dream, the image must be built before it can be construed.

Synesius sees dreams as the highest expression of imagination and his text is an excursus on the excellence of the imaginative life. The analogical domain selected to explain the faculty of imagination is the realm of light. This is the light-emanating *phantastikon pneuma* (translated into Latin as *spiritus phantasticus*). This powerful and luminous spirit irradiates beams of light that allow dreams to be seen during and within the nocturnal theater of sleep. The *phantastikon pneuma* lives between the rational and non-rational worlds. This *pneuma* is the powerful agent that captures the *eidola* that wanders throughout the universe, and their construction in the mosaic of a dream metamorphoses our understanding of reality.[35]

Oneiric images show the possibility of transformation, a translation that makes visible the invisible. A dream is the first step toward an understanding of the invisible. Father Florensky considers dreams to be something on the threshold that joins and separates the visible sphere of the real and the invisible sphere of the imaginal. Dreams are our sensing and making sense of the imaginal because they enable a connection between the visible and the invisible. They are the inverse perspective that allows the translation of the imaginal into the real.

Florensky sees the dreams of the night as psychological, but the hypnopompic dream, which is the awakening dream, is the one that accomplishes the translation from the sphere of the imaginal to the sphere of the real, and vice versa. A dream, in itself, can last a short instant in time, but the corresponding dreamtime can last from seconds to millennia. In dreams, the speed of the vector of time can be infinite and its direction can be inverted by moving from the future to the past. This inversion of time is essential to Florensky's understanding of the role of dreams as icons that hang on the wall, enclosing the imaginal. This inversion corresponds to the inverse perspective of the icons looming on the iconostasis of Orthodox churches. Dreams and holy icons partake of the same ontology. Dreams and icons have the same causal inverse time. For Florensky, dreams are comparable to holy icons and holy icons are solidified dreams. Dreams are gates that cleave the imaginal and the real. Florensky provides an example of the causal inverse time of the dream as an opening in a wall enclosing the imaginal by telling the story of a person who dreamed of being active during the French Revolution. After intensely long and complicated adventures, this early morning dreamer finds himself in front of a Revolutionary Court. At the end of the proceedings, being sentenced to death by guillotine, he wakes up with the cold iron bar of the headboard pressing on his neck.[36] The inverse vector of time in dreams is a demonstration of how *tempus fugit* backward in the imaginal sphere.

> In the dream, time runs, and runs fast, toward the present, inverse from the awake consciousness ... We are brought onto the plane of an imaginary space, through which the same event perceived from the plane of the real space is seen imaginally as if it was taking place in teleological time.[37]

There are two cogent imagining elements that define the icons' vectoriality in inverse constructions within the imaginal. The powerful tools performing the inversion are the inverse perspective and the use of gold in both the background and the *lumeggiature*. Gold corresponds to the innate light of the dream, while the inverse time corresponds to the inverse perspective.

Florensky dedicated several reflections to the topic of the inverse perspective (*Obratnaya Perspektiva*). In a remarkable essay dedicated specifically to this ambiguous geometry, and in his lectures at the VKhUTEMAS (1923–1924), Florensky pointed out that through inverse perspective we are looking within the imaginal sphere of human understanding. In this essay, Florensky attempted to demonstrate the existence of inverse perspective. He called attention to the so-called perspective mistakes that can be seen in all the representations before the affirmation of the *costruzione legittima* and a few others, after the legitimization of this monocular view that took place during the Italian Renaissance.

The geometry of the inverse perspective is utterly visual and relates directly to light: not to external light, but internal light. Arthur Zajonic, a physicist interested in quantum optics, points out that there are two lights of vision: one exterior, the other interior. To explain this duality, he refers to clinical cases of individuals who were born blind and, after having regained perfect physical sight, yet cannot see what is in front of them.[38] Zajonic proves that this happens because they do not have the interior light. They see the objects but they do not know how to envision them. There are no images in their mind. He describes that they come to know objects only through touch. They have tactile images rather than visual images. The simple vision of an object is not enough to build an image of it. To have vision entails much more than having a functioning organ of vision: it is essential to know how to construct the image.

To demonstrate how the traditional perspective of the *costruzione legittima* fails to recognize vision as a necessary component of representation, Florensky analyzes four famous engravings in *Underweysung der Messung mit dem Zirckel und Richtscheyt ...* (1525), by Albrecht Dürer (1471–1528), showing the construction mechanisms of the *costruzione legittima*.[39] One of these illustrations has been misinterpreted lately by many interested in the gaze and the byproducts of the "scopic regime" that presently dominates the theater of a visual culture, which does not know how to visualize.

The first illustration of the sequence produced by Dürer shows a bedroom where an artist is making a perspectival portrait—probably a legitimate likeness—using a portable perspective machine. This portable machine consists of a table on which a pane of glass or a sheet of transparent oiled paper was set vertically into a frame. An adjustable contrivance holds the draftsman in a fixed position in front of it. This machine is a crude empirical rendition of the *mathesis* of the *costruzione legittima*.

The second illustration is the one that has been misread and misapplied by the pseudo-philosophical-gazers. It shows a working table on which a dead-looking lady reveals her nature through a "Lucinda" to a draftsman who is going to transcribe his view onto a piece of paper on which he has traced the grid of the Lucinda. In this case, the Lucinda is a square frame holding a grid of strings that divides the view into 36 squares. The eye of the draftsman is kept in the required position by a phallic miniature obelisk. There is already a reference in this machine to a coordinate system that will eliminate sight from the site of the perspective drawing.

The third illustration shows a bedroom—a dim room—where an artist is reproducing an urn on a luminous oily sheet using a singular apparatus, an optical pipe connected to a string fastened to a ring on the wall. In this case the artist's eye is still part of the process. It deliberately follows the tracing of lines by looking inside the narrow pipe, but it is no longer part of the construction. The real point of construction of the objective vision is beyond the head of the artist. It is located in a ring secured on a wall behind the artist.

The fourth illustration, the final and most explicit of the series, shows a narrow room with a pair of artists and a pair of windows. One window is open while the other is closed. One artist is standing and the other is sitting. In the center is a lute sitting on a huge working table and a special kind of apparatus where a movable Lucinda has been coupled with a frame holding a drawing sheet. The perspectival string is connected to a ring on the wall and is kept in tension by a counterweight, which is maneuvered by a wand held by the standing artist. The sitting artist uses an orthogonal coordinated device to record the points of the construction of the image. The point is then marked on the movable panel holding the paper for the drawing. No human or divine vision is needed in this perspectival construction. The two people presented by Dürer are both visually impaired artists making a Braille rendition of a lute. With their machine they can reproduce any three-dimensional object in a jiffy and probably with fewer distractions than two sighted artists executing the same task.

A powerful commentary on Dürer's drawing machines is a canvas painted by a Sicilian architect practicing the surrealistic vice. Entitled *Colloquio* (1970), this oil painting by Fabrizio Clerici (1913–1993) shows all the drawing machines presented by Dürer conflated in a super-drawing machine located within a perspectival box.[40] The characters presented are a mask and an eye. The eye is the eye of the draftsman and the mask is the object to be represented. Behind the mask is a mirror, revealing the other side of the mask. The converse side of the mask is visible to us as well as to the sublimated eye of the draftsman. The incidental presence of the mirror delegitimizes this view of perspective and projects the potentiality of this super-drawing machine as a key to the realm of dreams.

Although skeptical about creating a "key to dreams," Peirce was confident in the power of dreams as sources of meaning for human reasoning:[41] "A meaning is the association of a word with images, its dream exiting power."[42]

For Peirce, dreams are images devoid of any reference to actuality;[43] they are tools able to call up images from the realm of the imaginal. Vincent Colapietro, a scholar of pragmatism and psychoanalysis, has pointed out the importance of dreams in the philosophy and semiotics of Peirce:

While taken individually these references to dreams [by Peirce] may seem of slight significance, taken together, they add up to something of deep, if not obvious, importance. Moreover, when these references are connected with texts stressing the importance [of] imagination for inquiry, they cease to appear incidental. Finally, the fact that these references are found in some of Peirce's most important early writings as well as in some of his most brilliant later pieces contributes to our sense that dreams are not peripheral to Peirce's account of meaning (especially of how meaning emerges and evolves in the context of inquiry).[44]

For Peirce, icons are the most powerful expression of dreams:

Icons are so completely substituted for their objects as hardly to be distinguished from them ... So in contemplating a painting there is a moment when we lose the consciousness that it is not the thing, the distinction of the real and the copy disappears, and it is for the moment a pure dream—not any particular existence, and yet not general. At that moment we are contemplating an *icon*.[45]

An icon, a "vagueness," is a dream. An icon does not draw any distinction between the self and the Other.[46] "It is all one with the Object."[47] An icon as a "magic" representation constitutes and replaces any object. It is the perfect tool for our mental motions. Our mental images are icons and working with icons is the most powerful tool for communicating in a constructive way.[48] Imagining and imaging are, iconically speaking, the same activity, since both of them make visible the invisible processes of the human mind within its cosmic framework. The phenomenology of images is one of mediation and it is accomplished by what Peirce called "Existential Graphs."[49] These graphic tools are effective icons transcribing facts in such a way that "experimenting on them, [is like] experiencing the thing."[50] As conjectural tools, Graphs are written on the sheet of existence. Dreams and graphs perform the same function since both are illuminated by the *lume naturale*.[51] Both Peirce's and Florensky's icons are divinatory processes that originate in the realm of the imaginal.

Notes

1 Shakespeare (1892: Act 4, Scene 1: 212, 217). [Cited in one of Frascari's sketchbooks for the Dream House (see Figure 74 in the Portfolio).]
2 [McCay, W. (1907-09-22) "Little Nemo in Slumberland". 38.8. *The New York Herald*. Available at: http://digitalcomicmuseum.com/preview/index.php?did=8851&page=38 (accessed March, 13, 2016).] [See Figures 47, 51 in the Portfolio.]
3 [Aphorism #237: "Unser Leben ist kein Traum – aber es soll und wird vielleicht einer werden." Novalis (1977: III, 281.]
4 [Latin for "after dinner".]

5 The connection between wine, food and dreaming, on the one hand, is a topic present in the writing of the great oneirocritics such as Aristotle (384–322 BC), Artemidorus of Daldis (lived in the second century), Synesius of Cyrene (ca.375–414), and Girolamo Cardano (1501–1576). On the other hand, this association is also a regular topic among the great gourmet critics such as Jean Anthelme Brillat-Savarin (1755–1826) and Pellegrino Artusi (1820–1911) or the great dieticians Hippocrates (460–between 375 and 351 BC), Galen (129–c.216), and Alvise Cornaro (1484–1566).
6 Novalis (2007: 57).
7 Novalis (1993: 82). [Wulf and Borsari (2007: 481).]
8 Gregory (1955).
9 Ibid. Lindberg (2007: 210–213).
10 According to Isidore of Seville:
> The ancients called every edifice (*aedificum*) a building (*aedes*). Some think "building" (*aedes*) took its name from "eating" (*edere*) something, giving an example from Plautus (cf. The Little Carthaginian 529): "If I had called you into the building (*aedes*) for lunch." Hence also edifice (*aedificium*), because it was first "made for eating" (*ad edendum factum*).
>
> (2006: 308)

For further information on the relationship between food and architecture, see Collins (1998), Frascari (1986), and Kunze (1994; 1996).
11 [Alberti (1997: 294, 302–303, 305, 309, 312).]
12 Monteil (1964: 170).
13 Alberti (1966a: 811).
14 Gordon (1949: 152–178).
15 Carême, Marie-Antonin and Fayot, Charles Frédéric (1842). Carême was the sixth child of an impoverished stonemason. He was abandoned in the street at the age of 11 after a plentiful meal. He found his way to the back door of a public eating house where he became one of the most important *chefs de cuisine*. In this position he could afford to turn down a permanent job offer from Czar Alexander of Russia, for whom he had catered a series of feasts. Carême, however, did prepare a book of designs for landmarks he thought were necessary to improve the architectural environment of Saint Petersburg, which he dedicated to the Czar.
16 The term generally used is macaronic language, but its inventor, Teofilo Folengo (also known under the pseudonym of Merlinus Cocaius), talks clearly of macaronic art and not macaronic language (Chiesa 1993: 57).
17 Frascari (1991: 13–32; 2003: 41–45).
18 Although, through several courses of decanting, editing, and rewriting, my language might have lost its original macaronic make-up, it has not forfeited its macaronic essence. The ideas mustering up this work are genuinely macaronic.
19 A non-reformed friar, Teofilo Folengo (1496–1544) was born in Cipata near Mantua in Italy on the other side of the Lago Inferiore, in front of Pietole (Andes), the place where Virgil was born. He used the name *Merlinus Cocaius* to sign his macaronic writing. The most famous among them is the *Baldus*. Folengo himself invented the word "macaronic." His *Macaronic Book* (*Liber Macaronices*), published in 1517, explains (2nd edn., 1521) that the macaronic art is so called from *macaroni*, which is "*quoddam pulmentum farina, caseo, botiro compaginatum, grossum, rude, et rusticanum*" ("a thick and unrefined rustic dish made of a mixture of flour, cheese and butter") (Folengo 1882: LXXV; 1911: vol. II, 284).
20 Lanternari (1981: 94–126).
21 States (1988).
22 The alchemy between architectural theory and practice can be understood by looking at the two red-headed figures in an illustration of the *Aurora Consurgens*—an alchemic manuscript of the fourteenth century. It is a perfect depiction of the union of theory and practice as the body of architecture. Architecture is analogous to these alchemic Siamese twins, who share the same digestive system and reproductive apparatus, even though they have separate conceiving organs and different mouths. This hermaphroditic image can be read as a representation of the complete identification between theoretical abstraction and empirical depiction. The hermaphroditic sum invalidates the complete absolutism of each one of the

two conceptions. Theory and practice are projected in a temporizing way that is extra-temporal. Theory and practice are metabolized into architecture, during that moment between the end of night and the beginning of day, when Carnival and Lent cannot fight each other.
23 This concept is presented in a dialogue entitled *Dialogo Facetissimo et Ridicolissimo*, dating from 1525. Ruzzante wrote many pieces to be presented at the house of Alvise Cornaro—mostly known for his treatise on sober life—who was interested in an architecture for a *vita beata*. For the role of architecture for a *vita beata* during Ruzzante's times, see Barbieri (1983). [See a recent translation of the *Vita Beata*: Cornaro (2014).]
24 [Tatarkiewicz (1976: 2). *Eudaimonia* can be loosely translated as contentment.]
25 North (1979).
26 Filarete (1965; 1972).
27 Peirce (1931–1958: CP 6.286: 189).
28 Peirce (1982: MS 614: 5).
29 Synesius of Cyrene (ca 370–414), a Platonic philosopher-bishop whose acceptance of Christianity was provisional and remained secondary to his commitment to Neoplatonism, wrote an influential work on the phenomenon of dreams before converting to Christianity. This work embodies a theory of allegory together with a study of the efficacy of dreams for the art of divination.
30 A notable figure in the history of logic, mathematics, metrology, and founder of Pragmatism, Charles Sanders Peirce (1839–1914) is nowadays a major figure in the academic realm of semiotics, a philosopher combining the reality of science with experience. However, during his lifetime, Peirce was a neglected genius, a pauper, and a recluse.
31 Born in 1892, Pavel Florensky, Russian theoretician of arts, theologian, and mathematician taught at the VKhUTEMAS in Moscow, and was an active intellectual figure during the Russian Revolution until 1933 when he was deported to a concentration camp. He was executed near Leningrad in 1937. Florensky's main concern was not in philosophy (filosofia) but in philokalia (filokalia). Very few documents are available in English on him, see the *Bibliographic Note* in Bychkov (1993: 101).
32 Synesius MDCXXXIII.
33 For the connection between Synesius and Artemidorus, see Le Goff (1988: 234).
34 [Cardano (1989: 11).]
35 Synesius (2014: 6–7, 145–151).
36 Florensky (1977: 28–30).
37 Ibid.: 30. [Frascari translated this passage. He might have used the first worldwide translation of "Iconostasis," which was in Italian (Florensky 1977) and of which he owned a copy in his library. Frascari also owned the first English translation of Florensky's text that was published in 1996 (Florensky 1996: 41).]
38 Zajonic (1993: 16–17).
39 Dürer (1977).
40 [Goldin (1999: 108); Troisi (2007). See also Mantura and Millesimi (1990: 111), in the MFLC.]
41 Peirce (1931–1958: CP 6.423).
42 Ibid.: CP 4.56.
43 Ibid.: CP 3.459.
44 Colapietro (1988: 72–73).
45 Peirce (1931–1958: CP 3.362).
46 Ibid.: CP 5.75.
47 Ibid.: CP 4.572.
48 Ibid.: CP 2.270.
49 [Roberts (1973: 20).]
50 Peirce (1931–1958: CP 4.86).
51 Ibid.: CP 1.80; 5.604.

2
TELLING AND CASTING

Marco Frascari

When practicing architecture, to dream is to make visible the invisible within the constructed world. The dream is the place where the ineffable is restated into a visible fable. To dream is a tectonic activity and within it takes place the construction of the intangible within a tangible world. Since biblical times, the telling of dreams has also been regarded as an act of casting. The narration of oneiric events has always been seen as an act of forecasting or an act of back-casting,[1] since we inject ourselves in our dreams all the time.

My visual and verbal fable of an ineffable house is the result of architectural labor and the narration of a dream. This "dream house" is a chimera composed of a project, a subject, an object, and also an inject. My drawings and the companion text result from the intertwining of these four procedures. These four words ending with 'ject' express launching acts of initiation that share a common etymological connection: they describe various acts of casting.[2] Project and object are parallel acts of casting forward, whereas subject is a casting beneath and injection is a casting into. These four ject-ending acts are an integral part of the architectural realm and the aim of these casting games, just like the purpose of dreams, is to cope with the fear of death and time.[3] The ontological nature of these multiple acts of casting is a process of fear removal. Architects forecast buildings; consequently, their designing is a project, an object and an inject resulting from the translations of their dreams. Through their multi-directional casting architects operate like dreamers who are able to exist within their own mental images. They inject themselves together with real and virtual clients within their projections of future buildings; *bona fide* architects deal with the objective and subjective presence of architecture. Architects exercise the capacity of waking up to their dreams through drawings and construction.

These architectural castings are acts of representation whose origin and nature can be explained as magical acts producing magic signs. Outside of anthropological studies, magic is a word that is no longer used in its technical meaning. It is generally used to indicate non-sensible practices of the human mind or its poetic expressions. Regardless of this negative condition, it is essential to give back to architectural signs and designs their magical status.

The results of the casting acts of architecture are magic signs traced on the ground or on the paper. Architectural dreams are expressed in drawings, a mix of conventional and natural signs. These drawings become magic tools. They translate dreams into a constructed world. As in primitive magic, they are not only an externalization of desire, but also practical signs of imagination.[4] An architectural sign or its expression in a drawing is magical, and, following philosopher Jacques Maritain:

> I call a sign "magical" when it occurs in a different functional state, in which it is a sign *for the imagination* regarded as the supreme or dominating controller of the whole of psychical life or of the whole life of culture. Whether the sign is in itself sensible or intelligible, it speaks ultimately to the powers of the imagination, it refers ultimately to a psychic regime immersed in the vital ocean of the imagination.[5]

These magical signs can be found in the true drawings, not the blueprints and the renderings that flood the commercial world of architecture. The semiotic of dreamed architecture is in the magic of drawings. These magical drawings are what Florensky and Peirce call icons.[6] Architectural drawings are icons where the gold background shows within the cut walls of the horizontal and vertical sections of edifices. These magic drawings, true icons of architecture, are expressions of architects' dreams, constituting the *mundus imaginalis* of architecture. The theory of the *mundus imaginalis* is closely bound up with a theory of imaginative cognition and of the imaginative function. This is truly a central position, a mediating place, owing to both the median and the mediating positions of the *mundus imaginalis*. The immediate mediating of the cognitive function ascribable to imagining takes place within the *mundus imaginalis*. The cognitive function of imagination provides the foundation for a rigorous analogical knowledge that permits us to avoid the dilemma of current rationalism, which only gives us a choice between two banal dualistic terms of either "matter" or "mind." The eminent Islamic scholar, Henry Corbin (1903–1978) defines the *mundus imaginalis* as an *intermondo*, a space where visual imagination establishes true and real thoughts: an imaginative perception and an imaginative knowledge that is an imaginative consciousness.[7] The *mundus imaginalis*: a world that is ontologically as real as the world of the senses and that of the intellect. This *mundus imaginalis* is an imaginal landscape. Corbin coined the term "imaginal" to discuss the realm of the cognitive imagination to avoid that this "world of images in suspense" be confused with the realm of the merely imaginary.[8] This world is ontologically above the world of the senses, and below the pure intelligible world.[9]

The validity of dreams depends upon this imaginal landscape. This world requires its own faculty of perception, namely, an imaginative power, a faculty with a cognitive function, a noetic value that is as real as that of sense perception or intellectual intuition. Its existence is a basis for demonstrating the validity of dreams. This world should not be confused with "fantasy," which is nothing but an outpouring of "imaginings."[10] The imaginal dream world of architecture can be explained by making a parallel to images in mirrors. In dreams and in drawings, buildings materialize as an image materializes in a mirror. The material of the mirror is not the substance of the reflected image, since it is always glass and silver independent of the reflected material. However, the image gives the subtle body of the reflected object and in this reflection the cognitive power of imagination is established as rigorous analogical knowledge.[11]

Within this imaginal world, the task of the architect is not to duplicate in graphic form a present reality (survey drawings),[12] or future reality (design drawings), but to offer a deeper understanding of the architectonic of material and numinous meaning through synchronic and diachronic views. The task is to translate the vision on paper and then into a built form. The same mixture of synchronicity and diachronicity, the same possibility of different spatio-temporalities, the same desire to make visible what is invisible, the same magic of dreaming are manifested in two specific graphic representations of architectural design: the plan and the section.

The contents of plans and sections integrate diachronically that which is present in a visible building, but is itself invisible in a synchronic manner. Different spaces are represented within the same framework concatenating in one vision a chain of different visions. Metaphorically speaking, the drawing of vertical and horizontal sections (the latter are generally called plans) represents the coalescence of the architectural dream, the writing and the reading of a possible architecture, in its imaginal realm. Presuming architecture ensues from an intangible super-faculty that arises from the property of a designing mind able to present graphically a future building by processes of imitation, the enigma of the spatial synchronicity and diachronicity of architectural sections presents a deceptive question. Entrenched in the theory of imitation is the magical belief in the identity of the represented with the representation: a belief that naturally results in attributing powers and capabilities to the likeness, which in a rationally ordered world would belong only to primary phenomena. However, if I consider the extraordinary capacity of architects to imagine, or better, to dream up a building by tracing horizontal and vertical sections of it, the enigma becomes real. It is the enigma of divination. Architectural divination is the tracing of the vestiges of phylogenetic and ontogenetic memory onto a piece of paper that will be translated into the constructed world. Architectural divination is a reflection through the tracing of sections. The tracing of a profile is the way of determining the character of a building that acquires its meaning not only through imitation but through the faculty of daydreaming in sectional vision. The phenomenal power of this imaginal faculty, a mirror

(Figure 62 in the Portfolio) of architecture, is clearly described by Steven Millhauser, in a passage of his short novel, *Little Kingdoms*:

> During three days a year, at the height of summer, the position of the sun and the position of the cliff combine to permit the castle to be reflected in the river. It is said that staring at the reflection one can see inside the castle, which reveals the precise disposition of its arched doorways, high halls, and secret chambers, the pattern of hidden stairways, the shadows cast by flagons and bunches of grapes on abandoned banquet tables, and there, high in the tower, the Princess pacing wearily, while far below, in the depths of the immaculate reflection, so deep that it is beneath the river itself, a shadow stirs in the corner of the dungeon.[13]

The requirements of the play

> Great is the architect who knows how to walk with the mind in the edifice yet to be erected.
> Simone Stratico[14]

A dream modifies the axis of time and space. In a dream, an *architectural vision* generates an itinerary that is not following the only possible path of the shortest distance between two points. An architectural dream is a *vision* of a building that cannot be and yet has within itself all the components of a possible reality. Dreams are not virtual reality; they are real illusions. They are illusions in the true etymological meaning of the Latin expression: *in ludere*, in play. When I am dreaming, I am playing. When the dream ends, I am banned from playing: *de-ludere*. The conclusion, the end of the play for architects, is the transcription in drawings, hopefully followed by the translation of the dream into a construction. In these illusions, reality is not imitated nor merely copied in a representation. During these dreams, identification takes place. Consequently, the self takes place in the action of becoming the other. This transformation of the self prevents its exclusion from the game and accordingly the self of the architect enters all subsequent transfigurations and renderings of a buildable dream. This is an unconscious process by which an architect transfers the response appropriate to a particular into a constructive mode.

As mentioned earlier, the work of Peirce plays a dominant influence on my design. The design of the house-tower is a 'play' that started in odd half-hour increments and has been converted into a 'scientific' study: a musing storytelling for the architects of the next millennium. Musement for Peirce is not a solitary meditation but a pragmatic habit and poietic that can be translated into graphic form.[15]

[Musement] is a certain agreeable occupation of mind ... [it] may take either the form of [1] aesthetic contemplation, or that of [2] distant castle-building (whether in Spain or within one's moral training), or that of [3] considering some wonder in one of the Universes, or [4] some connection between two of the three, with speculation concerning its cause.[16]

Wonder "consists in [the] active power to establish connections between objects, especially between objects in different universes."[17]

The faculty of musement is the art of dwelling in the imaginal since it is a faculty of thought tending to produce a belief, which is a reason for action. Musement is a highly tectonic activity since it is the construction of castles in the air reconciling the individual microcosms with the macrocosms of a society. It is a testing of imaginal structures through the disciplined procedure of visual reasoning:

> People who build castles in the air do not, for the most part accomplish much, it is true, but every man who does accomplish great things is given to building elaborate castles in the air and then painfully copying them on solid ground.[18]

The building of castles in the air is an activity constantly present in the tradition of architecture. Within the tradition of architectural treatises the most powerful castles in the air were those built by Giovanni Battista Montano (1534–1621).[19] To be more precise, they are temples built in the air. They are messages expressed through images, as Manfredo Tafuri has pointed out.[20]

Before embarking upon the narration of my dream, let me serve you up a thoughtful appetizer, an axiomatic statement and operative principle, which will prepare your mind for the savory main course of dream architecture.

> *Architects*
> *should never write and talk*
> *about their own architecture,*
> *and should never show it*
> *to other architects,*
> *or soon-to-be*
> *architects.*

This singular principle should be regulated by the professional organizations. Architects should explain their work only to clients but never to those engaged in the same or cognate professions. As intellectuals engaged in a constructive reality, they should talk and write about their theories and practices, always using someone else's architecture. Nevertheless, an interesting corollary must be added to this architectural principle of constructive unselfishness, an act of transmogrifying into the Other.

> *Architects can and must*
> *draw, write and talk*
> *about their own*
> *architectural*
> *dreams.*

In other words, they should present their castles built in the air. First, let's discuss the above-mentioned principle and then the corollary. On the one hand, the principle derives from a sound Vitruvian doctrine of Epicurean origin denying the role of *prima donna* to architects. In his treatise, Vitruvius mentions only one of his built projects, a basilica in Fano, and makes a point of complaining about his colleagues, prone to the unethical habit of professional vainglory, continuously pontificating on their own constructions, swanking and swelling about their own designs.[21]

A typical Florentine gainsayer, Alberti disliked most of the Vitruvius text written in a macaronic language that seemed Greek to the Romans and Latin to the Greeks. Nevertheless, Alberti, when writing his treatise on architecture, followed the same ethical principle and never mentioned his own architectural masterpieces.[22] It is logical to attribute to this modesty the reason why there is not a building tradition called "Albertian Architecture." On the other hand, the corollary is an unavoidable pendant and it can be easily deduced by looking carefully at Andrea Palladio's *Four Books on Architecture* (1570).[23] Palladio was the first architect to have an architectural tradition named after him—Palladian Architecture. Before this, the identification of a building tradition rested on the basis of nations and places (Doric, Gothic, Roman, etc.). In this treatise, the rustic Paduan, Palladio, talks profusely about his own either built or unbuilt buildings. This may seem to make him the perfect candidate for being a *prima donna* architect. However, examining carefully Palladio's *Four Books*, one realizes that he is not actually describing his own built buildings. He is not talking about the buildings that he had carefully and painstakingly, albeit often only partially, built. Palladio elucidates by narration and xylography the edifices he had dreamed up, the architectural visions of his *mundus imaginalis*, or, in other words, his castles in the air.

A simple and quick-witted procedure can be used to prove this very essential point by randomly selecting any plan of the private Vicentine palaces presented in the *Four Books*, and by placing it over a map of Vicenza. Immediately one ascertains that what Palladio had published is quite different from the urban reality of the constructed palace. To build Palladio's dream-palace, the family commissioning the palazzo would have had to be from the ruling party of the city government. Only from this dominant political position, could this family expropriate all the necessary ground required to erect such a paramount edifice. Palladio designed several city palaces for most of the leading families, representing all the possible factions of the oligarchic government of Vicenza. He was the favorite architect of every political group ruling the city. His architectural vision of classical temples transmuted for human habitation embodied the angelic longings of an Italic presence, establishing the urban configuration of Vicenza.[24] Palladio designed gigantic palaces but built only fragments of them. It would not have been possible to complete these dreamt-up mammoth palaces since his clients did not manage in the end to own enough land in the city. Another simple test is to compare the ground floor of the Vicentine Basilica, which was a public building, as it is presented in the treatise, with a survey drawing of the real condition of the actual building. It is evident that in his *Four Books*, Palladio did not represent the built entelechy but his dreams. The oneiric affection of this angelic architecture is attested by the use and abuse of the *Four Books*' edifices within the canonical iconography of the Venetian Capricci, a late eighteenth-century speculative Venice by Giovanni Antonio Canal, known as Canaletto (1697–1768) and Marco Ricci (1676–1730). It is a dreamed city that neither existed nor ever will exist.[25]

Another powerful proof of the dream-like nature of the plans of the Palladian palaces is found in the analysis of Palazzo Chiericati in Vicenza (1550), elaborated upon by Edward Casey in his philosophical discussion of the concept of place.[26] Casey's phenomenological understanding is a perfect demonstration of how the published plan of the palace is a dream, and how a dream is an architectural place. Palazzo Chiericati was not completed during Palladio's lifetime. The building was completed and enlarged during the eighteenth century. Casey uses this palace to discuss his concepts of walking alongside and walking around a place. Unfortunately for his own precision in scholarship but fortunately for the dream-building presented by Palladio, Casey discusses the images given in the *Four Books* as if he was experiencing a real construction. He dreams about walking around the building, ignoring the additional work done during the eighteenth century that makes it completely impossible to walk around the edifice. Furthermore, it is clear from Casey's text that he did visit Vicenza and he stopped by Piazza Matteotti, in front of the palace and under its loggia. Nevertheless, the dream embodied in Palladio's illustration is so powerful that Casey forgets his real experience of the place and he is completely seized by Palladio's dream. This does not take away anything from Casey's philosophical journey and his definition of the concept of *locus*, but it indicates that architectural dreams are *loci* so powerful that they can alter the memory of a very good philosopher and scholar. As another philosopher has pointed out "dreams are … digested, processed representations" of the imagination.[27]

The incubation

Omnis festinatio ex parte diaboli est.
[All haste is of the devil.]

Let us proceed slowly towards the main course and begin to single out the essence and the sapience of architectural thinking by avoiding the trap of envisioning dream architecture as an image of selfish and egotistical desires. To dream architecture means to conceive a building through an act of dreaming that is the longing of architects who are not interested in a one-person show. To dream architecture does not mean to conceive "the house of my dreams" as a conjecture of wish fulfillment. Avoiding this too narrow interpretation of the constructed world, ennobling architects can foster an architecture capable of changing the quality of life in an invisible but often touted way by constructing the "houses of dreams" or their "dreams of houses." Architects must privilege the unveiling architecture as a kind of philosophical divination, a divination by memory. Architectural divination takes place in a dream by using the gauge of the body to forecast or adumbrate possible constructions, since architecture is above all a maternal and therapeutic enterprise, which takes place through dream incubation, that is then expressed in drawings.[28]

Drawings are analogical procedures. Any analogy is a construction of images. Without an analogy, we cease to comprehend what we have seen. We need analogical thinking to really see "something." Analogy is the construction of images that give concrete coherence to highly abstract thoughts. Analogy is the vital spirit of any paradigm, perhaps even its basic organizing feature, because analogy is predictive. Analogical procedures, in architectural design, are not just pleasing comparisons. Analogy provides poetic boundaries to theoretical propositions and helps architects to push against these confines. A dream is analogical and, consequently, it is predictive. In almost every important literary work of antiquity, the interpretation of dreams substantially fosters the process of decision-making. The oldest interpretations of dreams are found in an Egyptian papyrus dated ca. 2000 BC. The sophist, Antiphon (ca. 470–411 BC), wrote the first Greek treatise of dream interpretation, and Pythagoras (ca. 570–ca. 495 BC) was the first to introduce the use of controlled sleep and dreaming as therapeutic tools. Among these oneirocritics, Artemidorus of Daldis was a most influential interpreter of dreams in Antiquity. He wrote a treatise consisting of five books on the topic of dreams and he sorted dreams into five categories.[29] These were later used by Ambrosius Theodosius Macrobius (fl. ca. 400) and formed the standard classification until Freud's work.[30] The Artemidorian oneiric categories are:[31]

1   *somnium,* a dream showing the future;

2 *insomnium,* a dream displaying the present;
3 *phantasma,* a dream demonstrating aberrant events;
4 *oraculum,* a dream manifesting an oral message from an authority or a god;
5 *visio,* a dream of a possible reality.

To further articulate the categories, Artemidorus distinguished dreams into five orders of signification: personal, strange, common, public, and cosmic; and six principles of dream interpretation: nature, law, tradition, time, art, and name. Analogically, the same categories, orders and principles can be applied to the interpretation and production of graphic expressions in architectural work. According to this group of divisive representations, architectural drawings can be sorted as follows:

1 drawings showing the future: the plan and section of a building to be;[32]
2 drawings showing the present: measured drawings showing images of an existing building;
3 drawings showing aberrant events: graphic analysis of disastrous conditions;
4 drawings of future construction handed out from an authority or a god, for example, the drawings of the temple given by God to Moses; dreams that initiated the erection of many medieval buildings;[33]
5 drawings showing a dream of reality, for example, Soane–Gandy's drawings of the Bank of England as a ruined building.[34]

These drawings can be further classified as:

1 personal: for example, Le Corbusier's matutinal paintings;[35]
2 strange: for example, Filarete's illustrations in his treatise;[36]
3 common: for example, Durand's axial graphic constructions;[37]
4 public: for example, Palladio's woodcuts for his treatise;[38]
5 cosmic: for example, Bruno Taut's watercolors for the glass architecture.[39]

A represented design can also be based on an interpretation of architecture according to the previously mentioned six principles of nature, law, tradition, time, art, and name. An analogous terminology is used by Vitruvius when explaining the design of temples.[40]

Francesco Colonna (ca. 1433–1527) stated the analogous nature between architectural imagination and dreams, in a critical and energetic manner in his extraordinary *rebus opus.* Carrying an idiosyncratic and lengthy Greek-Latin title, the *Hypnerotomachia Poliphili, ubi humana omnia non nisi somnium esse docet, atque obiter plurima scitu sane quam digne commemorat* was published by Aldo Manuzio in Venice in 1499. This has been one of the most influential texts in architectural theory. An in-folio volume with 170 woodcuts, this beautifully illustrated and printed text narrates the story of a dream within a dream full of architectural visions, using a juicy macaronic language, both graphic and verbal. This macaronic tale presents dreams as hypothetical tools of design for the unknown, and as important mental instruments of acquiring knowledge. The allegorical nature of the tale stresses this concept. The beloved Polia, the female character of the story, is a personification of knowledge. Her lover Poliphilus, the double dreamer, is desperately seeking her.[41] In reading the *Hypnerotomachia Poliphili*, it is essential to understand that Poliphilus' love for Polia metaphorically represents not only the love for knowledge, but also the love of thinking. Poliphilus, the slumber-jack of the *Hypnerotomachia Poliphili* fell asleep a first time dreaming of being lost and bewildered in a forest where he plunged into a deep sleep for a second time. During this double poetic stupor, he dreamt a rewarding architectural adventure. Descriptions of double dreams are rarely told in Western culture and Colonna uses the device in his dream-tale to indicate that it is not a wish fulfillment of Poliphilus' personal desire for Polia, instead it is a dream of knowledge twice removed from an egotistic reality. Images of dreams are closely linked to images of thought. The act of dreaming is the creation of a *locus* of thought; it is what in Italian is called *far mente locale*, which is a form of reasoning done in a regional manner. Any dream is an act of construction that must be construed. Dreams are *loci* of narration developed within the labyrinth of reflections between the physical and metaphysical possibilities of things. These oneiric *loci* of reflection are the places where geometry, philosophy, and architecture discover their common origin or "nature," i.e. their roots in human imagination. The world of dreams is a living forest in which fantasy dwells and solves the riddle of architectural corporeality.

Little Nemo in Slumberland, an astounding comic strip charmingly created by Winsor McCay (1867–1934), is another demonstration of the strong ties existing among dreams, infraordinary reality and architectural imagination (see Figures 47, 51 in the Portfolio).[42] Son of a lumberjack, essentially a self-taught graphic artist, McCay developed a dainty and precious comic strip based on the reoccurring dreams of a little Victorian boy named Nemo.[43] The adventures of Little Nemo take place in a peculiar dream-place, Slumberland. In this dreamland, the great architecture of Classical America prevails in a powerful surrealistic dimension. In his short dreams—a tabloid-page long—Nemo has the most visually wielding and intriguing nocturnal adventures. Changes of scale in the urban environments and continuously metamorphosing edifices dominate the architectural scene in Slumberland.[44] This alchemic and weekly mélange of a recurring architectural dream is the paradigmatic environment for understanding how, in any architect, there is always a little childhood self present. This childhood self is an essential part of any extended quest for architecture.

This *imago* of architecture, an idealized image of architectural bodies formed during childhood and persisting unconsciously into adulthood, is the motor of any successful design. As the Pythagorean mind of Vitruvius pointed out, in the First Book of his treatise, the education of an architect is a slow process that begins during childhood.[45] Little Nemo's architecturally overloaded dreams point to this beginning and, in themselves, they are part of the slow process of image construction required by proper architecture.

In the surreal nature of dreaming we must discover not the power of the extraordinary, but rather what Georges Perec (1936–1982) called the "infraordinary."[46] In architecture, the infraordinary is the source of detailing; it is the principal *locus* of meaningful events in architectural artifacts. The links between dream and the infraordinary essence of architectural imagination are unequivocally and intensely substantial; while the connections that architects and dreamers have traditionally made are ill-defined and tautological. To overcome these setbacks, I must contemplate dreams as a mode of thought. Architectural dreams are recurring dreams, which allow a slow construction of construed reality. They are a quest for an embodiment of the natural human thought patterns in stone, brick, glass, plaster, wood, and steel. Ordinary materials become extraordinary when emerging in the reality of construction if they have been part of a recurring dream.

The same surrealistically slow ambit was present in the dreams that originated the design of the *loci aesthetici* prior to the change of the end of the first millennium.[47] One of these *loci aesthetici*, which belongs to a great design tradition based on a dream, was narrated in an anonymous chronicle. One night the saints Peter, Paul, and Stephen appeared in a dream to a paralyzed monk, Gunzo, who was asleep in the infirmary at the monastery of Cluny. Using proper tracing tools, the three saints described in detail to the poor monk God's plan for a new cathedral. The spokesman of the group, Saint Peter, ordered Gunzo to report and to describe the plans for the new edifice to his ruling Abbot, the future Saint Hugh. A miniature in a Latin manuscript depicts the three saints showing the dreaming Gunzo how to lay out the proportions and dimensions for the plan of the future Cluny with the use of ropes (Figure 70 in the Portfolio). Saint Peter advised the monk that he would be cured of his illness if he reported their instructions. He was also to tell Abbot Hugh that, if God's mandate was not carried out, the Abbot himself would contract the disease that had paralyzed Gunzo. Of course, after hearing Gunzo reporting his dream, the future Saint Hugh erected Cluny III following the tectonic instructions of the three saints.[48]

The designing power of dreams is recorded in the liturgy of the dedication of the Catholic church and their anniversary celebrations. Several significant references to the biblical dream of Jacob are written in the solemn Divine Office prescribed by the Pontifical. When Jacob awoke from his dream of angels ascending and descending the heavenly ladder, he exclaimed: "How terrible is this place! This is no other but the house of God and the gate of heaven" (Gen. 28:17). Having taken the stone, he had used for a pillow, Jacob set it up as a sacred pillar and, pouring oil on it, called it the house of God (Gen. 28.18). This account from Genesis is an integral part of the dedication liturgy. The consecration of an altar suggests an overt connection between the liturgical function and its biblical precedent. Every Catholic church is built symbolically on the stone pillow where the dream of its construction took place. Reasoning by analogy, one can hold that the first stone of any successful building is the transfiguration of the pillow where the head of the architect laid upon and dreamt up the building.

Notes

1 [Forecasting is a process of reading signs that enables the adept, properly trained and experienced, to anticipate and foretell future conditions.]
2 [From the Latin verb *jactare*, to throw, to cast.]
3 [Revonsuo's scientific work led him to hypothesize that dreams are a tool inherited to "simulate threatening events" (Revonsuo 2010: 877).]
4 Beside the surrealist propaganda, many others have connected the drawing of images with magic casting. In her *Drawing on the Right Side of the Brain*, Betty Edwards talks about drawing as a magical activity (Edwards 1979: 2–3).
5 Maritain (1937: 5).
6 For the similarity between Florensky and Peirce's concepts of the icon, see Fabbrichesi Leo (1986: 10).
7 Corbin (1976: 9).
8 Ibid.: 10.
9 Ibid.: 11.
10 Ibid.: 9.
11 Umberto Eco (1989a) tried to rule out the images of mirrors as icons by arguing external optical laws. Nevertheless, in mirrors, imaginative perception, just as in the *mundus imaginalis*, does not follow physical laws, yet it is geometrical and not necessarily Euclidean. Both the geometry of mirrors and the geometry of the *mundus imaginalis* are based on the same inverted perspective.
12 Surveying an existing space and then translating it into a drawing accomplishes a form of graphic prognostication. Survey drawings are descriptions of the constructed world.
13 Millhauser (1993: 132).
14 [Stratico is cited in Cavallari-Murat (1966: 338): "Grande è quell'Architetto, il quale senza l'aiuto dei disegni e modelli sà passeggiare, per dir così, con la mente nell'edificio da erigersi, …".]
15 To understand this amusing path of interpretative play, see Peirce (1931–1958: CP: 6.458–6.463); Sebeok (1984); Bosco (1959) and Fabbrichesi Leo (1986).
16 Peirce (1931–1958: CP 6.458).
17 Ibid.: CP 6.455.
18 Ibid.: CP 6.286.
19 [Montano (1624).]
20 The drawings of Montano, besides using the traditional notation for buildings built in the air, edifices sitting on the clouds, they are, as Tafuri points out, a profound criticism of perspective naturalism. [See Tafuri (1966: 246–254).]
21 Vitruvius (1931: V.1.6; Vol. I: 552–555); Vitruvio (1997: V.1.6: 134).
22 For instance, Mark Jarzombek (1989: 154) notes that "Alberti never refers to his own architectural activity even in *De re Aedificatoria*, where, given his autobiographical propensity, this would be not only natural but expected."
23 Palladio (1570, 1997).

24 Andrea di Pietro Della Gondola (1508–1580) accepted his *nome d'arte*, Palladio, from his first powerful patron, Gian Giorgio Trissino (1478–1550). A cultured and refined man of letters, Trissino composed a tediously metaphorical poem entitled *L'Italia Liberata dai Goti* (Italy Freed from the Goths, 1547–1554). In this literary composition, an angel bearing the name Palladio helps the Italian heroes to escape from the dungeon of a Gothic castle.
25 Corboz (1985).
26 Casey (1993: 125–130).
27 Brann (1991: 337).
28 [Frascari (1995: 11) listed two types of drawings: design drawings and graphic dreams.]
29 Artemidorus (1975: 14–18).
30 Price (1986); Macrobius (1990: 88–89); Freud (1978).
31 [Artemidorus (1975: 14–18) lists them in the following order: *somnium, visio, oraculum, insomnium, phantasma*. The first three types of dreams are useful for divination, while the latter two are ascribable to physical and psychological disturbance and do not have a divinatory character.]
32 According to Blanc:
>En architecture, le dessin, c'est la pensée même de l'architecte; c'est l'image présenté d'un édifice futur. Avant de s'élever sur le terrain, le monument se dessine et se dresse dans l'esprit de l'architecte; il se copie d'après ce modèle médité, idéal, et sa copie devient à son tour le modèle que devront répéter la pierre, le marbre ou le granit. Le dessin est donc le principe générateur de l'architecture; il en est l'essence.
>
>(Blanc 1870: 23)
33 [Gunzo's dream is an example of future construction handed down in a dream by God. It is discussed in this text by Frascari.]
34 [In 1830, Sir John Soane commissioned Joseph Gandy to paint the "Bank of England as a Ruin." This work is kept in Sir John Soane's museum in London.]
35 [A copy of Curtis (1986) can be found in the Marco Frascari Library at WAAC. See also Le Corbusier (1995, 2013).]
36 Filarete (1965, 1972).
37 Durand (1805).
38 Palladio (1570, 1997).
39 Scheerbart and Taut (1972). [Taut (1919).]
40 Vitruvius (1931: III, 1, 1–9; Vol. I: 158–167); Vitruvio (1997: III, 1, 1–9: 236–243).
41 Alberto Pérez-Gómez (1992; 2008). Lefaivre (1997).
42 [*Little Nemo in Slumberland* ran in the *New York Herald* from October 15, 1905 until July 23, 1911.]
43 In Latin: *nemo* means nobody. Nemo is also Ulysses' alias, intended to make the other Cyclops think that Polyphemus has dreamt up the whole story. When blinded by Ulysses and asked by his peers who did this, the only answer Polyphemus could give was Ulysses' alias, Nobody (Nemo). Polyphemus was monocular, and perspective is essentially a monocular vision (for Polyphemus as king of perspective, see Florenskij (1983: 125; 2002: 262)). McCay (1959) was a great perspectivist, who constantly broke the static constraints of the *costruzione legittima*. He was one of the founding fathers of animated cartoons.
44 [This sentence has been modified from the latest English version to reflect the Italian version of Frascari's text (Frascari 1995: 15–16).]
45 Vitruvius (1931: I, I, 11; Vol. I: 16–17); Vitruvio (1997: I, I, 11: 20–21).
46 Perec (1974). [Perec (1997, 1989).]
47 A *locus aestheticus* is the touchstone of the artistic production of a culture and the construction of cathedrals has been the touchstone for any artistic production during the period of their erection. Every building and every object developed from the artistic production concerning the cathedrals. For example, the goblets of a private house derived from the form of the chalice used in the church.
48 Dreams served as vehicles for many other monastic constructions. The *Codex Benedictus* (Vatican, BAV, Vat. lat. 1202; 1072–1086) narrates how Saint Benedict appeared in a dream giving directions on how to build the monastery of Terracina to the newly appointed Abbot and Prior. The chronicler tells us that, in his dream demonstration, Saint Benedict showed them exactly where each part of the monastery should stand. Another monastic architectural dream is the one had by the future Saint Aubert. Around the year 708, the

Archangel Saint Michael appeared three times to this stubborn Norman Bishop. Finally, in the third dream, after the Archangel bored a hole in his head with one of his fingers, Aubert agreed to erect a monastery on Mont-Tombe, which later became known as Mont-Saint-Michel (see Figure 71 in the Portfolio). To tangibly prove this extraordinary origin of the monastery complex, the skull of Saint Aubert, which carries a perforation in the right parietal bone, can be viewed in a reliquary at the Cathedral of Avranches, a small town facing the island of Mont-Saint-Michel.

3
THE IMPORTANCE OF DREAMING IN ARCHITECTURE

Marco Frascari

I cannot actually build anything myself and I cannot afford to have it built for me. I am essentially and existentially a clever but clumsy person and, financially speaking, a bedlamite. I cannot drive a nail in the wall nor correctly balance my checkbook. Nevertheless, I am an architect and I enjoy erecting constructions. I cannot lay bricks to make walls, but I can dream up a building and I can tell others who are adroit and dexterous how and what to build. I know how to dream up a building. When I state that I dream up buildings, I am not merely using a picturesque way of speaking without a genuine content, a *façon de parler*, I mean it literally. I believe that dreaming is the crucial action at the groundwork of architecture: it is the act of casting a future building (Figure 1 in the Portfolio).

Dreamwork is also an important step in defining the field of the architectural discipline since it can allow a distinction between principle-based theories and constructive theories. The writing of principle-based theories is a self-gratulatory procedure used to demonstrate that the rational intelligence embodied in architectural artifacts and design procedures has been detected. The writing and drafting of constructive theories are not merely pragmatic and deal with the cunning intelligence necessary to devise and make buildings. Dreamwork casts future buildings, not through the discipline of principles but through the discipline of imagination. The discipline of imagination is an act of construction. This concept is embodied in the German word *Bild* and its derivatives, such as *abbilden*. A *Bild* is an image; it is not a mental proposition but something that we produce as an artifact. It is a concrete shape, which works as a model.[1] These images are not mental images; they are just as real as dreams are in the mind. A *Bild* is an icon, a magical icon.

According to Florensky, magical icons are technological outputs. The production of icons is a technology that, as with any other human activity, can be classified as a triad of functions. In any culture, there are practical, theoretical, and liturgical functions. The practical function of technology is to produce things or tools/machines. The theoretical function is to produce theories or concept terms, whereas the liturgical function is to produce things and thoughts by joining hard reality with subtle meanings. The construction of icons takes place within this triad of functions.

Liturgy is a technology of the infraordinary transformed into the extraordinary. It is a discipline based on iconic thinking that plays a major role in architectural dreaming. Liturgical transformation construes and constructs the space of the dream. The progress of this technology originates in the *mundus imaginalis* and is then translated into the sublunary world. This technological power of architectural dreams was acknowledged by Carlo Scarpa (1906–1978) in recounting one of his architectural dreams: "I always dreamed of building a house with moveable stone walls: vertical plans running on bearings in grooves."[2]

From the point of view of this surrealistic trophy, the technology of late night vision improves our capability to generate beautiful and topical images by giving us the possibility to blur the distinction between concrete and abstract, between dream and reality. The schismatic nature of dream and reality is perfectly expressed in a Chinese sacred canon: *Nan Hua Zhen Jing*. In this ancestral story, which indicates the importance of a surrealistic approach to architecture, Zhuang Zhou (ca. 369–286 BC) narrates that he dreamt of being a butterfly and that when he awoke, he asked himself if, instead, was he not a butterfly dreaming of being a man?[3]

The magic threshold

> Magic is ... affirming man's autonomous power of creating desired ends.
>
> Bronislaw Malinowski[4]

As an act of magic, an architectural dream casts forward and backward rhapsodies of images. As Bronislaw Malinowski points out: "Magic, from many points of view, is the most important and most mysterious aspect of primitive man's pragmatic attitude towards reality."[5]

Magic is made by tradition,[6] and the meaning of this 'trade' is based on the belief that hope and desire can neither fail nor deceive. To be precise, architectural dreaming is a golden gate into magic. It is an act of imagination taking place on a threshold. This is illustrated in *The Architect's Dream* (1840, Toledo Museum of Art, Ohio, USA), a well-known painting by Thomas Cole (1801–1848) presenting architectural dreams (see Figures 72 and 73 in the Portfolio), as well as in two drawings by the Turinese architect, Carlo Mollino (1905–1973) (Figures 1, 63, 66 in the Portfolio).[7] In both of these dreams it is clear that the architect is dwelling on a threshold. A threshold is generally considered a kind of passage, something to go through, not a place in which to dwell. Nevertheless, an architectural dream acts as a threshold for dwelling. In a mantic dream, the architect dwells on the threshold of dwelling and also, consequently on the threshold of architectural construction and architectural construing (see Figure 57 in the Portfolio). Cole's painting shows an architect lounging on an impressive pile of oversized architectural pattern books within a theatrical proscenium. The books are located on top of a stone-slab placed on the abacus that completes the capitol of a huge column, which is placed at the center of a perspectival background composed of buildings ranging from the Pyramids to a Gothic steeple. In the oration for Cole's funeral, William Cullen Bryant described this painting as a reverie of building, "such as might present itself to the imagination of one who had fallen asleep after reading a work on the different styles of architecture."[8] The painting was commissioned by Ithiel Town in 1839, and then rejected. The heavy curtains framing the *visio* seem to suggest that it is a theater of the dream. Furthermore, this magniloquent painting suggests that in a dream the organization of space-temporality is different. In this *visio*, as well as in other paintings of architectural dreams, buildings belonging to different spatial locations share the same space. Also, buildings destroyed by the unyielding nature of time are presented in a pristine condition. The buildings of this architectural dream are diachronically and synchronically located within the same light.

This light, an expression of the *lume naturale* or of the *spiritus fantasticus*, is an allusive aspect to see the invisible within the visible. Besides being a restatement of the role of the architect—to make visible what is invisible— the light reveals the ambit of a future design leading our imagination towards an act of material construction. The light in the dream reveals that the dream is a *Bild*. The dream is a visible occurrence that, like a model on the threshold of a Gothic or a Renaissance cathedral, is the factual source of the construction. The stone threshold is a covenant and the architect is the *magus* or priest celebrating upon it.[9] This synchronic diachronic amalgamation is typical of the magic dimension since "magic moves in the glory of past tradition, but it also creates its atmosphere of ever-nascent myth."[10] The threshold is the gate to the imaginal world of architectural imagination. Although Cole's painting is traced within the structure of the *costruzione legittima,* it is actually an inverted perspective of the dreamwork.[11]

In 1940, Carlo Mollino designed a dream house that he called the *Architect's House*.[12] The drawings and the title of this design are ambiguous. This design can be a design for a house to house an architect, or it can be the ideal house to be designed by an architect. In the Mollino archive, only two perspectival drawings of this design exist. One is a classical central perspective, representing an interior view that opens onto an industrial urban-edge landscape. It shows two service-tables located at the sides of a tilted drawing table equipped with a drafting machine; this is the architect's dreamed house (Figures 63, 66 in the Portfolio). The main table faces a modern large-pane window that extends at the corner of the ceiling and becomes a skylight. Beyond the window, at the center of the view, one sees a tower; this is the house of dreams. The other drawing is a bird's-eye view of the same tower in the forefront of an old vernacular construction to which a modern room with a window-skylight has been added. These two drawings were used to illustrate the third installment of the *Vita di Oberon* (Life of Oberon), a philosophical architectural tale, written by Mollino in a surrealistic mood and published in *Casabella* magazine in 1933.[13]

> Oberon bought a piece of land, the fragment of a farmhouse and the subsidized housing that was shaped like a gasoline tank, located on the other side of a backyard ... he settled opposite it, on the side of the road, within the ruin of the original farmhouse, to which an addition was made toward the backyard. The addition is a large glazed parallelepipedal room, with a northern exposure, which emerges from a leprotic ruin and protrudes into the void of the yard ... The parallelepiped, the baroque fragment of the ruin, the yard and the side of the large dwelling shaped the studio of the "mad architect". Looking out of the glazed wall, as if from a signal-box, Oberon would search for proportions, colors, and dimensions on the converse side of the public-housing building. The edifice had become a monstrous display of a real size sampler, inclusive of all colors and elements, of all pieces used to assemble architecture, an architecture that is all the same, and that everyone is now capable of designing ... From my studio I see all the measurements, the solids and the voids, the meters and feet intersecting in a grid and the color choices. These, commercial elements (pillars, cantilevers, studs in marble, stone and steel) are "standards" that come in progressive sizes. I dissolved them in daylight or pinned them to the obtuse and large wall beyond the field lawn. On the wall I marked perimeters and measurements that could be arranged in different ways and in different angles. As the musician draws from the orchestra, among the multitude of instruments, the voice of his favorite, and is consequently the only instrument he hears. In the same way, I draw from intricate and successive dimensions of true size pieces placed on the wall, choosing images for my construction. If necessary, I separate them from the others or I compare them using the appropriate template held to my eye, and finally I draw them in their proper place on the paper. Always, when I lay out spaces, I relate myself to the distant statues that I can raise against the wall at different heights. I do this because architecture is for humans and depends on their dimensions. Next to my drawing board lays the image of the wall, reproduced on a chart showing all the measurements in meters and feet. Finally, using these measurements, I draft the drawing in scale.[14]

In telling this philosophical tale, Mollino moves from the third to the first person. In a Wittgensteinian language game, Oberon, the sovereign of Slumberland, the "magus-architect," moves from being the object to being the subject. The story becomes a dream reported by Mollino himself. Oberon's Palace is transformed into the Mollino Room, where the constructive images of the imaginal world become the corporeal reality of one's tectonic world.

The story of this dream began with the Oberon Palace designed by Inigo Jones for the staging of Ben Jonson's Masque entitled "Oberon, the Fairy Prince" (1610–1611). The palace is like a wonderful machine that dances in front of its audience. It acts as a monstrous edifice at the rear of the backyard. The window of the architect's room becomes the iconostasis through which the architect has a vision of a dance taking place within an imaginal world, which he then uses to construct the icons of design at the drawing table (see Figure 66 in the Portfolio).

The dreaming and corporeal dimensions of the dance and its translation into tectonic movements are revealed in Mollino's tale.[15] Dance is the art of movement and, through transfiguration, it introduces time in a-temporal conditions. The translational movement of dance amplifies time. Dancing is learned and practiced in front of a mirror, analogously, architecture is learned and practiced through the mirror of the imaginal world. Mollino enters his future buildings with the analogy of the mirrored wall of the dancers.

Many architects enter the dream of their designs through the use of scale figures, but Mollino does not.[16] The geometry of the body enters in a different manner within his architecture. Photographic reflections are his tools of transmutation. The latent image of the body is revealed after the piece has been constructed, and becomes the projected embodiment of future pieces. In Mollino's photos, the corporeal metaphor secures a magic strength, consisting in the mirror-like power of creating and extending a new presence. The presence of the body in the photos raises a question about the completion of the act of divination in architecture.[17] Is a piece of architecture complete when its construction is finished or does it continue into the photographic realm? A divination by reflection, as a result of catoptromancy,[18] the geometry of Mollino reveals the bittersweet nature of the practice of architecture and the potentiality of every design to become another design. Mollino appears only once in his drawings, in a theoretical design, for a bedroom in a farm house, that was published in *Casabella*.[19] He does not appear directly, but is seen as a reflection in a mirror, at the center of the perspective, stressing again his catoptromancy approach. The story of Mollino's dream and photographic reflections gives a durable and subjective value to images that are often perceived to have only an ephemeral objectivity.

A mantic view

In practicing the architectural profession, following tradition, I evoke buildings on paper for clients. I draw horizontal and vertical sections so that they can decide if what I have envisioned is precisely what they want built. By this act of magic conjuring that reveals the profile of a building, they can imagine their future and possible life within it. As a next step, I conjure up the same building through a new set of detailed sectional drawings for a contractor and subcontractors who can then imagine how it should be built in the most socially conscious and economical way.

Recently, there have been two types of reactions to this non-scientific condition of conjuring images. On the one hand, there are architects who become design-build professionals in order to avoid dealing with the imagination of the builder. To increase their prestige with clients, they argue that what they are designing results from functional thinking since they know how to physically author a building. On the other hand, there are architects who run what they improperly call a critical practice. To acquire authority in the conjuring of future buildings and to avoid the effort of producing a building thaumaturgically, they begin their professional activity by designing buildings for acquiescing relatives, friends and acquaintances. Their products are offered to critics for praise and wide dissemination in authoritative magazines. Their authority derives from the critics and a marketing of information that is overloaded by fast-consumed images. Both procedures make authors out of architects, with a consequent perception of authority. The result of the acquisition of these unquestionable positions of authority is that the labor of architectural conjuring is no longer necessary and images become a substitute for imagination. Having been recognized as cutting-edge architects, the process of evoking buildings for both clients and contractors becomes completely unnecessary. Following this path, the outcome is the same: future construction results from pseudo-artistic intuition. This justifies all possible forms of building production, which no longer belong to an imaginative universal of a civilization, i.e., the imaginal sphere, but to a fictitious imaginary. Within this double-faced condition, the non-scientific conjuring up of a building could be solved with a baroque and jurisprudential equation of simulation and dissimulation as a matter of verisimilitude. Resemblance is the necessary condition.

Different theories of *mimesis* have ruled the architect's documents. Nowadays, a drawing is like a future building. Looking at a drawing is a form of "seeing as."[20] The verisimilitude between drawings and the resulting building is accomplished through prescriptive construction drawings. This legal resemblance makes buildings look as they appear in the critically acclaimed presentation drawings. This purely visual fulfillment, a legitimizing *mimesis* is not only done by commercial firms, but also by the so-called avant-garde architects, when they finally get a commission to build one of their unbuildable buildings. The authority of architects is based upon documents produced during the design stage, which consist of drawings and models. The traditional interpretation links these products to the constructed environment through the goggles of *mimesis*, where the built artifact should look exactly like the drawn expression of it. For centuries, this parroting condition has been quite acceptable because drawings and models were quite impure, imprecise and not directly related to a specific stage of design imagination. It was commonly understood that they were not completely veracious and were to be taken with a grain of salt. Unfortunately, nowadays, fidelity has become the key requirement, the dictum of likeness has become reciprocal: the building should look like the drawing and the drawing should look like the building. From this point of view, the illustrations in Palladio's *Four Books* would be rejected as false and incorrect, because they demonstrate proportions, angles, and dimensions that are not in the actual built pieces.

Although they had been built following sets of carefully constructed measured drawings from prototypes, many "Holy Sepulchers" and "Loreto Houses" do not look like the originals at all. They had been accepted as honest representations of an idea, rather than the particulars, on the contrary, the present condition of architecture would probably give them the label of fraudulent parroting. The condition of representation in which the drawings do not look like the constructed pieces and the buildings do not look like the design drawings, is no longer possible today. The draftsman's contract obliges architects to produce imaging without imagination. The association between authority and legitimization has completely parted documents from authors. The result is that the act of reading a drawing is no longer an act of imagination. The reading of drawings and models has become a most unimaginative routine in current practice. These architectural readings have moved from the intangible ambiguity of the realm of discernment to the tangible precision of the realm of contingency. The representation of dream has become illegitimate.

Drawings are mechanical representations done by an objective machine. Computer Aided Design (CAD) is the legitimate child of the draftsman's contract. A computer station for CAD is a drawing machine, a direct descendant of the drawing machines conceived by the objectionable desire for objective exactness in recording our three-dimensional space in two-dimensional representations: a dreamless condition. These machines have put to rest all the imaginative undertakings of the people involved in the making of architecture. The current act of reading drawings does not entail the great labor of imaginative construction that was required before the invention of drafting machines. These drafting machines, be they electronic or not, are equivalent to those dreadful children's coloring books, which are merely authoritative instruments to teach neat exactness. The completed picture of a coloring book brings about a feeling of having imagined an image, whereas in fact it has been merely a following of guidelines.

THE IMPORTANCE OF DREAMING IN ARCHITECTURE

The strength of imagination has been ruled out by the use of the machines that are required by the draftsman's contract. What is the contract of the draftsman? The answer is abecedarian. *The Draughtsman's Contract* is a 1982 movie, directed by Peter Greenaway for the British Film Institute. The action takes place in seventeenth-century England. The movie describes the affairs of an architectural draftsman engaged to produce a set of drawings for a country house by using a drawing machine. Mr. Neville, the draftsman, does not believe in human fidelity. He is a strong believer in the trustworthiness of graphic recordings. When the owner of the house is murdered, the fidelity of Mr. Neville's drawings is brought into question: are they truthful and legitimate evidence? Are the perspectival drawings legal evidence of reality?

Within the oral history of architecture, there is a general agreement that perspectival drawings are not proper and legitimate drawings for construction and tectonic conceiving, but the use of CAD has transformed in accepted reality the preposterous statement made by Dr. Brook Taylor, who, in his famous book on perspective, wrote:

> A Picture drawn in the utmost Degree of Perfection, and placed in a proper Position, ought so to appear to the Spectator, that he should not be able to distinguish what is there represented, from the real original Objects actually placed where they are represented to be. In order to produce this effect, it is necessary that the Rays of Light ought to come from the several Parts of the Picture to the Spectator's Eye, with all the same Circumstances of Direction, Strength of Light and Shadow, and Colour, as they would do from the corresponding Parts of the real Objects seen in their proper Places.[21]

The recognized outcome is that perspective, a machine product, is an objective viewpoint for casting a legitimate outlook of a building. This perspectival machine generates a blindfolded vision, a trivially unimaginative, and visually impaired view of the constructed world.

To explain the condition of an architect, such as myself, who is not willing to prescribe verisimilitude, nor intends to design his/her 'mother's house' or learn how to drive a nail into a wall, I must take an intellectual gamble and seek out the fundamental features of architectural existence. Architectural existence falls within that set of human conditions that the Germans call *Existenz*. The word *Existenz* appeared during the Modern Movement and it is generally related to the minimum standards of living. *Existenz* is a peculiar word that made its way into architectural thinking with the locution *Existenzminimum* and it cannot be translated into the English cognate locution "minimal existence."[22] The fundamental feature of architectural *Existenz* is to be found not in perception but in dreams and it is the role of the architect to translate these architectural dreams into reality. Architecture is not merely an oneiric interpretation: it is the discovery of the virtues of dwelling through the surrealistic dimension of dreams that leads to meaningful construction.

There are three key actors in the present condition of architectural production. There is the client, on one side, the building contractor, on the other, and the architect, constrained between the two. This tripartite relationship determines the responsibilities of the architect and is fundamental to understanding the present condition of the profession. Within this scheme, a second triadic order is inserted. This triadic order consists of three kinds of architectural drawings necessary to evoke a building: design drawings, presentation drawings, and construction drawings. Traditionally design drawings are for the architect, presentation drawings are for the client and construction drawings are for the builder. The design drawings offer the "seeing in" of the building, whereas the renderings and the construction drawings accomplish the "seeing as" of the future building. On the one hand, presentation and construction drawings are descriptive and prescriptive representations: the seeing of a likeness is the basis for projecting a drawing of a future building, a mimesis based on appearance. On the other hand, a design drawing is a cognitive representation of something that does not yet exist. They are drawings of productive representation resulting through a constructive eidetic process. Unfortunately, the request for a codified mimesis, realistic in the case of presentation drawings, or conventional in the case of construction drawings, has now become the parameter for design drawings. Design is a competitive activity and requires architects to showcase their graphic abilities. Consequently, the skill sets required for the production of the presentation and construction drawings have been transferred to the design drawings. The result of this inverted influence is that design drawings are no longer graphic representations analogically related to the built world, when in fact design drawings should be the ones casting their influence over the other two modes of production.

To understand the phenomenology of representation in architecture, I must set out an analogical path, which sees every architectural drawing as a divination activity. A design, a divination describing a future edifice, is a graphic prognostication knowingly translated into a building through specific descriptions. In Latin, the idea of *descriptio* is inseparable from the idea of *scriptura*, as Dario Sabbatucci suggests in his auspicious interpretation of divination as a form of writing and reading the world.[23] The Romans understood descriptions as translations of objects in graphic narration capable of depicting them. As a powerful form of semiosis, divination is a description of the world, a writing of the world. It is generally considered negatively because it is thought of as being based on a semiotic fallacy, a misjudgment of the pragmatic effect of signs and their semiotic relation to objects. However, divination presents itself in front of the world in two ways: on the one hand, there is a world to be written, and, on the other, a world to be read. Both worlds are to be imagined. The portrayal of divination as an imaginative reading and writing disallows the present negative interpretation of the idea of divination. Architecture is a reading and writing of the constructed world through architectural drawings. It is a divination done by casting figures of the constructed world and its proper *Existenz* is in the oneiric realm. The divination paradigm has been understood in two different ways, through the concept of the mad seer and the wise magus. Consequently, there are two manners of practicing architecture, either as a mad architect or a wise architect. The mad architect is a gifted designer, whereas the wise architect is a magus. Plato provides us with the key to understanding the tradition of the mad seer:

> But there is also a madness, which is a divine gift, and the source of the chiefest blessings granted to men. For prophecy is a madness, and the prophetess at Delphi and the priestesses at Dodona when out of their senses have conferred great benefits on Hellas, both in public and private life, but when in their senses few or none. And I might also tell you how the Sibyl and other inspired persons have given to many an intimation of the future which has saved them from falling. But it would be tedious to speak of what everyone knows. There will be more reason in appealing to the ancient inventors of names, who would never have connected prophecy (manticη), which foretells the future and is the noblest of arts, with madness (manicη), or called them both by the same name, if they had deemed madness to be a disgrace or dishonor; – they must have thought that there was an inspired madness which was a noble thing; for the two words, manticη and manicη, are really the same, and the letter τ is only a modern and tasteless insertion."[24]

The magus is a designer who composes images, signs, and ideas and sets the future of construction. For a magus, "to think is to speculate with images."[25] For the architectural magus, the art of designing buildings is a syncretic art. Architectural artifacts do not receive meaning from the things they signify, but rather from the conditions that do the signifying. Architectural drawings are drafted to make visible the invisible. They are what Polish philosopher and historian Krzysztof Pomian calls *sémiophores*: objects that are valued or praised not for their utilitarian function, but for the wonder they create, a wonder that can only be explained by making reference to the invisible.[26] Therefore, the architect is a magus who relates visible signs with invisible signifiers. Architecture, an extensively graphic divinatory activity, is the noblest of prophecies since it is an elegant translation of both the construed and constructed world of a culture and their proper *Existenz* is within the oneiric realm. Construction is the construing of a dream and architectural dreams are a form of maieutic.

The mystery of architecture is all about the divinatory nature of mirroring metaphors that rule the acts of translation. The translation of buildings into drawings is a backtelling, and the translation of drawings into buildings is a foretelling. This speculative chiasm is a hypogeal structure on which the contemporary project of architecture must be erected. This is a project that recognizes architecture as a trade with an intellectual tradition, which began earlier than the Enlightenment. Architecture is the result of an infinite mirroring of translations. The dream is the locus where the transmutation of backtelling into foretelling intelligence takes place.[27] The quasi-architecture of the dream, the Heraclitean *idios kosmos* undercuts the phenomenology of perception by refusing the scientific separation of past, present, and future.[28] In one of his superb *Illuminations*, Walter Benjamin (1892–1940) affirms that to a degree all great texts contain their virtual translation.[29] The projection of an interpretative scheme in a drawing or a building is a constitutive act of the drawing or the building itself. To translate an image is to recognize or guess what has made it into an image. This entails instituting an interpretation. A translation is the result of the univocity of the interpretative scheme and the ambiguity of the image. The architect who translates a building into a drawing or a drawing into a building proceeds by alternating schemes and corrections. Translations are not abstractions; they are successive steps towards definition. This is the cleverest aspect of the process of translation by which our constructed world comes about. The architectural imagery that is embodied in the drawings acts as a gelling agent of the architectural expression and constitutes the beginning of the architectural dream. Unfortunately, nowadays, these intriguing and desirable operations have been badly disguised within the meandering backrooms of professional practice. This phase of the art of architecture, which goes under the heading of "production drawing," has become a prosaic activity. This negative connotation originates within the educational realm. Students of architecture consider the translation of buildings into drawings to be a frustrating procedure. They consider these drawings to be merely a disciplinary demand that delays the growth and blooming of their individual design abilities.

The present condition of architecture is dominated by two different graphic procedures. On the one hand, there are the design drawings, while, on the other, there are the construction drawings. The making of the design drawings is considered to be the most prestigious act of the profession. It is an artistic effort that carries a vision. The dominant mode of production in design drawings is a rhetoric based on a desire for imitation. They are not based on a magical mimesis; conversely, they seek professional authority through imitation. The source of authority is not the designer but the subject of imitation: the original hut, the style, etc. Consequently, design drawings by a sole author have become authoritative documents, whereas construction drawings, drafted by multiple hands, are considered mere protective legal documents, which translate a design construct into prescriptions for construction. An unacknowledged rhetoric of mono-directional visual translation is the mode of production in construction drawings. Professors and professionals of architecture regard this part of the graphic transaction as a necessary but prosaic part of the making of architecture that can be deferred to construction management. It is a problem for project management to make the building look like the drawings. Nevertheless, in the past, these graphic transactions, between designing and building, were the most poetic ones since they were based on a magical mimesis. In these drawings, the relationship between the signs on paper and the buildings is not based on efficient causality but on formal causality of knowledge.

The real signs of proper construction drawings are magical signs. Understanding the difference between the desire for imitation and the magic of translation is crucial to the use of drawings for dreaming up a building. On one hand, ideal imitation is an organic recreation from earlier texts or objects, in the sense of being a formal or substantive adoption, as in 'look-alike' contests. On the other hand, translation is recognized as repetitive when it aims to match form and substance in a different language.[30] Translation is not imitation, but a magic conversion of images. Imitation is solar and trivial, whereas magic mimesis is nocturnal and nontrivial. French philosopher, Jacques Maritain (1882–1973) reflected on the nature of magic in the work of the influential French philosopher Henry Bergson (1859–1941) and stated:

> Monsieur Bergson has shown very clearly that the primordial element discoverable at the source and basis of magic is the relation of causality ... 'Magic is therefore innate in man, being no more than the externalization of a desire (Bergson) ...'. The thing which we consider lacking in Bergson's theory is that it takes no account of the indispensable instrument of magical activity, that is to say the *practical sign* ... we are in the presence of an imaginary refraction of the practical sign considered in the order of the *relation itself of signification*.[31]

The drawings for the construction of an edifice are developed through a process of translation whereby the 'facts' of an architectural project become a real building. Through an act of construction—a poetic translation, a magic mimesis—drawings are transformed into buildings and buildings into drawings. The established construing of this process of translation has been based on the *costruzione legittima* of perspective. This condition of perspective generates only external, not internal, vision. Marked by its very name, the *costruzione legittima* has been established as the only legitimate perspective; this condition implies that all other forms of perspective are based on errors, or are generated by errors. The paradigm of the *costruzione legittima* has been the standard model for understanding the role of the architect. To further elaborate on a discussion by Florensky about the perspective machine illustrated in Dürer's wonderful woodcuts, it can easily be demonstrated how the architectural profession has been framed by the paradigm of the *costruzione legittima*. Mirroring Dürer's illustrations analyzed previously, I make the following analogies:[32]

1   *The architect is the person drawing the subject of construction on the Lucinda.*
2   *The builder is the character that is the maker of the object.*
3   *The client can be identified as the ring attached to the wall, the center of a blind projection.*

This triadic structure has been the model for the practice of architecture and a source of frustration for architects. It has generally been enforced as the only legitimate manner for practicing, and the only source of the rules of the 'serious' architectural game, which generated an understanding that, because of these rules, an architect can predict the outcome of every construction event.

The magic of translation

> The magic art ... like the other arts and crafts ... is also governed by a theory.
>
> Bronislaw Malinowski[33]

An extremely complex intellectual procedure is embodied in the act of architectural translation. To understand the complexity of this process of architectural interpretation, it is necessary to consider the mirroring act of translation upon which architectural education has traditionally been based in the past, i.e., the discipline of the translation of buildings into drawings. However, before examining the essential role of this magic mimesis-paradigm to understand the creative process in architecture, a discussion of the following traditional analogy will sanction the significance of the paradigm. A person learning another language must be taught the discipline of translation before being able to formulate a thought in a new language. Following a well-established didactic tradition, a language-learner must translate from the new language into the native, and from the native into the new. Currently, the dominant pedagogical trend demands of student-architects the aptness to design a new building, without having first translated any edifice into a set of drawings. This would be comparable to being able to think in another language without having first translated from that language into the native language and vice versa. The result is a pedantic

THE IMPORTANCE OF DREAMING IN ARCHITECTURE

imitation of graphic output of well-known designers, without having any real comprehension of what the transformation into the built world would be. Consequently, the dominant theoretical tendency is based on a concept of architectural representation, which favors an explanation of architectural events under the sign of verisimilitude: constructed buildings should appear like the design drawings produced by the architect. This tendency, which developed during the Enlightenment, and was fostered by heavy propaganda during the Modern Movement, is a nefarious paradigm of truthful representation and limits the richness of character and intensity of the universe of architectural inventions. Buildings no longer construe an architect's poetic understanding of human dwelling. They have become expressions of pseudo-artistic obsessions, which result from the architect's search for celebrity and individual fame. Under the influence of this preposterous paradigm, debates on verisimilar constructions and representations have unfolded, disregarding the fact that the signs of verisimilitude are part of a philosophical polarity. The opposite pole of verisimilitude is wonder. This philosophical polarity recalls and intersects with a few others, viz., real and fictitious, credible and incredible, authentic and false, rational and non-rational.[34] The Gnostic architect, Louis Isadore Kahn (1901–1974), stated:

> Form comes from wonder. Wonder stems from our 'in touchness' with how we are made. One senses that nature records the process of what it makes, so that in what it makes there is also the record of how it was made. In touch with this record we are in wonder. This wonder gives rise to knowledge. But knowledge is related to other knowledge and this relation gives a sense of order, a sense of how they interrelate in a harmony that makes all the things exist.[35]

This enigmatic, poetic statement shows that in architecture, wonder is central to any intellectual and design search, due to the fact that wonder is a state of desire. According to Kahn, wonder is human desire in its beginning, an almost erotic search for knowledge:

> Wonder is the forerunner of all knowing.
> Wonder is the primer. It primes knowing.[36]

Wonder is a faculty that has completely disappeared from contemporary architectural discourse. In the present practice of architecture, it is realized only by accident. The word "wonderful" has become almost meaningless, an expression of praise and celebration, used to avoid the expression of a deeper and more specific comment.

The translation of a building into a drawing is the necessary act to perform a graphic divination of a building. Architecture produces buildings that are poetic artifacts. These artifacts cannot be easily translated and maintain the same expressive configuration. Buildings can be translated into drawings and drawings into buildings, yet the result of this process generates a different building. Humorously, Mark Twain (1835–1910) demonstrated this point by having one of his stories, *The Celebrated Jumping Frog of Calaveras County* (1865), translated into French and then translated back into English as *The Jumping Frog: in English, then in French, and then Clawed Back into a Civilized Language Once More by Patient, Unremunerated Toil* (1875).[37] The difficulty arises when buildings are translated into other buildings, the problem being one of replication. The essence of this theoretical tangle is described beautifully in the paradox presented by Jorge Luis Borges (1899–1986) in a short story entitled *Pierre Menard, autor del Quijote* (1939).[38] Menard did not want to write another *Quijote* but 'the' *Quijote*. Menard's aim was to produce a text, which corresponded word for word to that of Miguel de Cervantes, but which was not a mechanical transcription of the original. The nature of this paradox is revealed by the incongruity that exists in the concept of a perfect replica. Evidence of problems found when translating within the same expressive mode can be seen in the dislikable and prosaic replicas of the Parthenon built in Nashville, or the half-scale dreadful replicas of famous buildings at Disney's Epcot Center in Florida. However, these artifacts can be truly replicated when the cunning intelligence of the architect is challenged by the request for replication through the use of other materials to achieve the desired expressive configuration. This is the case with many replicas of Christian Holy buildings that were built between the medieval and Baroque ages. A marvelous example of the medieval ability for translation can be seen in the building complex of Santo Stefano in Bologna. This aggregation of religious buildings is an architectural digest of the most important Christian monuments in Jerusalem, which do not look like the original edifices at all. The Sacri Monti are a series of religious buildings on top of a series of individual hills. They are Manneristic instances of translation of the history and landscape of Palestine transmuted into the landscape and history of the Brianza region, at the foot of the Alps in Piedmont and Lombardy, Italy. A similar form of translation is seen in the Villa Duodo (1593), designed by Vincenzo Scamozzi (1552–1616), which translates the seven churches of Rome onto the hill of Monselice, near Padua.

For Benedetto Croce (1866–1952), an Italian Idealist philosopher, prose is translatable, whereas poetry is untranslatable. Croce divides translation into two realms. On one side, there are the *belle infedeli* (unfaithfully beautiful) and on the other, the *brutte fedeli* (faithfully ugly).[39] In contrast to Croce's position, another Italian philosopher, Giovanni Gentile (1875–1944), holds that translation is the basic condition of any thought and learning.[40] For Gentile, the act of translation encompasses not only the translation from foreign languages, but also occurs within native languages.

Translation is a mental activity that takes place in a continuous manner. For Gentile, anyone who is reading this sentence, even when the person is a native English speaker, is in essence translating it. In other words, there is no possibility of a definitive translation because every expressive occurrence is different. Paradoxically, when I combine the idea of Gentile with the terminology of Croce, I can affirm that the same duality exists within the realm of architecture. On one hand, there are the *belle infedeli* of Palladio who translated his own church of San Pietro di Castello into the Church of San Francesco della Vigna, San Francesco della Vigna into San Giorgio Maggiore, and San Giorgio Maggiore into the Redentore, or any of his villas into any other villa he designed. On the other hand, there are the *brutte fedeli* of Aldo Rossi (1931–1997), who translated the drawings of his *Monumento alla Resistenza* in Cuneo (1962) into the architectural reality of the *Monumento a Sandro Pertini* in Milan (1988–1990). Therefore, it can be stated that a reformulated construction of an edifice is an analytical procedure based on a paradox: to be truly faithful to an original, it is actually necessary to be unfaithful. The act of translation is the key factor to understanding the tradition of production and reproduction in Western culture. Translation is a trade—a *techne*—based on tradition that can also be betrayed. Two puns, in Italian, translate this concept into an easily remembered form, viz., *traduttore = traditore* (translator = betrayer) and *traduzione = tradizione* (translation = tradition).[41]

The trade

Science is born of experience, magic made by tradition.
Bronislaw Malinowski[42]

Survey and construction drawings are in themselves poetic texts that reformulate other poetic texts. They are the result of analytical processes that aim to reconstruct, through interpretation, the specific manner in which meaning has been developed. In the architectural trade, the Western tradition begins with the Greeks,[43] who considered the languages and the architecture of other peoples barbaric and, therefore, they were not interested in translations. Nevertheless, in their notion of hermeneutics, one could find the beginning of the Western concept of translation in architecture. Hermes was the Greek god who translated for the humans the hermetic language spoken by the Olympian gods. The etymology of the word *hermes* is uncertain but it belongs to a semantic family that indicates a deep insight into the unknown.[44] The story of the invention of the Corinthian capital, as told by Vitruvius, provides important clues to understanding the process of translation that took place in Greek architecture. Vitruvius narrates that Callimachus, a renowned artist, saw the tomb of a young Corinthian maid, on which a basket was placed containing her favorite objects. The basket was set on an acanthus bush plant, and its leaves grew and coiled around a square lid. Callimachus thought that this form was original, and beautiful, and he translated it in stone.[45] In his mind, the decoration of the tomb became a *paradeigma*.

For the Romans, the phenomenon of translation is more familiar and habitual, although the "translation" is generally from the Greek language. The terms used by Latin writers are *interpres, interpretari, interpretatio*. These terms have an economical-juridical origin since they describe an act of mediation between two price figures (Lat. *inter-pretium*). From the Romans' point of view, interpretation is an act of figuring out.[46] A translation is the reconciliation between the buyer's price and the seller's price. Every interpretation is an economic event, a transaction. Palladio transacted the stone columns of Antiquity into the less expensive plastered brick columns. In Colonial America, Palladian columns were translated into the cheaper wood form. By assimilating acts of interpretation the Romans figured out the written and built texts of the Greeks. This is demonstrated, for example, in the work of Vitruvius, who began the transformation of the architectural discipline by writing his treatise on architecture. He had difficulty with the translation of Greek terms into Latin. In reality, the Romans based translation on the concept of emulation (*aemulatio*).[47] In an attempt to legitimize architecture, Vitruvius traced the path for the transformation of the art of building, from a profession *sine litteris*, to a discipline that can be explained with encyclopedic knowledge. According to Vitruvius, architecture is a *techne* (art) among the *technai* (arts), and the literary *techne* is the paradigm at which the Vitruvian act of emulation was aimed.[48]

Emulation, a magic mimesis based on a challenge, is the basis of many architectural productions. For instance, Renaissance princes, in their constructive urge, tried to emulate Classical Roman architecture, while the English gentry emulated Venetian aristocrats in the building of their villas. During the apogee of the Roman Imperial Age, the dominant term used to indicate the act of translation was *mutare* (to transmute), a term favored by Lucius Annaeus Seneca (ca. 4 BC–65 AD).[49] In architecture, a transmutation is a change whereby the actual and symbolic building materials are traded in for other, more precious, building materials, for example, plaster is transmuted into marble by using Roman stucco. *Mutare* was a process of innovation, which allowed the building trades to rediscover their alchemic tradition. Clay was transmuted into bricks and bricks were transmuted into glazed tiles, and so forth, in the search for an ever-lasting material.

During the Alexandrine Period, the Greek word for "translation" was *metaphoro* and the Latin word for "translation" (emulation) was *transferre*.[50] The concept embodied in this Hellenistic act of translation is a carry-over or transportation of meaning. The equivalent concept in architecture is literally a physical transport of building elements to convey meaning. The Romans transported columns and many other architectural artifacts from Greece to Rome, the Venetian transported spoils to Venice from all over the Mediterranean Basin. The Europeans brought elements from the Old Country to the New World. The great power of this building tradition is demonstrated by a well-known Christian story. Mary's house of the Annunciation was miraculously flown by angels from Palestine to Italy. Known as the flying house of Loreto, it is now enclosed in the Basilica by the same name. The term *translare* (to transport) dominated Middle-Latin tradition. It was then converted to *tradurre* (to bring) in the Late-Latin tradition.[51] The Holy House of Loreto was angelically transported from Palestine to Loreto, and disseminated all over Europe through replicas. *Traducere* is metonymical whereas *translatio* is metaphorical.[52]

Architectural translations are based upon acts of conversion of Roman buildings into Christian buildings. The Christian version of the trade is based on conversion. The basilica, a Roman administrative building, was converted into a religious edifice. The term *uerto* indicates a concept of translation revealing complex and subtle articulations.[53] The conversion of a building is a translation of a building type into its opposite. The discriminating nature of this translation is the basis for a long chain of building types. The basilica, as the etymology of the word itself suggests, began its chronicle of magic mimesis as the "place of the king" (Lat. *basileus*, from the Greek: βασιλεύς). Transmuted into a marketplace, it was later transformed into a place for the administration of justice, and finally it was converted into a religious building. During the Middle Ages, administrative buildings emulated religious buildings, however, the name "basilica" in this last conversion was lost. This traditional building type became known in Italy as "*Palazzo della Ragione*." Only in one case did the name "basilica" return to a building. In Vicenza, the *Palazzo della Ragione* is called the "*Basilica*." This name change occurred after Palladio's exterior transformation of a medieval civic hall within a Mannerist *loggia*.

In the Middle Ages, the theory of translation abandons the notion of imitation and develops the notion of metamorphosis of the text. An example of this process can be found in the history of the hospital, which has a long record of conversions that began with the translation of the monastery cloister into the hospital courtyard. The preference is for what the Germans define as *Umarbeitung* (reworking) rather than *Übersetzung* (translation). The *transferre* is therefore identified with the *tradere*.[54] Translation is one of sense rather than the literal word by word. In the Middle Ages, the word "Latin" assumed the generic meaning of "language," especially in Anglo-Norman writing, which evolved into the English *latimer* (*ni = m*).[55] The story of the *lingua tosca*, as told by the Austrian philosopher Ivan Illich, can be compared to the story of the *maniera tosca* in the architectural translation of a building into another building, or the transcription of a building into a drawing; as opposed to *volgarizzare*, which is a translation by the use of local materials.⁵⁶ The opposition is between oral translation and written translation: between *transcribe* and *translate*.⁵⁷ Joseph Rykwert's reflection on the oral tradition in architecture explains it wonderfully. To translate a building into a drawing and a drawing into a building means to induce (to infer general laws from particular cases), to deduce (to verify that what has been hypothesized at a certain level determines successive levels), and to abduce (to test new codes through interpretative hypothesis).⁵⁸

Both construction and survey drawings should be glamorous descriptions of a building since visual perception is constructive in character.⁵⁹ The analysis of the rabbit-duck illusion by the architect-philosopher, Ludwig Wittgenstein (1889–1951) proves this constructive character, however, the best proof was given in his discussion of the visual interpretations of a triangle:

> Take as an example the aspects of a triangle.

> This triangle can be seen as a triangular hole, as a solid, as a geometrical drawing; as standing on its base, as hanging from its apex, as a mountain, as a wedge, as an arrow or pointer, as an overturned object which is meant to stand on the shorter side of the right angle, as a half parallelogram, and as various other things ...⁶⁰

The projection of an interpretative scheme onto a drawing or building is the constitutive act of the drawing or building itself. To translate an image is to recognize, or guess, what has instituted it as image and to institute an interpretation. The translation results from the play between the ambiguity of the image and the univocity of the interpretative scheme. Whoever translates a building into a drawing or a drawing into a building proceeds by alternating schemes with corrections. These translations are not abstractions; they are steps of successive definition. The translation between drawings and buildings is a manifestation of the architectural faculty of instituting and recognizing equivalencies between different objects. For example, two parallel lines can be equivalent to a wall. This equivalence is the fundamental objective of any architectural representation.

Three kinds of translation are possible in architecture.⁶¹ The first is a translation within the system of buildings or drawings themselves. This reformulation consists, on the one hand, of the replacement of building elements with other building elements and, on the other hand, of the replacement of graphic marks with other graphic marks. For example, the substitution of one building element with another occurred in Greek temples, where the original wooden columns were replaced with marble ones.[62] The substitution of graphic marks takes place, for example, when penciled-in drawings are inked. The second kind is the translation of buildings into survey and construction drawings and vice versa. The third is the translation of concepts into architectural elements and vice versa, through the sophisticated art of architectural detailing. The actual theory of architecture is always hidden in the details.

Notes

1 In the imaginal world, architects can dream a building or its *eidolon*. i.e. a model of it. In dreaming the *eidolon*, they are dreaming its icon, in other words, its drawings or its model or the constructing procedures. According to Artemidorus (1975), to dream a god or its image is the same thing. For a discussion of the equivalence between icons and images, see Barasch (1993: 32).
2 [Pietropoli (1983: 90–97).]
3 Focchi (1981: 241).
4 Malinowski (1948: 56).
5 Ibid.: 114.
6 [Latin *trans-dare*, to give across.]
7 Mollino was deeply interested in magic. See Gabetti and Irace (1989) and [Brino (1987: 79)].
8 Bryant (1848: 27).
9 The magic importance of the stone threshold is interchangeable with the cornerstone as discussed in Trumbull (1896: 22, 54–55).
10 Malinowski (1948: 63).
11 A *costruzione legittima* can easily be inverted with the help of a secondary view. Florensky (2002: 233, 236–238) discusses this and draws attention to a painting by El Greco entitled *The Dream of Philip II* (1577–1580), and a few other works by the same painter.
12 [Mollino's two drawings for the architect's house are published in Brino (1987: 79).]
13 [*The Life of Oberon* was published in a few episodes in *Casabella* from July to November 1933.]
14 Mollino (1933: 44).
15 The powerful connection between architectural imagination and corporeal imagination is made in a 1986 ballet entitled "The Mollino Room," which was conceived by Mikhail Baryshnikov for the American Ballet Theatre [(Banes, 2007: 317–318)].
16 For the use of scale figures in the dream drawing of architecture, see Frascari (1987).
17 [Frascari (1991: 61).]
18 [Catoptromancy is a form of divination through the use of a mirror.]
19 Brino (1987: 156).
20 Wollheim (1980: 205–226) developed the concepts of "seeing as" and "seeing in."
21 Andersen (1992); Taylor (1719: 1–2).
22 [Mumford (2000: 27–44).]
23 Sabbatucci (1989: VII–VIII).
24 [Plato (1892: 449–450). A copy of the *Phaedrus* by Plato (1975) can be found in the Frascari library.]
25 [Aristotle (1965: 140–141); Yates (1964: 3350; Aristotle, *De Anima* 431, a, 17.]
26 Pomian (1987: 12).
27 [Frascari (2011: 148–150) discusses the process of transmutation in relation to architecture, introducing Exercise #9 "The Single Drawing."]
28 [Heraclitus: Diels-Kranz B89. See Heraclitus (1987: 55). See also Frascari's Foreword in Corona-Martinez (2003: IX).]

29 Benjamin (1968: 69–82).
30 Copeland (1991: 30).
31 Maritain (1937: 6–7).
32 [Florensky (2002: 250).]
33 Malinowski (1948: 66).
34 For a discussion of this polarity and its philosophical implication, see Lanza and Longo (1989: 5–6, 10–11).
35 Kahn (1962: 91).
36 Kahn (1986: 218).
37 [Drury (2015: 181–189, 261).]
38 Borges (1964: 39).
39 Croce (1902: 71).
40 Gentile (1920: 369–375).
41 For a discussion of the Italian paranomasia, i.e. *traduttore* equals *traditore*, and the quibble, i.e. *traduzione* equals *tradizione*, see Folena (1991: IX, 3–5) and Lepschy (1981: 457).
42 Malinowski (1948: 3).
43 Snell (1953).
44 Folena (1991: 6).
45 [Vitruvius (1931: IV.1.8–12; Vol. I: 206–211); Vitruvio (1997 IV.1.8–12: 372–375).]
46 Folena (1991: 6).
47 Ibid.:10.
48 For a discussion of Vitruvius's attempt to legitimize architecture through the literary analogy, see Romano (1987: 81–141).
49 [Folena (1991: 38). Seneca, *Epist.*, 107.10.]
50 Folena (1991: 8).
51 Ibid.: 9–10.
52 Ibid.: 71–72.
53 Ibid.: 8.
54 Ibid.: 10.
55 Ibid.: 19.
56 [*Volgarizzare* is Italian for "to translate into the vernacular" (Illich 1988: 52–83).]
57 The tradition of architectural notebooks is based on this opposition. See the famous Villard de Honnecourt's notebook (ca. 1230, Paris: Bibliothèque Nationale de France, MS. Fr. 19093) and the Taccuino Vaticano (Rome: Vatican Library, Urb. Lat. 1757) of Francesco di Giorgio Martini (1439–1502).
58 [Rykwert (1984: 14–27).]
59 The Latin *grammatica* becomes the French *grimoire*, a magic and mysterious book of sorcery. The English *glamour* is a powerful visual spell that, at the present, unfortunately means merely an empty look (Folena 1991: 20).
60 Wittgenstein (1953: 200).
61 In this passage I am converting the linguistic concepts of Jakobson (1959: 232–233, 232–239) on translation into concepts of architectural translation.
62 [Rykwert (1998a: 204).]

4

THE ORIGIN AND BEGINNING OF THE DREAM HOUSE

Marco Frascari

> 'Enter your skiff of Musement, push off into the lake of thought, and leave the breath of heaven to swell your sail. With your eyes open, awake to what is about or within you, and open conversation with yourself; for such is all meditation.' It is, however, not a conversation in words alone, but is illustrated, like a lecture, with diagrams and with experiments.[1]

Although the sketching and drawing on paper began in August 1993 with the invitation to design a *Dream House for the Next Millennium* from the Contemporary Art Center in Cincinnati, the story of this design began several years prior, while I was one of the assistants in the Interior Architecture group of Professor Carlo Scarpa, at the IUAV (Istituto Universitario di Architettura di Venezia) in Venice (see Figure 26 in the Portfolio). One day in early Spring, at the usual weekly meeting with his group of assistants, Scarpa announced that, even though he was not a registered architect, by virtue of his position in academia, he had been selected to administer the professional registration exam. In addition to chairing the committee of examiners, it was his specific duty to write the design brief. He asked for our advice and suggestions. The group proposed themes that were all institutional, such as libraries and schools. However, he commented that we were all wrong; that a real design test should be something of a dream, or a personal longing, from which any architectural quest originates. The topic that he chose for the design portion of the test challenged future professionals to dream up a house-tower for an architect, to be located on the prosperous hills near Asolo (Treviso in Italy). This wonderful countryside had been celebrated in several paintings by Giorgione (ca. 1477–1510), Carpaccio (ca. 1460–1526) and the Bellinis, as well as in Colonna's literary, double-oneiric descriptions of architecture in a landscape. The unspoken client for this enigmatic edifice was actually Scarpa himself. Without a doubt, this was one of the most difficult design tests ever assigned at a registration exam. The questions that arose in my mind upon considering the design program established by Scarpa for the test were as follows:

1 Why should an architect, in order to prove professional competency, have to design such an odd building, like a tower, for a client, who is also an architect?
2 What makes this theme peculiar as a design test?

These questions puzzled me for years, until I discovered the dwelling-tower constructed by Carl Gustav Jung (1875–1961). The story of the design and construction of this tower, on the edge of upper Lake Zürich at Bollingen, is narrated by Jung in his autobiography entitled *Memories, Dreams, Reflections* (1961). Jung relates that the tower is a representation in stone of his "innermost thoughts" and the "knowledge" that he had acquired.[2] Jung points out that in the tower, thoughts rise to the surface and, in reaching back centuries, they anticipate a distant future. In such an edifice, creativity and play act together and lighten the torment of creation. Through my discovery of Jung's tower, I came to realize that Scarpa was asking for a real architectural dream: a demonstration of architecture through a graphic evocation of the magic embodied in thaumaturgic and therapeutic design. Asking future architects to dream up another architect's dream was equivalent to asking them to design for the 'Other.' The drawing boards in the test room were like altars for these new architects to inaugurate their ability to deal with the difficult realm of alterity. In effect, to begin their design careers, Scarpa invited them to imagine and bring forth a numinous building.[3]

A numinous building is a phenomenal construction that deals with the sacred dimension of inhabitation. The numinous manifests itself as a power or force, which is quite different from the forces of nature. Musical instruments, architectural forms, beasts of burden, even vehicles of transportation are numinous objects. A hierophany separates the things that manifest the numinous from everything else around them, because they embody the spirit and the power of transcendent beings.[4] A beatific life can be had in numinous rooms. The main role of the art of building is to make our life congenial and satisfying, in other words, a *vita beata*. Numinous architecture increases our ability to invest in psychic energy and thereby fosters a *vita beata*.

Jung's tower in Bollingen, just like Scarpa's tower in the Veneto dreamscape, is a place where it is possible to be "harmonized" with "the ephemeral conditions of the present."[5] Scarpa's tower is also a search for the "infinite possibilities" of dwelling, a search for a "possible architecture."[6] The professional exam written by Scarpa was a perfect test to demonstrate professional competency in the design of a possible architecture. Incumbent in this design provocation, everyday experience and dream experience are conflated. The design process of this tower was an act of communion with the self and an act of communication with the Other through a waking meditative activity of imagination, akin to dreaming. It was a request to express the architectural Other through the self. Since then, this design pursuit has been in the back of my mind or, better yet, deep within the meanders of my architectural memories. This event came back to me when I was challenged by the dream house project. I realized that I had been waiting for just such an occasion to tackle the theoretical and practical design of a thaumaturgic and therapeutic building that would embody a theory and a practice for drawing up a numinous construction within possible infinities.

The tower is an emblem, a means of translating one of the many private architectural memories an architect has into the collective memory. These memories make up a building program and architects spend their lives construing and constructing insights embodied in their memories. This urge embodied in the construction of wonder is always derived from assumptions made by some Other architect. Architects in their building activity cannot really discover anything new. They can merely operate on the margins of construction events and prepare the ground for wonder to build marvels that will strike the imagination of another architect. These edifying visions of possible edifices mark the boundaries of any architect's vision.

They learn to understand obscure notions of the constructed world entrusted to them during their architectural education, that being their age of wonder. Like Theseus in the labyrinth, architects work to uncover amazing secrets, tracing their path with a thread and seeking a way out of the maze. Even so, the architecture they later generate will not completely reveal the obscure secrets of building. The extraordinary labyrinth is the place where the construction of architectural images and the construing of built events occur. Architecture comes out of the prudent manipulation of these constructs. The only way to develop an understanding of these constructs is to tell an amazing story, and in my case, the story of a triumphantly dreamt-up building.

The tower, a sapient artifice, is an architectural engram charged with vital tensions. The design of my tower is like the trump of 'The Tower' in the tarot deck. The French name of this card was the "House of God" (*Maison de Dieu*). A graphic association was made at some point with the Tower of Babel, which can be regarded as the origin of an architectural aporia. However, the trump card reveals that towers are numinous buildings. They are homes to a *numen* and are, at the same time, a true space for a divinity and the result of divination. The complex iconographic structure of this trump card suggests that a tower is a therapeutic construction. The tower is depicted being struck by lightning, which causes the falling of stars, stones and people. As in a dream, this card is not a still image; it is a triumphal image unfolding a mediation between feeling and perception. As philologist and philosopher Giambattista Vico (1668–1744) could have implied, the tower is a pneumatic building.[7]

The design of a tower in a dreamscape is a "monster of architecture."[8] These monsters are extraordinary events of representation. They are meaningful occurrences, which invite transmutations that merge the signified with the signifier through translation. Architectural monsters, like celestial novelties, are untouchable sacred signs of possible building elements for future constructions, that must be taken as prophecies against the conventional criticism of anointed and depressing design routines. Monsters are mantic *sema*, which foretell future events: they are *signs* that originate from analogic reasoning.

The practice of dreaming

The house-tower design was developed using tactics rather than strategies.[9] A few of these tactics have already been mentioned, such as day-dreaming. Day-dreaming applies a non-rational approach, and this attitude is not melancholic. Tradition tends to depict painters and architects as being melancholic figures governed by Saturn. Architectural day-dreams instead are jovial and full of gaiety. As an architectural student, I spent time admiring the Loggia designed by Fra Giocondo in Piazza dei Signori in Verona. While there, a puzzling consideration came to mind. How was it possible that Giocondo, a great architectural theoretician and elegant builder, who, from Rudolf Wittkower's point of view, should have been born under the sign of Saturn, had selected as his religious name, Giocondo? Giocondo means happily playful. Fra Giocondo probably had a spirited nature, the same nature that characterizes many renowned architects. I cannot imagine a gloomy Carlo Scarpa, a sad Alberto Sartoris, or a Saturnine James Sterling. Instead I can imagine Scarpa and Sartoris as sons of Mercury, and Sterling as a son of Jove. Summerson and Jencks singled out the jovial architectural wit of Sterling in an article sub-titled "*Vitruvius Ridens* or Laughter at the Clore."[10] The happiest of all, and a great master of humor, was *ser* Filippo Brunelleschi (1377–1446), who besides being a great architect, was an extraordinary practical joker.

Architectural tradition calls for a dyad to explain the origin of 'legitimate' perspective: Filippo Brunelleschi's experiments (shortly before 1413), and Alberti's book on painting (1435).[11] Alberti's theorization is the first written record of the *costruzione legittima*. Nevertheless, he attributes the beginning of perspective construction to Brunelleschi. In *The Life of Filippo Brunelleschi (Vita di Filippo Brunelleschi,* ca. 1482–1489), Antonio di Tuccio Manetti (1423–1497), an architect himself, wrote about Brunelleschi's experiments.[12] These experiments, shortly before 1413, were based on two tablets, which have been lost, representing respectively: first, the Baptistery of *San Giovanni*, and, second, a view of *Piazza della Signoria*, both in Florence. The mirror is the instrument that permitted the *costruzione legittima* to be challenged. Many art historians have attempted to reconstruct the intellectual conceptions behind the mental and corporal procedures and methods employed in the well-known baptistery tablet experiment. This experiment was conducted while standing three *braccia* (arm's lengths) from the *limine* (threshold) of the Cathedral of Santa Maria del Fiore in Florence. The reflected image of the baptistery was gazed at, by looking through a hole in a mirror at an opposite mirror. Scholarly discussion does not account for the arcane and occult nature of this experiment. The tablet's perspectival rendition of the baptistery, the 'omphalos' of the city of Florence, is a curious painting where a laminated silver sky reflects the clouds. As carefully described by Manetti, the mirror image of this representation was to be seen through a pinhole in the tablet itself. Whereas nothing is arcane in the monocularity of the *costruzione legittima*, everything is arcane in the paired images in Brunelleschi's experiment. The tablet of the baptistery is more akin to the metaphysical geometry of a medieval Byzantine icon than to the intelligible geometrical constructions employed in the *costruzione legittima*. The use of the mirror carries overtones of an experiment in the Etruscan discipline of catoptromancy (divination with the use of a mirror).

Brunelleschi's reflective experiment suggests that architectural imagination is a form of divination through the use of a mirror. The mirror is the gate to the *mundus imaginalis*. It is the imaginable place of perspectival construction as well as the imaginal place for the fabrication of a building's image. Filarete, in his *Treatise on Architecture*, acknowledged that "Ser Brunellesco" initiated the whole affair of perspective through the use of a mirror and stressed the analogical relationship between the construction of perspective and the construction of a building.[13] The magic wand in common shared between the two events is a divider or pair of compasses. The mirror is a powerful tool, having the capacity to make a designer gaze clearly through a reflection, even better than by directly staring at something.

Brunelleschi, the mirror gazer, was a cunning architect. He was gifted with what the Greeks called *metis* and the Latins called *sollertia*. *Sollertia*, the act of cunning judgment, is an essential intellectual procedure for architectural making. *Sollertia* is a fundamental virtue of a resourceful and ingenious architect. Architecture is only possible when the architect is an expert (*peritus*), gifted with a quick and artful intelligence (*ingegno mobili sollertiaque*).[14] Brunelleschi not only cunningly conceived devices for casting images or erecting domes, he also conceived practical jokes and played pranks. His jokes are essential to understanding his way of working. He was a singular character who liked to clarify his ideas by means of artfully constructed, metaphorical, and allegorical pranks.

Of note is the story of Brunelleschi's egg in the context of the erection of the dome of the Florentine cathedral. When Brunelleschi was invited to present a model of his proposal to the competition committee, in charge of appointing the architect, he refused to fulfill the request. Instead, he gave the members of the committee an egg and asked them to make it stand upright without visible support. After their failed attempts, Brunelleschi crashed the bottom of the egg on the table, which made it possible for it to stand up vertically. When the committee remarked that anybody could do it that way, Brunelleschi cunningly answered that if anybody had seen his model, they would have made the same comment and anyone could be appointed. As a result of this cleverly staged act, he was chosen for the job. However, the committee did not trust Brunelleschi completely and co-appointed Lorenzo Ghiberti (1378–1455), who was an artist with less cunning, who lacked construction knowledge. Brunelleschi hatched a plan. By feigning an illness after the construction started, he left poor Ghiberti alone to direct the work. This revealed Ghiberti's incompetence and consequently Brunelleschi was left solely in charge.

These few episodes demonstrate the musing character of Brunelleschi's mind. To better discern the architectural implications of the baptistery tablet experiment, it is essential to reflect on another practical joke by Brunelleschi (1409), narrated in the short tale entitled *La Novella del Grasso Legnaiuolo* (*The Fat Woodworker*), which was handed down for posterity by Manetti in 1489.[15] The execution of Brunelleschi's joke is based upon a dream, and is similar to the plot later used by Pedro Calderón de la Barca in his *La Vida es sueño* (1635). The *novella* states that in the month of January, Brunelleschi and a few friends decided to chastise Manetto, the Fat Woodworker, who did not show up for a dinner held by his friends, with a practical joke.[16] The joke aimed to trick Manetto into believing that he was someone else, to be more precise, that he was his friend Matteo, who was out of town at the time. The joke concludes when Manetto is utterly convinced that he is Matteo. To persuade him of this, Brunelleschi and his friends used a series of mirror dreams. The play of mirror events in this story can be related to the use of the mirrored images of the baptistery experiment. A key passage to understand the relationship between dream, mirror, and imagination is where Brunelleschi has Manetto, who is finally convinced that he is Matteo, brought back to his house.

> They entered the Fat One's bedroom, where he was lying in a deep sleep, and they put him on a stretcher with all of his clothes. They carried him to his house – where, by chance, his mother had not yet returned from the villa, which they knew since they kept a close watch over everything – and they put him in his bed and put his clothes where he usually put them. But since he usually slept with his head at the head of the bed, they left him with his head at the foot of the bed.
>
> Once they did this, they took the key to his shop and went inside. They took all of his hardware and moved it from one place to another. They did the same with his tools, leaving the wood planes with the edges up, and the saws with the teeth down. They did this with all the items in the shop that they could, so that the shop was so mislaid and in such turmoil that it seemed demons had been there.[17]

The inversion of position is completely superfluous to the carrying out of the joke. Yet Brunelleschi cunningly elaborated this ending to leave a substantive clue for posterity in order to show that his baptistery tablet experiment with the mirror is the inverse experience of the *costruzione legittima*. It is an experiment of perceptual epistemology in the realm of the imaginal.

Description of the design of the house-tower

The site selected for the design of the house-tower is located in the heart of the Amish and Mennonite country near the village of Intercourse, Pennsylvania (see Figures 25, 2, 7, 8 in the Portfolio).[18] I always considered this area to be a dreamlike landscape. I selected this location for its pleasant agricultural landscape, but also and foremost for my admiration for the stupendous geometric compositions employed by the Amish in their quilts. The geometric designs of these quilts and the geometry of the tower belong to the same semantic field (Figure 27 in the Portfolio). Amish quilts are semiophors. They are objects of high compositional quality and sophisticated tectonics, which result from piecing together remnants of cloth from various provenances. A quilt is an object of material quality, which has the same conceptual origin as spoil-architecture. A quilt is sewn from fabric spoils of other artifacts that have ended their practical utility or symbolic value and are translated into another artifact, which carries a new meaning. The making of a quilt is a social and collaborative process, not only in the collection of fabric pieces, but also in its production. Many hands are involved in quilting and sewing.

In quilt making, a construction is always a construing. For example, a quilt may embody memories of joy (as in marriage quilts) and sorrow (as in mourning quilts). A quilt is a representation that is not necessarily verisimilar. One classical quilt pattern called "log-cabin" represents the tectonic process of the construction rather than the final appearance of a log cabin. In another pattern, called "court-house steps," the image sewn from the pieces of fabric shows the urban tectonics of a small town county seat, and not monumental stairs. I decipher the nature of quilt construction by using the ritual event of the barn raising for a newly married couple in the Amish community. Barn raising requires a day's work, a bountiful meal, and the participation of the entire local Amish community. This communal event weaves together both a specific and general story, which deepens the meaning of the manufactured artifact.

To paraphrase one of the *Pensées* of Blaise Pascal (1623–1662), I can say that if a craftsperson dreams about being an architect for twelve hours every day, that same person would be happy to be an architect who dreams about being a craftsperson for twelve hours every day.[19] This chiastic interpretation is the basis for the selection of materials and the construction technology of the house-tower. The dominant theme is one of a game of words that might be termed "pneumatology": both the process of construction and the materials used are selected for their breathing capability. The house-tower is built with different kinds of massive masonry work. Stone is used for the corners, and bricks for the walls. The front columns are constructed from alternate layers of shallow pink marble drums (*rosatello di Verona*) and gray concrete, cast in metal formwork to make it shine (see Figures 42, 48 in the Portfolio). The interior walls are finished with *stucco lucido* of different colors, using the same palette as in the paintings of Roberto Matta (1911–2002). In the heavily trafficked areas, a simpler plaster, made with quicklime and marble dust, is applied with a trowel over a brown undercoat. The ceilings are made out of a stretched linen fabric. The exterior brick walls are either plastered using a mix of old tiles, dust, and quicklime, or left exposed. The basement and ground floors are finished in polished stone, while the upper floors are hardwood. The top loggia is paved in terra cotta with the insertion of one 11 x 11 cm tile in polished brass (see Figures 78 and 79 in the Portfolio). The window frames are made of steel, wood, and felt, with brass hardware (see Figure 33 in the Portfolio).

The geometric relationship between the square plan of the building and the square format of the paper used in the final drawings is a quintessential rhetorical portrait device, whereas technological tactics govern the tectonics of construction. The ground floor of the tower is the threshold to the upper and lower levels. This floor in its entirety becomes the access room for the whole building. There is a duality of purpose to the moving doors on this floor: when the doors are open, they form closed closets, and when the doors are closed, they form open closets. This duality relates this threshold to the tradition set by the myth of Janus and his temple. In the temple of Janus, the doors are kept open during a time of war and closed during periods of peace. It also makes reference to Cardea, the wife of Janus and goddess of hinges,[20] who is credited with having a cardinal role in the beginning of architecture. Thus the cardinal floor of the design, and the first to be delineated, is the ground level. The key building element of the tower derives its meaning from the weaving of the pattern of this floor. The main structural elements of the tower are a ponderous column (see Figures 29, 48, and 64 in the Portfolio), three massive walls, and a swift staircase.

Below the ground floor there are two vaulted levels of cellars dedicated to the preservation and aging of wine and food. The pneuma of the house originates in the lower level which is a wine cellar. In it dwells the *spiritus phantasticus*, which presides over the numinous nature of the building.[21] The upper cellar level is dedicated to the storage of food. Ascending above the main level there are two bedroom floors and then the floor that contains the library and a studio (Figure 60 in the Portfolio), followed by the kitchen and dining room floor (Figure 59 in the Portfolio), and, finally on the top floor, an open loggia covered with a double-pitched roof.

The main façade consists entirely of windows for looking in and seeing out. The window design is very important as their purpose is not only for ventilation, illumination or views onto the landscape. Windows are powerful tools for the graphic forecasting of past constructions and for the backcasting of future buildings. Indeed, the most popular DOS operating system is called Windows. In the Western tradition, perspectival construction is based on an understanding of the role of windows in unifying the field of perception. In the house-tower, windows are powerful analogical tools, which become instruments to counteract the objectification of reality. These machine-windows allow one to see in and out while mirroring oneself in the surrounding reality.

There are several analogical machines embodied in the house-tower. A crane and a built-in sextant are incorporated into the structure of the roof (Figure 36 in the Portfolio). A water wheel at ground level (west orientation) produces energy and motion for the contrivances of the house. Stoves for heating and open fireplaces are located in the kitchen and on the loggia (Figures 34 and 59 in the Portfolio). The last, and most important, analogical device is an angelic compass on the roof, which operates as a weathervane (Figures 35 and 38 in the Portfolio).

Notes

1 Peirce (1931–1958: CP 6.461).
2 Jung (1973: 223).
3 Pioneers who formulated ideas about the numinous element are Carl Jung, Lawrence Kuber, Thomas Troward (1847–1916), and Rudolf Otto (1869–1937). Otto, a German theologian, coined the term "numinous." He derived it from the Latin *numen*. The word *numen*, in Latin, is connected with the word *sacer* (holy), indicating the holy dimension of magic (Otto 1950: 5–7, 117–118).
4 [The word hierophany derives from the Greek and signifies a manifestation of the sacred.]
5 Jung (1973: 237).
6 The idea of a possible architecture and infinity is encapsulated in the title of a piece of music composed by Luigi Nono (1924–1990) to remember Scarpa's œuvre: *A Carlo Scarpa, Architetto, ai Suoi Infiniti Possibili* (1984).
7 Vico (1984: 181–182, 274–275, 285–286).
8 [Frascari (1991).]
9 For the difference between tactics and strategies, see de Certeau (1988: XIX, 36–38).
10 Summerson and Jencks (1987: 45–46).
11 Alberti (1966b).
12 Manetti (1992). [Manetti (1970).]
13 Filarete (1965: 304–305) (XXIII f. 178 r./v., f. 179 r); Filarete (1972: 651–654) (XXIII f. 178 r./v., f. 179 r).
14 Vitruvius (1931: V, 6, vii; Vol. I: 286–287); Vitruvio (1997: V, 6, vii: 570–573).
15 Manetti (1991).
16 The time of year can be deduced by the fact that people wish each other Happy New Year.
17 Manetti (1991: 29–30).
18 [Frascari (1995: 25) explains that Intercourse was named after the fact that it was the social "meeting place" of the Amish and Mennonite communities.]
19 [According to Pascal:
If we dreamt the same thing every night, it would affect us as much as the objects we see every day. And if an artisan were sure to dream every night for twelve hours' duration

that he was a king, I believe he would be almost as happy as a king, who should dream every night for twelve hours on end that he was an artisan.

(2009 129)]

20 [The term hinge in Italian language is "cardine" from the name of Cardea.]
21 This design for the cellar contains references to the first building I designed in 1970 as an independent professional. I designed a house for a vintner on the Morainic hills beyond Lazise, a small, medieval-walled town on Lake Garda near Verona. I was proud to take on the latere (modern) tradition for vintner house designs as in the Dionysiac tradition of Ignazio Gardella (1905–1999) and Alberto Sartoris (1901–1998), and not the tradition of the Sanatoria. Consequently, I thought this was my opportunity to design the *architettura metafisica* catechized by Sartoris. Nevertheless, during construction I discovered that my dream for a metaphysical cellar was a selfish dream, not a dream cellar. The client was present every day during the construction of the cellar, but only occasionally during the construction of the upper floors. His aim was to provide a perfect cellar for his wines, and he was closely involved with the selection of materials, the dimensions, the proportions, and the construction methods. For the tradition of wine cellars in Veneto architecture, see Frascari (2008a: 24).

5

THE PRESENT ARCHITECTURE SMELLS BAD

Marco Frascari

Designers, in their sermons about architecture and urban environments, often define spaces using opposing binomials. This is a system where the nature of the rapport between parts in the constructed environment is explained using pairs of opposite principles. Urban designers concern themselves with the relationship between collective and individual spaces. Architects trouble themselves in determining the actual dimensions and points of contact between public and private spaces. If they are ecologically minded, they worry about artificial spaces overtaking natural spaces. If they are piously oriented, they concern themselves with profane spaces taking-over the sacred spaces of religion, culture, and civilization. The result of this setting of polarities is that they are bound to design spaces that stir up feelings of tension and uneasiness.

The result of a design process based on dualistic choices is that spaces are considered either good or bad according to their performance in relation to binomial limits. The analyses of design performance are made through scientific pre-evaluation and post-evaluation. Constructed spaces are considered subordinate to other tasks for which they become the means. In describing his own experience as a member of the Planning Commission of Puerto Rico, Leopold Kohr (1909–1994), suggested that the pre-design studies elaborated by design professionals were merely attempts to discover the direction in which the wind is blowing. He went on to say that they completed their projects following the wind, the tide, and the alleged will of the future users. Furthermore, he pointed out that, after the completion of the project, people preferred to return to the old city of San Juan and to leave behind the new, rational, and fashionable building complexes.[1] Unlike the newly designed city, the old city of San Juan, dating back one hundred years, evolved without concern for social and behavioral objectives, or the planning of design phases that aim to produce an urban space.

Following pre-design and post-evaluation studies, rational and critically-minded designers tend to refuse the non-rational, 'wondrous' nature of architectural forecasting. They cannot accept that a dream is a phenomenon that surpasses any scientific experiment. The realization of a dream offers a durable and subjective value to the built environment that otherwise might only have a "doubtful or ephemeral objectivity."[2] In their verbal, graphic, and numeric estimates, architects should be concerned with numinous constructions instead of hiding the absence of a dream behind scientific or pseudo-scientific procedures. Numinous constructions uniquely emanate a sense of well-being and deal with the sacred dimension of inhabiting. The numinous realm is a special ambit that defines a holy space and is devoid of moral and rational aspects. Numinous spaces cannot be functionally labeled; they are non-rational spaces where a beatific life can be achieved.

Vita Beata

The main role of the art of constructing architectural and urban spaces is to make our life congenial and satisfying or, in other words, to create numinous places for the enjoyment of a *vita beata*. In professional foretelling, architects should be concerned with the making of such numinous places. The plans of Palladio's villas are ideal demonstrations of the attainability of a numinous space. They are perfect *loci* for a *vita beata*. No single room is functionally or rationally labeled in Palladio's *Four Books*.[3] Palladio's numinous rooms result from the triple integration of measurement, decoration, and proportion. They assimilate time, space, and individuality into one spatial unity. They are poetic rooms, i.e., true stanzas.[4] Stanzas are therapeutic spaces where one can find respite from human and environmental concerns. They are places for reverie, daydreaming, and dreaming. They are the places dedicated to the non-rational activity of *otium* (leisure), which is a necessary condition for a *vita beata*. Analogously, numinous 'urban stanzas' are places where one can experience a *vita beata*.

A negation of the idea of a *vita beata* takes place between floors, in the *mezzanino* (mezzanine) of Venetian palaces. The mezzanine, a half-height floor in between regular height floors, is an interstitial architectural space that Venetian merchants exported to other cultures. The mezzanine is a service space in-between two floors dedicated to the work of the servants where the negation of *otium*, i.e. *nec-otium*, takes place. The mezzanine is a place of negation, where a person cannot ever stand in a vertical position, but must always bend the shoulders. The same condition is true for interstitial urban spaces. Life negotiations take place within the in-between spaces of the urban environment, i.e. beyond or between colonnades, surrounding a square, in a back alley or in other interstitial spaces. Mezzanines and urban interstitial places are the *loci* where the meeting of private and public, individual and collective, sacred and profane takes place.

Pantaloon, a Venetian merchant in the *Commedia dell'Arte*, demonstrates a character who cannot enjoy a beatific life. This character, with hunched shoulders, holds his private office and the public reception room in a mezzanine, as well as his personal bath and employee rest-room. His revered boardroom is enveloped by mundane hallways and profane waiting-rooms. This dual condition of the mezzanine floor as opposed to the main floors can be compared to urban spaces in Victorian England that were used as private gardens in the center of public squares. This negation of numinous space is achieved by inserting traffic infrastructure areas along public gardens. A corresponding dual opposition might be found in suburban America between private houses and public urban renewal projects. Similarly, sacred spaces of historical importance, such as the City Hall of Philadelphia or Boston, used to be contrasted by the surrounding profane and mundane spaces of red-light districts.[5]

A proper method to figure out the non-rational approach to the design of numinous rooms is to consider the way Camillo Sitte (1843–1903) looked at urban rooms. In his theoretical city planning work, Sitte does not define spaces in rational and functional terms; he merely lists a sequence of urban ideograms. His book, *The Art of Constructing Cities*, is a grammar for the divination of civic spaces, civic stanzas delineated to understand changes.[6] The basic technical distinction between analog (continuous) and digital (discrete) representations is crucial since Sitte's ideograms of urban spaces must be read like the hexagrams of the *I Ching, The Book of Changes* through analogical procedures and reverberations.

Although designed in particular ways and used in specific manners, urban stanzas are numinous architectural spaces that have ineffable aspects. In a Palladian villa, for example, numinous rooms are not indicated by their function or purpose, such as bedrooms, living rooms, etc., but by mythological names that reveal their numinous ideograms, such as the "Room of the Muses" or the "Room of Morpheus." On the other hand, as in the case of the White House in Washington, DC, the formal office of the President named the 'Oval Office', is a room based on a Pythagorean oval. This denomination would remain with the room even if its purpose changed. Numinous urban and dwelling spaces allow one to "take a breath." This is not true of most contemporary built environments. Today's architecture does not have *pneuma*: it consists of the glamorous apposition of seductive glossy and chic decoys. In Italian, an architectural critic might refer to a building as having a "large breath" (*un edificio di largo respiro*). Numinous spaces are of "large breath": they are a truly pneumatic architecture. By the term "pneumatic," I do not mean inflatable architecture, but a space where a *pneuma*, or élan resides. The building then becomes either a deity or a machine, a *pneumatic machine*, i.e., a construction with an aura. The building has a *spiritus,* and it "smells good."[7]

Most designers conceive ostentatious buildings flaunting luster-laden surfaces and trammeled geometries, when, in fact, the outcome is just dull, prosaic, and obtuse. These buildings are above all inhuman acrid utterances. The piercing smells inherent in the chemical adhesives and polymeric substances employed in their construction, in order to make them look exactly like the drawings, dominate the scenery of today's built environment. These malodorous constructions demonstrate that the great art of building well is long gone. New buildings are mephitic: they smell bad. They have lost their *pneuma* or *spiritus*, *ch'i* or *aura* and they no longer have the presence of a pneumatic machine. Although regarded as an artifice, the art of building well is the natural cornerstone of the art of living well. It has become bereft of its original intention to generate and abet a beatific life.[8]

At the end of the first book of his *De Architectura,* Vitruvius discussed the construction procedure for an urban pneumatic machine.[9] As a demonstrative contrivance to explain the consequential role of winds in designing a city to be congenial to its inhabitants, he suggested the use of the aeolic engine, a pneumatic toy, invented by Hero of Alexandria (10–70 AD). This pneumatic machine, put into motion by the *spiriti flati*, is an instrument that reveals the latent empyrean ratios of the divine (*aeolipilis aereis licet aspicere et de latentibus caeli rationibus | artificiosis rerum inventionibus divinitatis exprimere veritatem*).[10] These *spiriti flati* were demonstrated in Athens by Andronicus of Cyrra who built the Tower of the Winds and capped it with a bronze merman weathervane. On the walls of this octagonal building were representations of the winds, personified as angels, as well as angles of direction casting shadows. The pneumatic flow detected by the tower is equivalent to the flow of the Chinese life-giving energy, *ch'i*. This energy is the basis of *Feng Shui,* the art and science that has influenced the shape and orientation of many Far Eastern cities, palaces, and cemeteries.[11]

Architecture is a virtuous art that has been divested of its exemplary status.[12] Nowadays, it is seldom the case that any ethical scope or moral standard is embodied in buildings. Constructions are presently the expression of dull, prosaic, obtuse, and above all discomforting architecture. They have become tedious and boring for their users. The aim of my project for a house-tower is to demonstrate that architecture can startle boredom. Real architecture should return to being the result of macaronic thinking.

The happiness of bathroom imagination

> Here he must drink what is called the water of Forgetfulness (Lethe), in order that he may forget everything he has hitherto thought of. After that he drinks another water, to wit, the water of Memory, whereby he remembers what he sees down below.
>
> Pausanias[13]

Contemporary architecture, although seductive, exhales toxic odors. This mephitic fact is understandable, but not acceptable. This curious event is neither a deduction nor an induction, but an abduction à *la* Peirce and part of an intellectual process he calls musement.[14] Progressing in my play, I propose that the real value of a bathroom for human existence can only be understood through the power of the *ars macaronica*. Ostensibly, at this point, I should summon the powerful muse invoked by Giordano Bruno in his *La Cena delle Ceneri*:

> By now I really need thee, sweet Mafelina, who art the muse of Merlin Cocaio.[15]
> *Or qua te voglio, dolce Mafelina, che sei la musa di Merlin Cocaio.*[16]

To give me the oratorical flair necessary to carry on this 'exercise,' I need the gift of Mafelina, the euphonious muse of the contriver of the macaronic art, Merlinus Cocaius (the pen-name of Teofilo Folengo), to unfold my musing and analogical thoughts on plumbing. These considerations on plumbing, were elaborated graphically during the design process for the bathrooms of the house-tower. These drawings are a pretext for construing architecture as a source for a *vita beata* and to re-inspire the idea that the role of the architect is to design places for 'happiness.' Through these reflections on the bathroom, unfolded in a macaronic manner, I aim to reveal the pneumatic core of a house for a *vita beata* and to stimulate the architectural spirit of others.

Under the spell of the modern goddess "Hygiene," the design of bathrooms has lost the capacity for being the locus for a relaxing psychic activity.[17] It has become merely a space, or better yet, a metonymic closet for secret constraints.[18] Bathrooms are no longer considered ennobling places where a sacred spring or a *mundus* is located, but rather a space where the presence of waste is swiftly removed by hydraulic means. It is a space that can be determined either through the rules of the *Existenzminimum,* or through a partial or total refusal of that very code by constructing the space with a "*De Luxe*" design mandate of lavishness.[19] In other words, a bathroom can be conceived with Spartan rigor or by tasteless and ostentatious material wealth. This dual design approach reveals an attitude towards bathrooms that is manichaeistic in nature and demands a new way of thinking about bathrooms entirely, what Louis Kahn may have called "volume zero."[20]

My curiosity for the nature and the design of bathrooms originates from my early professional training in Verona, a city of plentiful Roman hydraulic dreams,[21] when I worked in the studio of Arrigo Rudi (1929–2007) *Architetto*.[22] Rudi's initial undertaking in any design project was a meticulous refinement of the plan and sections for the bathrooms, as well as the layout of the ceramic tiles.[23] None of these bathrooms was derived from the simple plan and section diagrams published in the Italian graphic standards manual, the *Manuale dell'Architetto*. Each was custom-designed and resulted from a slow refinement process that often required the same time it took to develop all the rest of the design. At first, I was annoyed by what seemed a waste of time. However, a few years later, during one of my after-dinner contemplations I came to realize the transcendence and the importance of the design of bathrooms, when I happened to glance at the plans of the Fondazione Angelo Masieri, in Volta de Canal, Venice, by Carlo Scarpa.[24] Just like Paul on his way to Damascus, I underwent a conversion; in my case, I came to believe that the bathroom is an ideal place to foster a beatific life. The bathroom is the last 'metaphysical' *locus* in the mundane, where the architectural union between *voluptas* and *venustas* and between the sacred and the profane is possible.[25] In current architectural design, the bathroom is the last place left where the *pneuma* may lead our lives toward a beatific stage. It is the last domicile of Synesius' *phantastikon pneuma* or Bruno's *spiritus fantasticus*.[26] The *pneuma* or *spiritus* that dwells in the bathroom is the last reminder of a time when *pneuma* permeated freely through the entire house and made human dwellings numinous places.

The bathroom is a numinous place, with numinous objects, where hierophanies may unfold (see Figure 51 in the Portfolio).[27] A hierophany separates that which manifests the sacred from everything else around it. Hierophanies can become symbols that signify symbolic forms. These forms become sacred, because they embody the spirit or power of transcendent beings. For example, throughout history, pearls were considered symbols or numinous objects that represent a cosmological center, and were associated with the moon, women, fertility, and birth. With respect to the bathroom and its fixtures, they can be symbolic of initiation, love (sacred and profane), beauty and ugliness, mutation, transformation, birth, and the center of the house. The bathroom is a representation of the *mundus* (Greek κόσμος).[28] One walks in "unclean" (Italian *immondo*) and walks out "clean" (Italian *mondo*).[29] Today, the bathroom is the last architectural artifact where an understanding of the cosmos as a symbolic expression of human cosmogony and "cosmetic" (*kosmos*) can be manifested in its quintessence.[30]

It was with the advent of the Industrial Revolution and the invention of plumbing and bathroom fixtures that the bathroom became a fixed entity: a necessary space almost relegated to the back. There was no longer a need to carry hot water from the kitchen to a portable bathtub, or to retrieve the chamber pot from under the bed or nightstand. Consequently, the house was no longer understood to be a pneumatic machine. Yet, a 1915 advertisement put out by the Trenton Potteries Company demonstrates the latent presence of a *pneuma* inhabiting the bathroom. It shows a luminous, ethereal bathroom as the heart of a house. The advertisement enlarges the bathroom in relation to the house, playing with scale and central perspective. The bathroom seems to be illuminated by the divine radiance of the *spiritus fantasticus*, rather than by daylight coming from the window or from an electric fixture. This advertisement visually suggests that the bathroom can still be a numinous place.

In Palladian villas, the majority of rooms were numinous; no single room was labeled "bathroom." Consequently, the ritual of bathing or other bathroom activities could take place in any room. The virtuous inhabitants of a Palladian villa enjoyed beatific ablutions and discharges, which could be performed, for instance, in the "Room of the muses" or the "Room of the Seasons." These rituals could take place while looking out in any direction that was visually and thermally delightful. It was even possible to have a slipper-bath or the commode dragged in front of an open fire.[31]

The bathrooms of the Fondazione Masieri (1968) by Scarpa are exemplary pneumatic machines; each is a small room of "large breath." The original program, to house architectural students, required an environment that would foster creativity. The cylindrical shape of the bathrooms determines the upper floor spaces of this small building. In these bathrooms, fixtures become sacred fonts, the springs where the nymph Egeria displays her phenomenological expression. These womb-like cylindrical bathrooms, which are finished in a radiant-colored *stucco lucido*, are a means for creative egresses.[32] By the use of this lustrous plaster, the bathroom reveals the spiritual, lustral power of a water font that is analogous to the amniotic fluid from which life originates. It is a perfect building detail for a lunar building consecrated to the training of mother-architects.[33] The extraordinarily scented spirit of architecture dwells in these bathrooms. Water is treated as a sacred element in these inner *aediculae*. The detailing of the upper floors relates to that of the ground floor with regard to dealing with the *"acque alte"* caused by possible shower or toilet overflows. The bath is a microcosm, a counterpart of the macrocosm, of the edifice.

Scarpa knew how to deal with the element of water within a building. Unlike some of his peers, he never forgot the "joy" and "fear" of water.[34] His design allows for the *acqua alta* (the high-tide water of Venice) to enter the building through visible and invisible waterproof means. His architecture lets the water in gently, makes it a joyful event, and then allows the water out when the tide drops.[35] The combination of shower, basin, and toilet bathrooms of the cylindrical *bagni* of the Fondazione Masieri becomes a *stanza da bagno* (room for bathing). In a superficial reading of the triangular plan of the existing shell, the circular baths may appear to be prefabricated modular monoblocs or like interstitial spaces that have become overgrown columns. Instead, they are the "stanzas" for and of thought, just like the stanzas that compose a poem.[36]

This idea of the room for bathing as a *stanza* is revealed clearly in the Villa Ottolenghi (1974–1979), another design by Scarpa, in Bardolino near Lake Garda. To enter this chthonic dwelling, it is necessary to descend into mother earth. The room for bathing is the poem of the house, the "stanza" of the stanzas. The Villa Ottolenghi is a therapeutic edifice. The cosmological representation of the roof of this dwelling is like a threshing floor, under which dwelling takes place.[37] The bathroom design for the master bedroom was achieved through three stages of refinement. The initial solution was a traditional one, a closet added to the bedroom, such that it had no presence within the body of the house.[38] It eventually evolved from being a private space to being a numinous place that interacted with the house as a whole.

Having had ablutions in memory and forgetfulness let us now move on to the odoriferous throne of memory. The locution "odor of sanctity" (*odore di santità*) has always fascinated me and it now puts my macaronic thinking to work. Advertising campaigns frequently remind us that we live in a society that is superciliously proud of being odorless. Through this redolent paranoia, hundreds of synthetic products that claim to sanitize air and surfaces emit an odor of sanity in order to eliminate the odor of sanctity. Such habits created miasmic buildings, an unwholesome architecture, hard to deplore because it is odorless. In our contemporary culture, scent is good: odor is bad (most deodorants are scented, even unscented ones, which have always some presence of scent). We deodorize our houses the same way that we deodorize our bodies.[39]

What kind of smell is the odor of sanctity? When I raised this question with my macaronic grandmother, who supervised my religious education,[40] her answer was: the fragrance of roses and incense. However, while visiting the churches in Mantua, during the annual celebration of *Ognissanti* (All Saints' Day), my sense of smell led me to conclude that the odor of sanctity was not a particularly fragrant scent, but a musty odor mixed with the scent of old incense and cleansing oils. This unusual odor is like the one of the pneumatic beginning of humanity. One of the principles of Giambattista Vico, presented in his *New Science*, is the burial of the dead and the immortality of the human soul.

> Afterward, the god-fearing giants, those settled in the mountains [377], must have become sensible of the stench from the corpses of their dead rotting on the ground nearby, and must have begun to bury them.[41]

According to Vico, our being human began by the act of covering the putrescent bodies of ancestors with *humus*. The emanating smell of the remains is their spirit, their immortal soul. Pneuma is the sacred odor of memory. The sense of smell, one of the strongest links to memory, holds the key of the door to the *mundus imaginalis*. From this point of view, bathroom odor is the current version of the odor of sanctity, the aroma for physical and mental sanity of a modern pneumatic iconostasis: the current golden gate to a beatific life.

All these concerns about odor and the numinous nature of the bathroom have been condensed in the design of my house-tower for the next Millennium. The pneumatic spaces in the dream house have ineffable and impersonal qualities, although they were conceived in a particular manner and can be used in a specific and individualized way. The plan geometry of the numinous bathrooms is maternal and womb-like, and their materials and lines are ruled by the same geomaternal procedures that order the design of the tower (Figure 80 in the Portfolio).[42]

A design epiphany occurred while sketching a bathtub and writing a declaration of intention for the project. This was followed by a study of the geomater as well as the details of bathroom fixtures. My first sketch shows a means of entering the pneumatic world of architectural imagining through an angelic vision of the *mundus imaginalis*: a *mundus* that is as ontologically real as that of the *mundus* of the senses and the *mundus* of the intellect (see Figure 39 in the Portfolio). Like Scarpa, I refused the closet solution or the interstitial place. I played with the geomater and treated the bathroom as an enhancement of the *stanza* in one case, and as a counterpart of the main column of the structure in the other (see Figures 39, 48 in the Portfolio). The anthropomorphic geomater of these two numinous spaces is based on the use of curved lines that reference organs and skin. The study drawings for the bathrooms focus on individual details, such as the basin and the mirror, which are emblems of the numinous. In the final presentation drawing, a detailed section of one of the bathrooms is paired with a study of the compass weathervane, which is located on the roof (Figures 5 and 6 in the Portfolio).

In the bathroom of the master bedroom, the bathtub interacts with the main column and together they form the transitional space between the bedroom proper and the elongated bathroom niche (see Figures 39–41 in the Portfolio). Both spaces are vaulted and finished in *stucco lucido,* while the transitional space has a flat, mirrored ceiling. This connects us with the *mundus imaginalis* of architecture that was expressed in the first sketch, which showed the angelic vision of the world of the image. In this setting, the bathtub is a place which evokes a faculty of imaginative power, a cognitive function with a noetic value that is as real as that of sense perception or intellectual intuition. Lying in this bathtub, *ubi* (where) becomes *ubique* (anywhere). The mirror above this transitional space is analogous to the one used by Brunelleschi when he conjured up the invention of the *costruzione legittima*.[43] An active imagination is a mirror *par excellence*, an epiphanic place where images are born.

The aim of these bathrooms is to promote a beatific existence, a *vita beata*, and to put aside for a time the trials of living. The attainment of a *vita beata*, a good spirit, is the goal of human existence. The house-tower is an ensemble of places for lovers of virtue. Its bathrooms are the *loci* where the pneuma, or spirit, of virtuous happiness dwells. By investing in psychic efficacy, this architecture provokes a beatific life and amplifies the latent talents of her inhabitants. The body of the dream tower is bathed by the pneuma arising from the angelic plumbing of the bathrooms.[44]

Notes

1 Kohr (1976).
2 [Bachelard (1971: 1).]
3 Palladio (1570 and 1997).
4 The word "stanza" in English is used only for a unit of a poem; it hardly connotes a room. In Italian, the word *stanza* denotes a unit of a poem as well as a unit in a building. The latter usage is derived from the Arabic term *bayt*, meaning dwelling place, verse, as well as tent (Agamben 1993: 130). In an architectural dream, a *stanza* is both a locus of word play and bodily play.
5 There is a corresponding contrast between the scents of old wax or incense and the foul smell of urine.
6 Sitte (1980). [Sitte (2013).]
7 During the twelfth century the term *spiritus* acquired new meanings in psychology and cosmology. It stressed the coherence between the macro and the microcosm (Chenu 1957). Vico, in his *New Science*, indicated that reaction to smell is the origin of the most archaic of human institutions—the inhumation of bodies—an act that made us human (Vico 1984: 184–185) [(Boyle and Frascari 2009).]
8 [Rykwert (1982).]
9 Vitruvius (1931: I, VI, 4–8; Vol. I: 56–61); Vitruvio (1997: I, VI, 4–8: 48–51).
10 Vitruvio (1997: 1, VI, 2: 46–47). "That this is true we may see from Aeoluses of bronze, and by the craftsman's inventions of things which express the truth of the divinity, about the causes which lurk in the heavens." From Vitruvius (1931: 1, VI, 2: 54–55).
11 *Feng shui* literally means wind and water. These forces shape both the human landscape and fortune. To practice *Feng shui* is to read the fortune of a place. In Italian, *fortuna* (fortune) is etymologically related to *fortunale*, a meteorological wind and water disturbance.
12 Daniele Barbaro, Giovambattista Caporali, Andrea Palladio and many other Renaissance theoreticians personified the discipline of architecture as the Queen of Virtues (Frascari 1988a: 20); [(Frascari 2011: 57)].
13 Pausanias (1913: 494).
14 [Peirce (1931–1958: CP 5.171: 105–106).]
15 Bruno (1995: 113).
16 [Ibid.: 36.]
17 Georges Vigarello (1985) wrote the first monograph that dealt with the changing relationship between body perceptions and social cleanliness. His study focuses on the evolution of the "bathroom" in France since the Middle Ages. During the Middle Ages the bath served a hedonistic purpose for pleasure and relaxation, rather than for hygiene. During the Baroque period, hygiene was perceived to be a threat to the porous skin of the human body, the interior of which was in constant flux. Vigarello's work is important regarding seventeenth- and eighteenth-century documentation.
18 Stewart (1995).
19 The idea of "*De Luxe*" and this dual canon of bathroom design can be explained by understanding that the idea of luxury (It. *lusso*) is generated from the idea of lechery and lust (It. *lussuria*).
20 [Anderson (1995).]
21 Seppilli (1977) analyzed the numinous nature of Roman hydraulics.
22 Upon my graduation from the IUAV in Venice, I worked for two years in Arrigo Rudi's studio. [See Los *et al.* (2011).]
23 Rudi assisted Carlo Scarpa during the renovation of the Museum of Castelvecchio, in Verona (Los *et al.* 2011: 49–57). There was the belief among those working in his studio that this fascination with bathrooms was one of the many "*Scarpismi*" that Rudi held in his bag of design-tricks. Indeed, Scarpa was enamored with the design of bathrooms. In fact, one of his favorite dinner stories relates how wonderstruck he was by the bathrooms in the Four Seasons Hotel in New York.
24 Angelo Masieri, a pupil and collaborator of Carlo Scarpa, died in a car crash in Bedford, Pennsylvania, in 1952 while on his way to study architecture with Frank Lloyd Wright in Arizona. His parents had commissioned Wright to design their house in Volta di Canal on

the Grand Canal, in Venice, but after their son's death, they changed the scope of the design, and decided to build a residence for students of architecture. Wright's design was not approved by the city administration; they failed to understand the importance of architecture for the future of the city of Venice. The building stood unoccupied as an empty shell and was at risk of collapse. At this point, Valeriano Pastor, one of the first pupils of Scarpa, was commissioned to preserve the building. A few years later, Scarpa was entrusted with the design of the student residence, but he died before its completion. Franca Semi, who had collaborated with Scarpa on this project from its inception, completed the work. Its current use, however, as a museum and exhibition space, alters the magical qualities of edification as originally intended for this edifice.

25 A numinous bath is part of what Alberto Sartoris calls *architettura metafisica* (Sartoris 1984; 1986).
26 In his *De Magia*, Bruno (1986: 54–55, 96–97) follows the thesis of Synesius and relates *pneuma* with the subtle body (*corpo sottile*) of angels. See Klein (1979: 51–61) and Klein (1975). For a historical account of *pneuma*, see Kessling (1922) and Osler (1991). [See also Emmons and Frascari (2006: 87–102) in the edited volume by Kenda (2006).]
27 Otto (1950: 1–7) stated that the idea of "numinous" does not exist in modern religion; by extension I affirm that the idea of a numinous space is a concept that does not exist in modern design. Modern designers discount the subjective nature of numinous space.
28 [Vico (1984: XXI–XXII: 274–273).]
29 For the opposition between clean and unclean, see Bleeker (1968).
30 [Vico (1984: XXI–XXII).]
31 The mobile nature of bathing was very comfortable (Rivers et al. 1992: 86–95).
32 Egeria and "egress" share a common root: "to carry out." Egeria is derived from *egerere*, meaning "to push out." Egeria was the nymph invoked for a good childbirth.
33 In the second book of his treatise, Filarete follows the animalistic footsteps of Leon Battista Alberti and suggests that buildings are alive just like human beings. The architect is the mother, while the client is the father, of the edifice. During "architectural pregnancy," the mother/architect grows the baby building in his/her memory by using the light of *pneuma* (*fantasticare*). After seven or nine moons the baby building, in the form of a small wooden model, is born. With proper constructional care this monster (*sema*) will grow into an adult building (Filarete ca. 1461–1464: II, f. 7v; Filarete 1972: II, f. 7v: 39–41; Filarete 1965: II, f. 7v: 15–16). To understand the maternal aspect of architecture in Scarpa's work, see Braham and Frascari (1995: 16–27). See Figure 80 in the Portfolio.
34 For the fear and joy of water, see Auer (1995).
35 The first expression of this Zen-like approach to the predicament of high-tide water is found in Scarpa's restoration of the ground floor and garden of the Fondazione Querini-Stampalia (1959–1963) in Venice, as well as in the Brion-Vega Cemetery in San Vito d'Altivole (1969–1978).
36 According to Dante:
> And here one must know that this term (*stanza*) has been chosen for technical reason exclusively, so that what contains the entire art of the canzone should be called *stanza*, that is, a capacious dwelling or receptacle for the entire craft. For just as the canzone is the container (literally the lap or womb) of the entire thought, so the stanza enfolds its entire technique.
>
> (*De Vulgari Eloquentia* II. 9, cited in Agamben 1993: VII)
37 The origin of the roof design can be found in the threshing floor courtyard of the Villa al Palazzetto in Monselice (near Padua). This floor, which Scarpa himself called "The moon and the sun," became a fully developed cosmological floor under which the aspects of the house are configured in the Villa Ottolenghi.
38 The architecture of the closet and its cultural influence are discussed in Stewart (1995). Closets are private places, which promote a total withdrawal from the public sphere of the house. This condition was imposed upon bathrooms by the theoreticians of architecture that Rykwert (1998b) labeled the "First Moderns," and by the German idea of *Existenzminimum*.
39 Contemporary architecture smells bad. It is malodorous and it needs to regain a pleasant odor. An analysis of this topic is beyond the scope of this work. For a further understanding

of the relationship between smell and architecture, see Le Guerer (1992); Ackerman (1990: 24–39, 59–60). [See Boyle and Frascari (2009).]
40 For instance, my grandmother's explanation for the acronym *DOM*, found on the doors of many churches, was like a Mantuan imperative: "*Done Omeni Marieve*" (women and men get married), instead of the official: "*Domine Omnia Mundi,*" (God cleanses us all).
41 Vico (1984: 184).
42 I called the tool for the pursuit of a *vita beata* in architecture "geomater." This term was coined by James Joyce (1976: 297), who combined *matrix, mater* (mother) and *meter* with *geo* (earth) into a "pregnant" metaphor, which describes geometry as a discipline based upon measurement, prediction, and genesis (see Figure 80 in the Portfolio). I am an image-maker, one who constructs and construes "geomaternal" figures in and upon the world. These maternal figures express the materialistic nature of the "graphplot" (the full-bodied science of architectural representation). I structured this "graphplot" into three parts, according to the nature of architectural imagination: first as a "mantic geometry": a projective geometry that makes visible the invisible; second as a "body geometry": a metric geometry that makes tangible the intangible; and third as a "color geometry": a topical geometry that makes material the immaterial. These categories can be used to manifest the image-making potential of architecture, both historically and didactically. They are not so much a division of kind as they are aspects of the imaginative metaphysics of the geomater. They overlap in procedure and share the same logic as magic and poetics. For a complete discussion of the idea of geomater, see Braham and Frascari (1995: 16–27).
43 [Millon (1994: 449–451).]
44 [Frascari (1987: 123–142).]

6

THE ANALOGICAL MONSTER

Marco Frascari

Mantic architectural procedures are founded upon analogical thinking in its most refined forms. Analogical thinking yields to our perceptions of what we see, smell, taste and make. Analogies allow us to discern the semantic relationship in formless matter by using our bodies as the basis for construing. For example, the construction of historical geographical maps (*mappa mundi*) resulted from a reading of anthropomorphic forms in a landscape. The resulting teratology through collages of body parts satisfies our expectations.[1] Analogies bestow visibility on the invisible through mental leaps. Mantic architectural processes are based upon analogical mimesis, which unifies through similarity and contiguity, because in an analogy all the elements are grasped simultaneously.

The house-tower is based upon this mimesis of similarity and contiguity. It is a result of analogical thinking and a demonstration in a dream. Otl Aicher (1994) points out: "In dreams the visual structure of thinking and the icons dissolve as abstractions and move back into the realm of illustration."[2]

Architectural dreams are meaningful and useful demonstrations to architects. In one of his aphorisms, Nietzsche stated that pure and simple dreaming is not the same as dreaming that you are dreaming.[3] The latter is the fundamental rule of this demonstration of architecture. Nietzsche also affirmed the need to rediscover the truth in the mythopoetic, and to preserve "the universality of dreaming ... and the continuation of the dream." Tactics that generate actual architectural demonstrations should be developed.[4] In a dream, I know that the room within which I find myself has no walls, nevertheless, I definitely know that I am in a room. The importance of dreaming for architects is embodied in this description of a dreamscape. The dream is a demonstration and a hypothetical design of the unknown; thus, it is a substantial tool for acquiring knowledge. The dream is a *logos,* a rhetorical procedure, for wondering within the labyrinth, where the dialogue between real and hypothetical possibilities takes place. In an autobiographical account, Alberti explained how this act of architectural imagination occurs:

> During the night specially when the anxieties (*stimoli d'animo*) keep me restless and awake, I used to survey and build in my mind an unheard-of machine able to lift and to carry, to consolidate and to erect (*statuire*) tremendous and inestimable things ... Sometimes being deprived of these images, I created or built in my mind few well-composed edifices, with their Orders arranged in several columns, with unusual capitals and bases, and with proper ties and a new grace in cornices and entablatures.[5]

Being half-asleep (Latin *sopor*) and induced into a dream-like status, Alberti designs tremendous machines and unusual building details. This soporific mental activity moves from a confused state of anxiety to a clearly formed image of construction. This constructed fantasy embodies the human condition in the monstrous expression of building details.[6] A theorization latent in this passage by Alberti is that dreaming about architecture produces monsters that are imaginative concepts. These representations, born under the aegis of Hypnos, provide a further clue to the character of a theory of images based on monstrous demonstrations, where meaning is generated by the coupling of fantasy and wisdom.

Macaronic speculation is a monstrous way to demonstrate that the corpus of the discipline of architecture is and will always be, by nature, compressible, resilient and resourceful. Its inherent grotesque nature is the most proper form in which to think and write in architecture. The marvelous taste of architecture and macaronic sapience can be discovered through a careful use of the imagination and by the assimilation of its pantagruelic nature.[7] Macaronic thinking is organic and "alive" and is based on pending thoughts. This figurative procedure, at the same time both sublime and subliminal, can weave the fabric of architectural theory within the marble loom of its construction (see Figure 50 in the Portfolio). In Italian and French, the verbs *pensare* and *penser* mean to hang something, which relates to a pending thought. It means to think with pause. This suspension of time is an elegant notion that ties together hesitation and wonder, and defers the desire to make present. The condition of pending thoughts is one of being "in-between," or being located on a threshold. The marvelous produces an in-between perception that is outside standard awareness and challenges the limits of consciousness. The marvelous alters the conception of transcendental imagination, wherein perceptions are ascribed to one consciousness.

THE ANALOGICAL MONSTER

The drawings of the house-tower

The Door to the invisible must be visible.

René Daumal[8]

Novalis structures the narrative of his tale about *Heinrich von Ofterdingen*, in such a way that "the shape of the future is divined, then telescoped and projected backward into the past."[9] In this tale, the dreaming Heinrich finds an archaic book, which contains images of a time yet to come, in a cave. In this dream-tale, marvel and wonder are coupled together, without regard for the orderly passage of time: the past and the future are interchangeable. "A dream is often significant and prophetic, because it is a natural effect of the soul – and *hence* based on ordering of association."[10]

The laws of association are not bound by the temporal order of cause and effect. Actual architectural design is free from temporal effect. Once built, a virtuous edifice looks as though it has always been there. Its design is a combination of past designs already constructed and future designs yet to be commissioned.

The drawings for the house-tower share the nature of the images in the tale of Heinrich. The pictures in the book by Novalis, just like the house-tower drawings, work by the laws of association. In a dream, an archangel, a heavenly spirit, handed down to me the model for the house-tower (Figures 44 and 45 in the Portfolio). I was given an icon, an eidolon, of an edifice that betrays its humanity through its structure, its plan, and even its cornerstone. Drafting architectural drawings became an attempt to make sense of this prodigious eidolon. The model was constructed after the drawings; nevertheless, it retained the three-dimensional likeness of the original model in the dream that inspired the drawings (Figures 19–23, 56, 64, 75 and 76 in the Portfolio). In this design process, just as in a dream, the arrow of time is inverted (Figures 64, 65, 77 in the Portfolio).[11]

Two types of drawings were made. One type of representation manifests the invisible in the visible (see Figures 1–6 in the Portfolio). The other transubstantiates the recto into the verso to produce a chiasm of theory and practice (see Figures 7–18 in the Portfolio). In both types architecture has been represented in a subjunctive mode. The practice of architecture should not be subordinated to any other enterprise. Many architects impose use of space rather than exemplify or suggest possible uses with their building designs and urban manipulations. The end product of their activity is not a design in the true sense, but a rigid predetermination of use. They carry out a professional duty, whereas they should enjoy the delight of a demonstrative realization allowing their drawings to evoke future buildings. These drawings are a process of urban and architectural divination (see Figure 52 in the Portfolio). A true architectural drawing is a graphic divination describing a future construction. Graphic prognostication begins by surveying an existing space and translating it into a drawing.[12] Divination is a sophisticated form of semiosis. Divination is generally judged negatively as it is thought to be based on a semiotic fallacy, as a misjudgment of the pragmatic reading of signs and semiotic relationships. However, the interpretation of divination, as an imaginative form of reading and writing, overturns this negative rendition. Following this non-rational method, architects become augurs and trace spaces to mirror the needs of future inhabitants. To be non-rational does not mean being irrational, but it means following an ineffable procedure to understand the *ratio aeterna*, the eternal tale of a miraculous urbanity.

The recto and the verso

I dragooned Claudio Sgarbi, a friend and former pupil, to follow my dream in the design of the house-tower according to my preparatory drawings (Figures 1–6 in the Portfolio). Alice Min Soo Chun and I drafted the recto-design drawings (Figures 32, 7, 9, 11, 12, 13, 15, 17, 18 in the Portfolio), while Claudio drew the verso-design drawings on Mylar (Figures 8, 10, 14, 16 in the Portfolio).[13] Both sides are mantic projections, since they transform non-semiotic materials (stone, wood, glass, textiles, angles, joints) into symbols allowing mental joy and despair; while also constructing an imaginary reality of the second order out of those symbolic materials. In other words, these representations suggest a union between the signifier and the signified and between a symbol and its meaning. Like icons, they bear a direct affinity to the object and therefore they ensure a greater truthfulness and intelligibility. However, they were not designed to produce constructible verisimilitudes.

The aim of a recto/verso drawing is to make visible that which otherwise would be invisible. Graphic representations, from this point of view, can be subdivided into two categories. On the one hand, there are drawings that are the result of perceptual description: "seeing as."[14] Their nature can be explained in an elliptical manner: I see a plan as a representation of "David's house." On the other hand, there are drawings that are cognitive representations that express a graphic concept of construction: "seeing in." The physical act of drawing is the only tool that can be used to develop the capacity of "seeing in," as has been stated by Scarpa:

> If I want to see things, I don't trust anything else. I put them in front of me, here on paper, to be able to see them. I want to see, and for this I draw. I can see an image only if I draw it.[15]

The twofold nature of representation implies both likeness (seeing-as) and a constructive eidetic process (seeing-in) as the basis for drawing. This twofold nature can also be interpreted by the concept of *disegno* elaborated by Federico Zuccari (1542–1609), a late Mannerist painter and architect, working in Rome. In *L'Idea de Pittori, Scultori et Architetti* (1607), Zuccari discusses the notions of *disegno interno* and *disegno esterno*. The *disegno interno* is "the concept originated in our mind to know everything and to act, in accordance with the envisioned thing."[16] *Disegno esterno* is born out of *disegno interno*. *Disegno interno* is concerned with conceiving and *disegno esterno* is its practical expression. The *disegno interno* is the instrument of intellectual representation, be it theology or carpentry, which is used to develop the tangible lines of the *disegno esterno*. The "seeing-in" (*disegno interno*) is a cognitive representation that results in physical and metaphysical perceptions under the *lume naturale*. In this light (*lume naturale*) not only do objects leave impressions on the percipient, but the percipient leaves an impression on the objects as well.

The scopic character of mantic images rules both the recto and the verso of the architectural projections of the house-tower. To contrast the trump-like quality unfolded on the recto side, the verso discloses the "virtual wickedness" given in the visual representation of architecture.[17] In the verso-tower drawings,[18] the recto-tower is rarefied and reversed.[19] However, the recto and verso drawings are conjoint projections of horizontal and vertical cuttings (sections) through the edifice.[20] This recto/verso technique of representation of a future building is *"une petite bouchée"* derived from the discussion of musement by Peirce.[21]

Notes

1 [Whittington (2013).]
2 Aicher (1994: 60).
3 Nietzsche (1974: 54).
4 Ibid.
5 Mancini (1911). [Mancini (1967: 183); Alberti, 1973: I, 120.]
6 [Frascari (1991; 1987: 123–142).]
7 [Frascari (1991); Bakhtin (1984: 133, 167–168, 339); Ridgway (2015: 61–62).]
8 Daumal (1992: 9).
9 Pfefferkorn (1988: 170–171).
10 [Novalis (2007: 169), aphorism #959.]
11 [Florensky (1996: 41–43).]
12 Construction and survey drawings are descriptions of the constructed world.
13 [Frascari (1997: 176), footnote 5.]
14 Wollheim (1980: 205–226).
15 Sergio Los quoted Carlo Scarpa (Massironi 1982: 17).
16 ["*cosa, & operare di fuori, conforme alla cosa intesa, ...*" Zuccari (1607: 4). Biblioteca Hertziana 85 S.: Ill. - Mit Strukturdaten Gh-ZUC 931-2070 raro; accessed on February 15 2016 at http://eres.biblhertz.it/public/Gh-ZUC931-2070.pdf.]
17 For a conceptualization of virtual wickedness in architecture, see Tafuri (1990: 25–54).
18 The recto drawings show that water powers the house; it lifts weights and turns the water wheel located on the side of the tower. There are two cellars: one for wine, the other for salami and other food products. The top floor terrace which holds the two construction cranes is crowned by a compassed weathervane. The bathrooms are pneumatic places and

the kitchen is the most important room in the house-tower (Figure 59 in the Portfolio). The remaining spaces exemplify or suggest possible uses, rather than determine or impose one.

19 Regarding the verso design, Sgarbi explained to me that:

Imaginative plans for a vague house that will last forever, never to be completed, always quasi-built. One corner of the dwelling is situated on a *mundus* next to a fig tree and an apple tree. The footprint of the house-tower is approximately 21 ft. x 21 ft. and is 72 ft. high. The house is designed to be self-sufficient. High tech solutions furnish the house and feed the *mundus*. Living activities are not bound to one predetermined location and can take place anywhere in the tower. The underground level is permeated with steam. The walls on the ground floor respond to the revolving sun. Here objects lose their names and salamis hang everywhere. On the top floor an Eolic organ plays under an ark.

20 The etymology of the word "science" can help us understand the ontology of cutting. It is derived from the Latin verb *scire*, which means "to cut" (Vico 1988: 48).

21 [Peirce (1966: 360).]

CONCLUSION

Marco Frascari

Dream long and hard enough

At this point I hope that you, the reader, are properly digesting my architectural dream. Allow me to now serve up a tantalizing dessert, a concluding statement: architecture's latent reality is made up of prosperous visions and dreams (Figure 53 in the Portfolio). The edifices in our constructed world are fabrics interwoven with dream stuff to form a latent presence. It is believed that architects turn an idea into a sensory phenomenon. On the contrary, they actually shape the sensory phenomenon into an idea. Architects don't open the doors for the spirit to enter everyday life with their dreams. Conversely, they elevate the mundane to a spiritual plane, to release the spiritual content of the physical reality. One cannot thematize architectural design procedures. They can only be represented by means of tropes and analogies. These procedures are fluid mental attitudes dwelling between the classical dichotomies of Western philosophy and the confused structure of image construction. The dream is the established locus of this condition between rationality and non-rationality. Designing architecture is akin to dreaming, however, dreaming is not like designing architecture.

It is high time to heed these lines to release the freedom of spirit through dreams, and to compose the last "stanza" for the survival of architectural culture (see Figure 61 in the Portfolio),[1] a culture that may be quashed by the unforgiving business-like environment in which professional architects have to move today.[2] In their search for aesthetic, anti-aesthetic or hyper-aesthetic outcomes, architects design buildings that often generate discomfort or tension in the users. Furthermore, frustrated by the lack of status of the architectural profession, many designers use architecture to inflate their egos. Both of these approaches to design can generate neurosis and an array of mental and somatic ailments in the users as well as in the designers. The majority of architects deal with an array of dubious values rooted in fashion, corporate image, and dashing publicity. In the present ambiguous condition of the profession, architecture has lost its thaumaturgic and therapeutic dimensions.[3] Architects can overcome this quandary through a proper theory of dreaming as the one pointed out by William S. Burroughs:

> Dream long enough and dream hard enough, You will come to know
> Dreaming can make it so ...[4]

Notes

1 [In a short file in Frascari's digital archive entitled "Last House," the author writes another possible ending for the Dream House and discusses ideas for a competition entitled "The Last House/Das Letzte Haus" (1995). He described an heptagonal tower made of 3780 blocks of cast glass (1' x 1' x3').]
2 The house-tower, this last "stanza," is related to the XVI trump card in the tarot's deck: The Tower. This trump card is positioned between the Tower of Babel, the last house of the past (Lat. *cave superbiam*, beware of pride), and the purification through fire (the lightning that made glass from the sands of the desert).
3 Frascari states, in a document entitled "Last House", which can be found in Frascari's digital archive:
   In 1913, a great German humorist and pacifist, Paul Scheerbart (1863–1915) published an "asteroid novel" entitled *Lesabéndio*. Lesabéndio is the protagonist and also the architect who built a tower that links the asteroid "torso" with its astral "head". Walter Benjamin interprets this dream-like fable about glass architecture to be an image of how humanity can achieve freedom: "Scheerbart's prose is of such transparency that one understands why he was the first to welcome the glass architecture which, after his death, would be banished from his country as subversive" (Benjamin 2003: 387). Benjamin points out that in Taut's "buildings, in [the] images and in [the] stories humanity prepares itself to survive culture, if there is no choice" (Benjamin 1977: 219) and, more importantly, this is done through laughter. Bruno Taut's Glass Pavilion at the Werkbund Exhibition (1914) reflects a similar dream. However, after Taut's advocacy for glass architecture, an expression of cast glass dreaming is found in *Dandanah, The Fairy Palace* (1919–1920), a toy cast in glass blocks, designed by Blanche Mahlberg. This colorful glass toy ought to be recast and given to architects to rediscover the play of musement. To live in this tower, or in any other numinous building, is a revolutionary virtue *par excellence*, and a badly needed form of positive intoxication.
4 Burroughs (1995: 158).

PORTFOLIO

Drawings, model, and sketchbooks
for the house-tower

PORTFOLIO: DRAWINGS, MODEL, AND SKETCHBOOKS

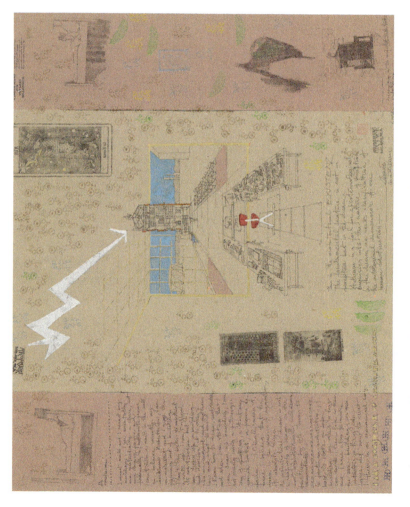

Figure 1 A *Dream House for the Next Millennium*. Preliminary design by Marco Frascari. Perspective of the house-tower. Hand drawing, transfers on colored paper (75 × 90 cm).

Source: © Marco Frascari Collection, The Architectural Archives, University of Pennsylvania (aaup.104_10.94.2273).

PORTFOLIO: DRAWINGS, MODEL, AND SKETCHBOOKS

Figure 2 A *Dream House for the Next Millennium*. Preliminary design by Marco Frascari. Plan of the ground floor of the house-tower. Gold marker, colored pencils and inks on colored paper (scale 1:25; 78 × 103.5 cm).

Source: © Marco Frascari Collection, The Architectural Archives, University of Pennsylvania (aaup.104_10.94.2276).

PORTFOLIO: DRAWINGS, MODEL, AND SKETCHBOOKS

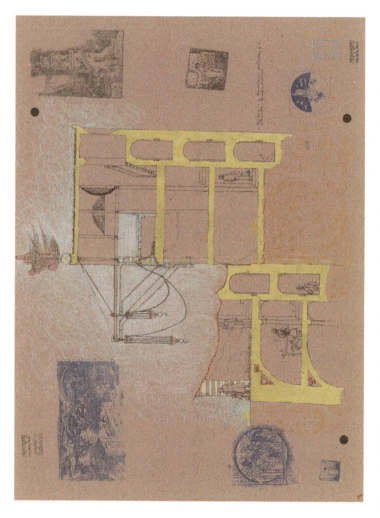

Figure 3 A *Dream House for the Next Millennium*. Preliminary design by Marco Frascari. Partial section of the house-tower under construction. Hand drawing with black and blue transfers on paper. Colored pencils and gold marker for the wall section (scale 1:25; 78 × 103.5 cm).

Source: © Marco Frascari Collection, The Architectural Archives, University of Pennsylvania (aaup.104_10.94.2274).

PORTFOLIO: DRAWINGS, MODEL, AND SKETCHBOOKS

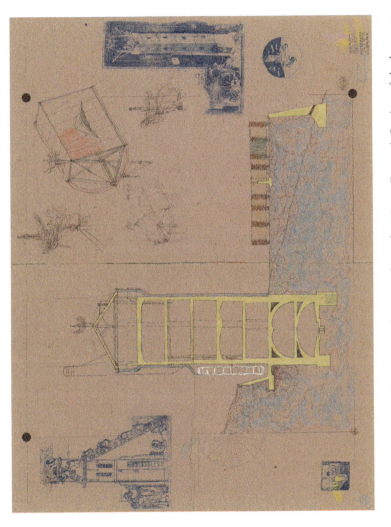

Figure 4 A *Dream House for the Next Millennium*. Preliminary design by Marco Frascari. Section of the house-tower. Hand drawing with black and blue transfers on paper. Colored pencils and inks. Wall poché in gold marker (scale 1:50; 78 × 103.5 cm).

Source: © Marco Frascari Collection, The Architectural Archives, University of Pennsylvania (aaup.104_10.94.2275).

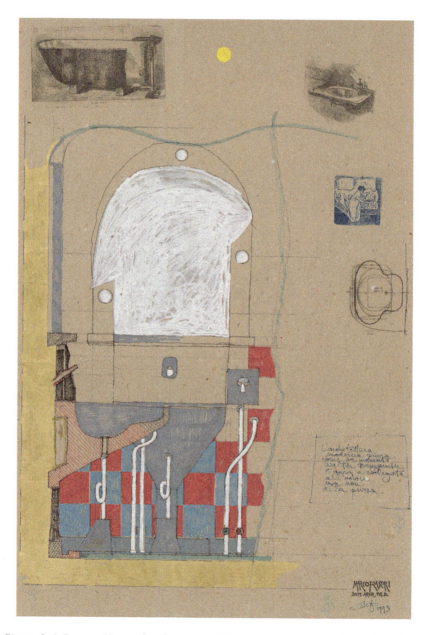

Figure 5 A Dream House for the Next Millennium. Preliminary design by Marco Frascari, 1993. Detailed design of the bathroom. Hand drawing with black and blue transfers on paper. Colored pencils and inks. Wall poché in gold marker. Pipes colored with a silver marker (scale 1:5; 52 × 76 cm).

Source: © Marco Frascari Collection, The Architectural Archives, University of Pennsylvania (aaup.104_10.94.2278).

PORTFOLIO: DRAWINGS, MODEL, AND SKETCHBOOKS

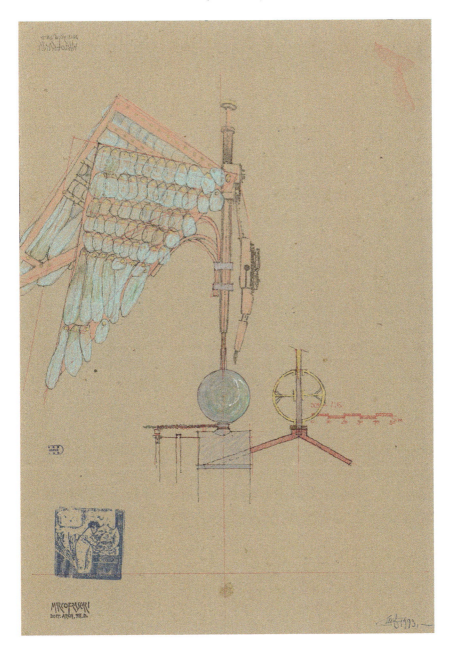

Figure 6 *A Dream House for the Next Millennium.* Weathervane detail by Marco Frascari. Hand drawing with black and blue transfers on paper. Colored pencils and inks (scale 1:5; 52 × 76 cm).

Source: © Marco Frascari Collection, The Architectural Archives, University of Pennsylvania (aaup.104_10.94.2277).

PORTFOLIO: DRAWINGS, MODEL, AND SKETCHBOOKS

Figure 7 *A Dream House for the Next Millennium.* Hand-drafted ground floor plan of the house-tower by Marco Frascari and Alice Min Soo Chun. Gold marker, colored pencils and inks on Mylar (scale 1:25; 76 × 73 cm).

Source: © Marco Frascari Collection, The Architectural Archives, University of Pennsylvania (aaup.104_10.94.2267, recto).

PORTFOLIO: DRAWINGS, MODEL, AND SKETCHBOOKS

Figure 8 *A Dream House for the Next Millennium.* Hand-drafted ground floor plan of the house-tower by Claudio Sgarbi. Colored pencils and inks on Mylar (scale 1:25; 76 × 73 cm).

Source: © Marco Frascari Collection, The Architectural Archives, University of Pennsylvania (aaup.104_10.94.2267, verso).

PORTFOLIO: DRAWINGS, MODEL, AND SKETCHBOOKS

Figure 9 A *Dream House for the Next Millennium*. Hand-drafted plans of the intermediate levels of the house-tower by Marco Frascari and Alice Min Soo Chun. Gold marker, colored pencils and inks on Mylar (scale 1:25; 76 × 73 cm).

Source: © Marco Frascari Collection, The Architectural Archives, University of Pennsylvania (aaup.104_10.94.2268, recto).

PORTFOLIO: DRAWINGS, MODEL, AND SKETCHBOOKS

Figure 10 A *Dream House for the Next Millennium*. Hand-drafted plans of the intermediate levels of the house-tower by Claudio Sgarbi. Colored pencils and inks on Mylar (scale 1:25; 76 × 73 cm).

Source: © Marco Frascari Collection, The Architectural Archives, University of Pennsylvania (aaup.104_10.94.2268, verso).

PORTFOLIO: DRAWINGS, MODEL, AND SKETCHBOOKS

Figure 11 A *Dream House for the Next Millennium*. Hand-drafted plans of the loggia, the cantina and the roof top of the house-tower by Marco Frascari and Alice Min Soo Chun. Gold marker, colored pencils and inks on Mylar (scale 1:25; 76 × 73 cm).

Source: © Marco Frascari Collection, The Architectural Archives, University of Pennsylvania (aaup.104_10.94.2269, recto).

Figure 12 *A Dream House for the Next Millennium.* Hand-drafted plans of the loggia, the cantina and the roof top of the house-tower by Marco Frascari and Alice Min Soo Chun. Mixed media on Mylar (scale 1:25; 76 × 73 cm).

Source: © Marco Frascari Collection, The Architectural Archives, University of Pennsylvania (aaup.104_10.94.2269, verso).

PORTFOLIO: DRAWINGS, MODEL, AND SKETCHBOOKS

Figure 13 A Dream House for the Next Millennium. Hand-drafted section of the house-tower by Marco Frascari and Alice Min Soo Chun. Mixed media. Gold marker, colored pencils and inks on Mylar (scale 1:50; 76 × 73 cm).

Source: © Marco Frascari Collection, The Architectural Archives, University of Pennsylvania (aaup.104_10.94.2270, recto).

PORTFOLIO: DRAWINGS, MODEL, AND SKETCHBOOKS

Figure 14 A Dream House for the Next Millennium. Hand-drafted section of the house-tower by Claudio Sgarbi. Mixed media. Colored pencils and inks on Mylar (scale 1:50; 76 × 73 cm).

Source: © Marco Frascari Collection, The Architectural Archives, University of Pennsylvania (aaup.104_10.94.2270, verso).

Figure 15 *A Dream House for the Next Millennium*. Hand-drafted, partial section of the house-tower by Marco Frascari and Alice Min Soo Chun. Mixed media. Gold marker, colored pencils and inks on Mylar (scale 1:25; 76 × 73 cm).

Source: © Marco Frascari Collection, The Architectural Archives, University of Pennsylvania (aaup.104_10.94.2271, recto).

PORTFOLIO: DRAWINGS, MODEL, AND SKETCHBOOKS

Figure 16 *A Dream House for the Next Millennium*. Hand-drafted, partial section of the house-tower by Claudio Sgarbi. Colored pencils and inks on Mylar (scale 1:25; 76 × 73 cm).

Source: © Marco Frascari Collection, The Architectural Archives, University of Pennsylvania (aaup.104_10.94.2271, verso).

PORTFOLIO: DRAWINGS, MODEL, AND SKETCHBOOKS

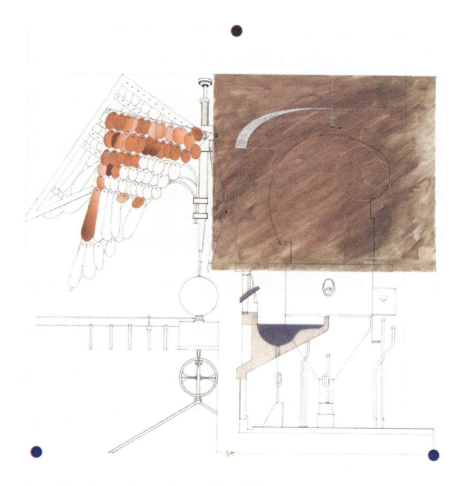

Figure 17 A *Dream House for the Next Millennium*. Hand-drafted construction details of the bathroom of the house-tower by Marco Frascari and Alice Min Soo Chun. Mixed media. Colored pencils and inks on Mylar (scale 1:5, 76 × 73 cm).

Source: © Marco Frascari Collection, The Architectural Archives, University of Pennsylvania (aaup.104_10.94.2272, recto).

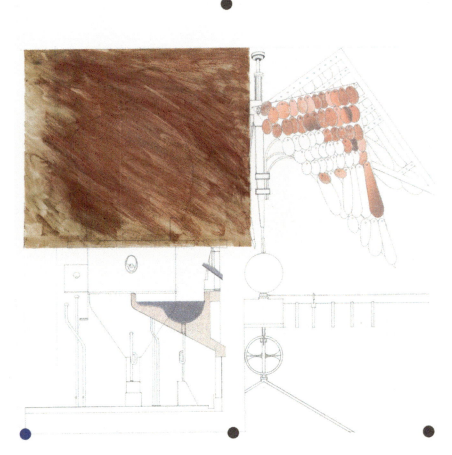

Figure 18 A Dream House for the Next Millennium. Hand-drafted construction details of the bathroom of the house-tower by Marco Frascari and Alice Min Soo Chun. Mixed media. Colored pencils and inks on Mylar (scale 1:5, 76 × 73 cm).

Source: © Marco Frascari Collection, The Architectural Archives, University of Pennsylvania (aaup.104_10.94.2272, verso).

PORTFOLIO: DRAWINGS, MODEL, AND SKETCHBOOKS

Figure 19 A *Dream House for the Next Millennium*. Wooden model of the house-tower by Marco Frascari and Alice Min Soo Chun.

Source: © Marco Frascari Collection, The Architectural Archives, University of Pennsylvania (aaup.104.21).

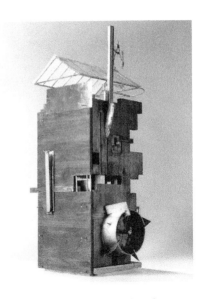

Figure 20 A Dream House for the Next Millennium. Wooden model of the house-tower by Marco Frascari and Alice Min Soo Chun. South-east view.

Source: © Marco Frascari Collection, The Architectural Archives, University of Pennsylvania (aaup.104.21).

Figure 22 A Dream House for the Next Millennium. Wooden model of the house-tower by Marco Frascari and Alice Min Soo Chun. North-west view.

Source: © Marco Frascari Collection, The Architectural Archives, University of Pennsylvania (aaup.104.21).

Figure 21 A Dream House for the Next Millennium. Wooden model of the house-tower by Marco Frascari and Alice Min Soo Chun. South-west view.

Source: © Marco Frascari Collection, The Architectural Archives, University of Pennsylvania (aaup.104.21).

Figure 23 A Dream House for the Next Millennium. Wooden model of the house-tower by Marco Frascari and Alice Min Soo Chun. North-east view.

Source: © Marco Frascari Collection, The Architectural Archives, University of Pennsylvania (aaup.104.21).

PORTFOLIO: DRAWINGS, MODEL, AND SKETCHBOOKS

Figure 24 Sketchbook 161, back and front cover (25 × 25 cm). August 1993. *The Architect's Dream, House for the Next Millennium* by Marco Frascari. Handwritten, mixed media.
Source: © Courtesy of Marco Frascari Estate.

PORTFOLIO: DRAWINGS, MODEL, AND SKETCHBOOKS

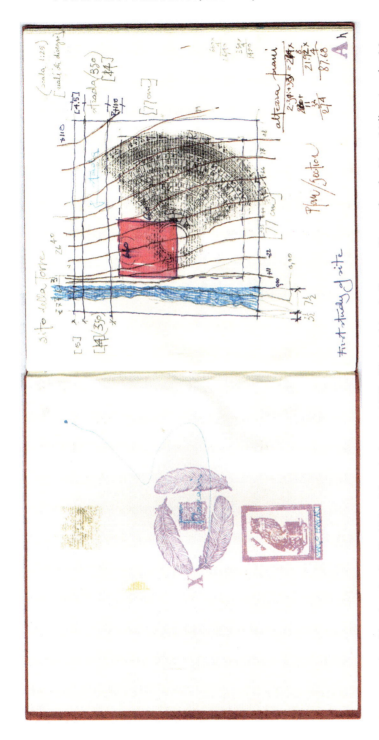

Figure 25 Sketchbook 161, f.1v/2r (25 × 25 cm). August 1993. *The Architect's Dream, House for the Next Millennium* by Marco Frascari. First study of the site. Mixed media. Transfers, colored pencils and inks.

Source: © Courtesy of Marco Frascari Estate.

PORTFOLIO: DRAWINGS, MODEL, AND SKETCHBOOKS

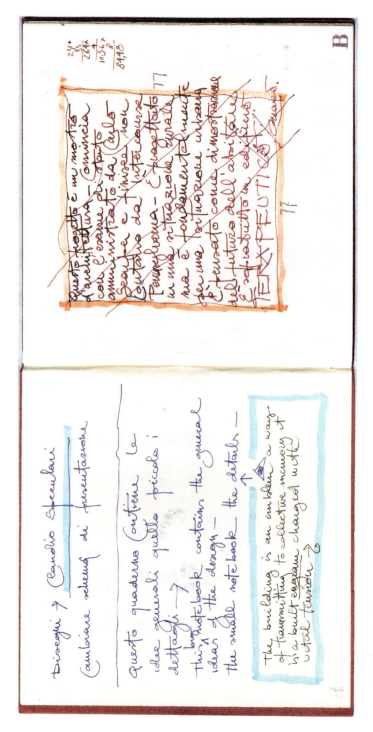

Figure 26 Sketchbook 161, f.2v/3r (25 × 25 cm). August 1993. *The Architect's Dream, House for the Next Millennium* by Marco Frascari. Notes about the sketchbooks and the nature of the project.

Source: © Courtesy of Marco Frascari Estate.

PORTFOLIO: DRAWINGS, MODEL, AND SKETCHBOOKS

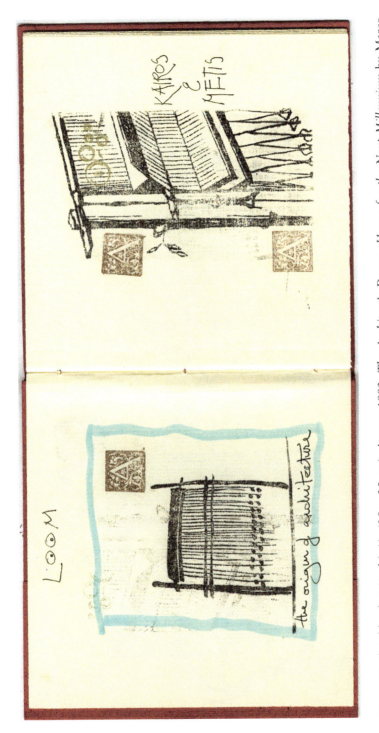

Figure 27 Sketchbook 161, f.3v/4r (25 × 25 cm). August 1993. *The Architect's Dream, House for the Next Millennium* by Marco Frascari. Study for the layout of the drawings and notes. Colored pencils, inks and markers.

Source: © Courtesy of Marco Frascari Estate.

PORTFOLIO: DRAWINGS, MODEL, AND SKETCHBOOKS

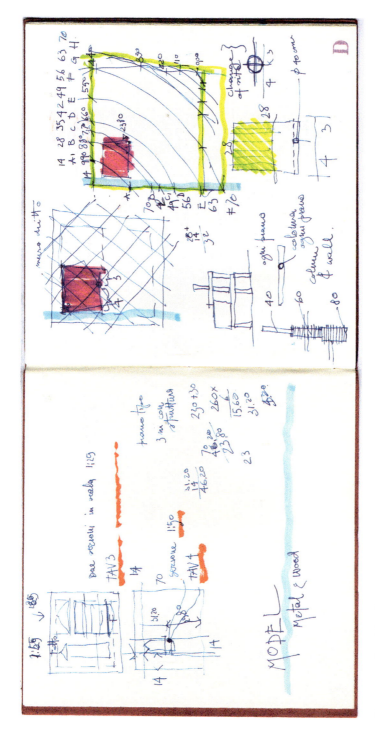

Figure 28 Sketchbook 161, f.4v/5r (25 × 25 cm). August 1993. *The Architect's Dream, House for the Next Millennium* by Marco Frascari. Study for the layout of the drawings. Colored pencils, inks and markers.

Source: © Courtesy of Marco Frascari Estate.

128

PORTFOLIO: DRAWINGS, MODEL, AND SKETCHBOOKS

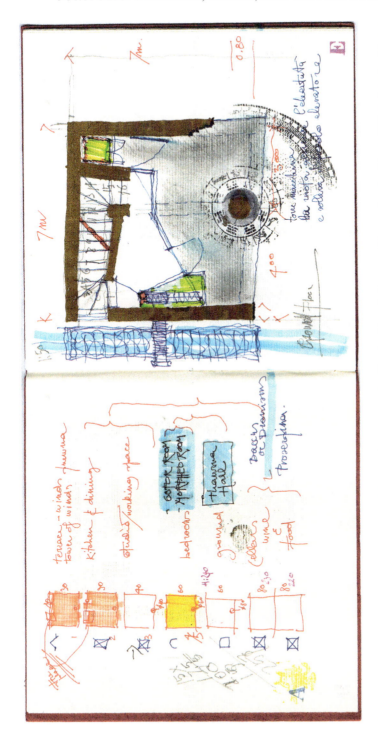

Figure 29 Sketchbook 161, f.5v/6r (25 × 25 cm). August 1993. *The Architect's Dream, House for the Next Millennium* by Marco Frascari. Study for the ground floor plan. A "ponderous column" determines the layout and orientation of the plan.

Source: © Courtesy of Marco Frascari Estate.

129

PORTFOLIO: DRAWINGS, MODEL, AND SKETCHBOOKS

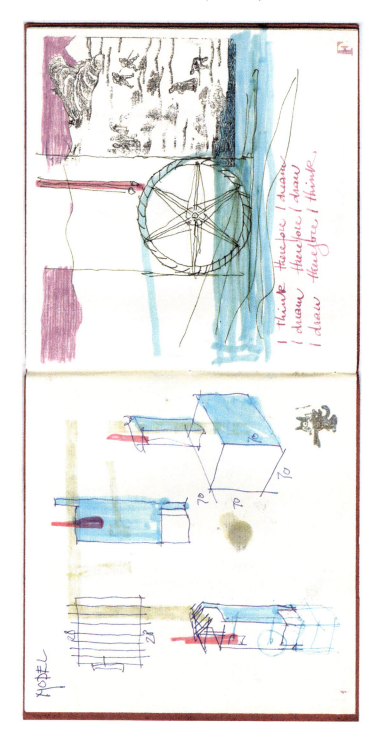

Figure 30 Sketchbook 161, f.6v/7r (25 × 25 cm). August 1993. *The Architect's Dream, House for the Next Millennium* by Marco Frascari. Sketches for the model and notes ("I think therefore I dream …"). Colored pencils, inks and markers.

Source: © Courtesy of Marco Frascari Estate.

130

PORTFOLIO: DRAWINGS, MODEL, AND SKETCHBOOKS

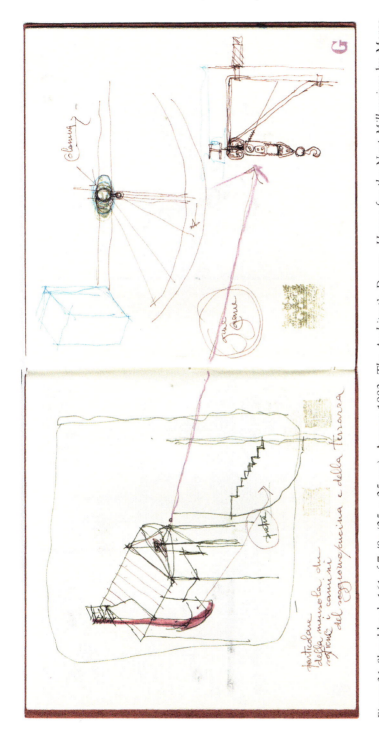

Figure 31 Sketchbook 161, f.7v/8r (25 × 25 cm). August 1993. *The Architect's Dream, House for the Next Millennium* by Marco Frascari. Design sketches. Colored pencils, inks and markers.

Source: © Courtesy of Marco Frascari Estate.

131

PORTFOLIO: DRAWINGS, MODEL, AND SKETCHBOOKS

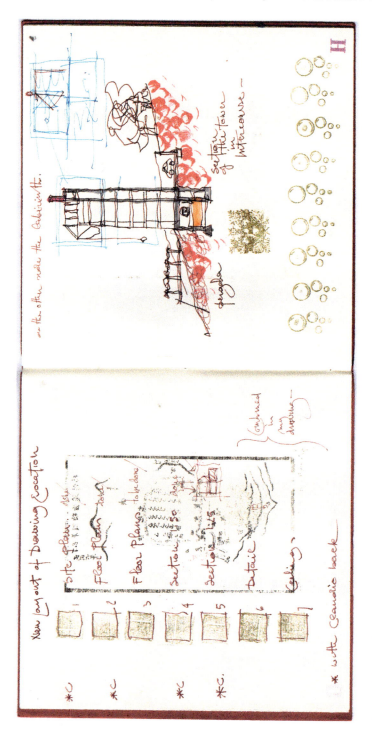

Figure 32 Sketchbook 161, f.8v/9r (25 × 25 cm). August 1993. *The Architect's Dream, House for the Next Millennium* by Marco Frascari. New layout of drawings evocation and sketch for the section of the house-tower. Mixed media. Transfers, colored inks and markers.

Source: © Courtesy of Marco Frascari Estate.

PORTFOLIO: DRAWINGS, MODEL, AND SKETCHBOOKS

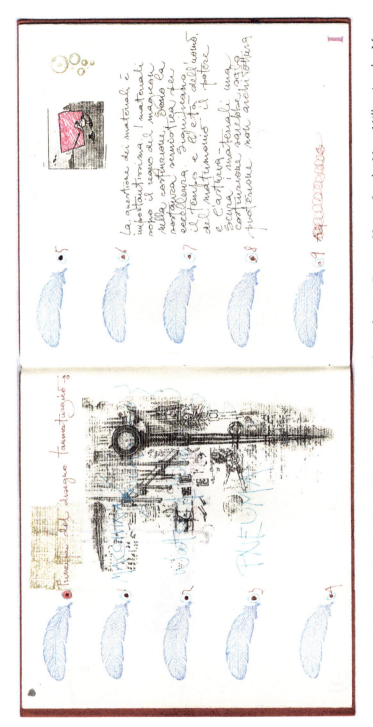

Figure 33 Sketchbook 161, f.9v/10r (25 × 25 cm). August 1993. *The Architect's Dream, House for the Next Millennium* by Marco Frascari. Notes on the materials of the tower. Mixed media. Transfers, colored inks and markers.

Source: © Courtesy of Marco Frascari Estate.

PORTFOLIO: DRAWINGS, MODEL, AND SKETCHBOOKS

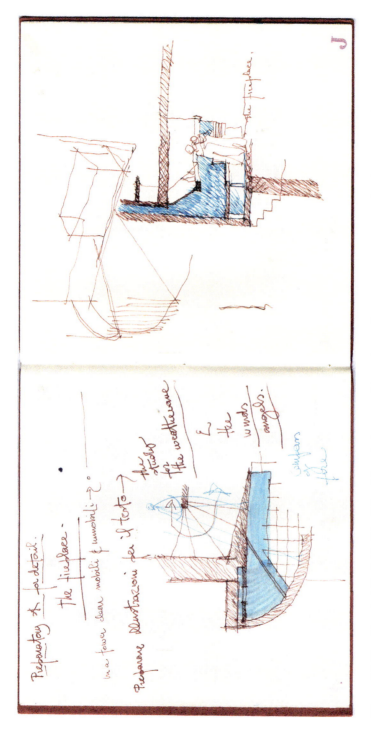

Figure 34 Sketchbook 161, f.10v/11r (25 × 25 cm). August 1993. *The Architect's Dream, House for the Next Millennium* by Marco Frascari. Preparatory sketches for fireplace details. Colored inks and markers.

Source: © Courtesy of Marco Frascari Estate.

PORTFOLIO: DRAWINGS, MODEL, AND SKETCHBOOKS

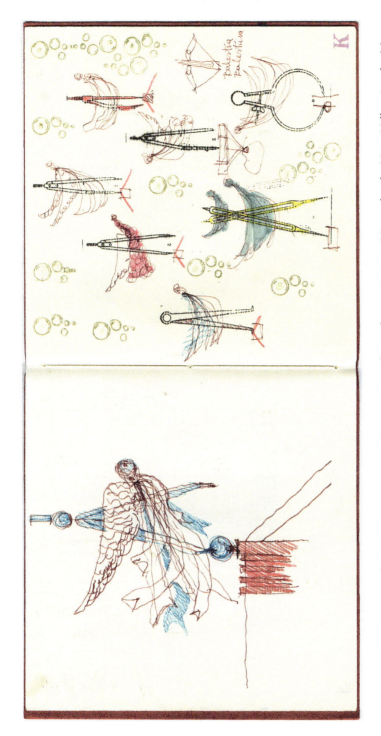

Figure 35 Sketchbook 161, f.11v/12r (25 × 25 cm). August 1993. *The Architect's Dream, House for the Next Millennium* by Marco Frascari. Weathervane sketches. Mixed media. Transfers, colored inks and markers.

Source: © Courtesy of Marco Frascari Estate.

PORTFOLIO: DRAWINGS, MODEL, AND SKETCHBOOKS

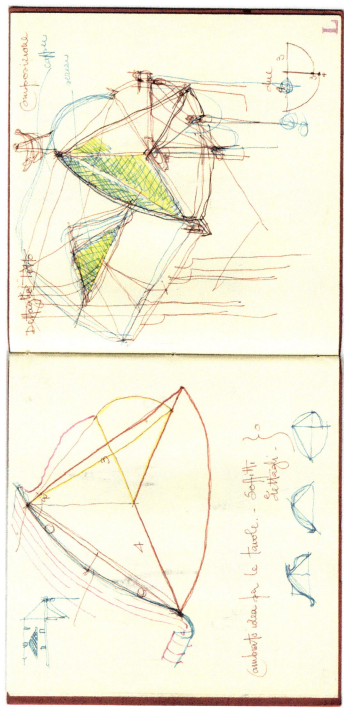

Figure 36 Sketchbook 161, f.12v/13r (25 × 25 cm). August 1993. *The Architect's Dream, House for the Next Millennium* by Marco Frascari. Sketches of the roof. Colored inks and markers.

Source: © Courtesy of Marco Frascari Estate.

PORTFOLIO: DRAWINGS, MODEL, AND SKETCHBOOKS

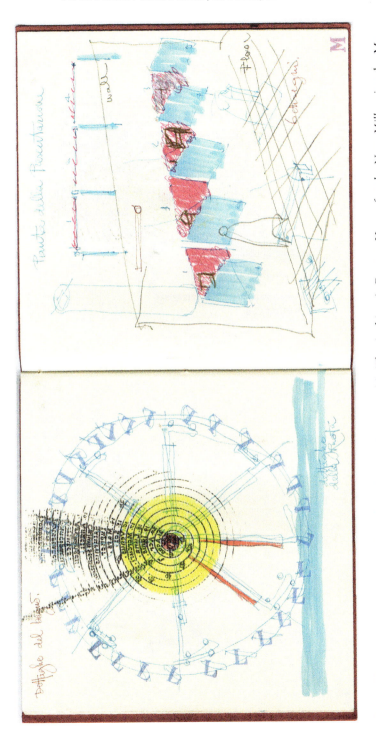

Figure 37 Sketchbook 161, f.13v/14r (25 × 25 cm). August 1993. *The Architect's Dream, House for the Next Millennium* by Marco Frascari. Detail of the waterwheel and sketches for the layout of the exhibition of the drawings. Mixed media. Transfers, colored inks and markers.

Source: © Courtesy of Marco Frascari Estate.

137

PORTFOLIO: DRAWINGS, MODEL, AND SKETCHBOOKS

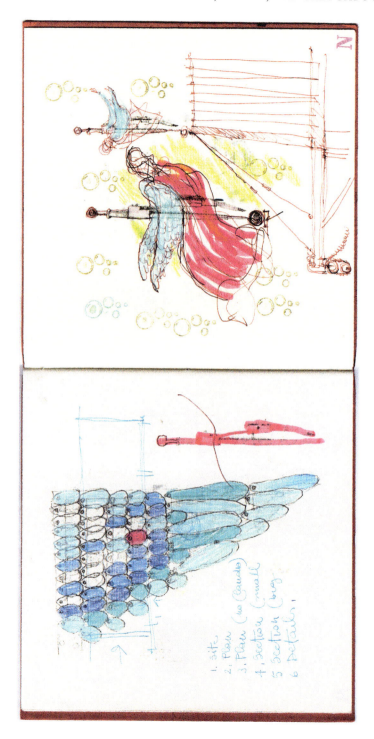

Figure 38 Sketchbook 161, f.14v/15r (25 × 25 cm). August 1993. *The Architect's Dream, House for the Next Millennium* by Marco Frascari. Weathervane sketches and list of the drawings to be drafted. Mixed media. Transfers, colored pencils, inks and markers.

Source: © Courtesy of Marco Frascari Estate.

PORTFOLIO: DRAWINGS, MODEL, AND SKETCHBOOKS

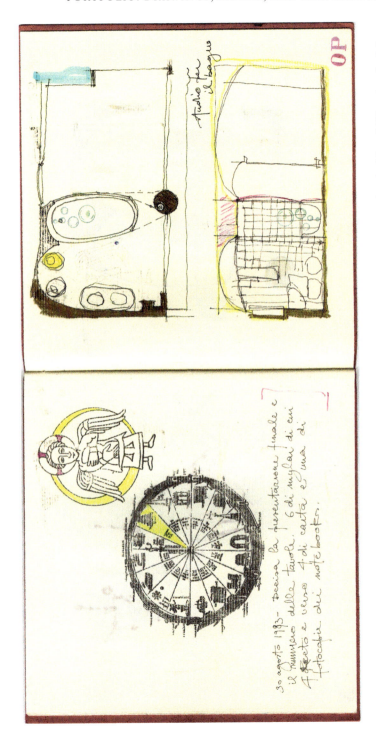

Figure 39 Sketchbook 161, f.15v/16r (25 × 25 cm). 30 August 1993. *The Architect's Dream, House for the Next Millennium* by Marco Frascari. Notes about the presentation layout of the drawings. Plan and section studies for a bathroom. Mixed media. Transfers, colored pencils, inks and markers.

Source: © Courtesy of Marco Frascari Estate.

PORTFOLIO: DRAWINGS, MODEL, AND SKETCHBOOKS

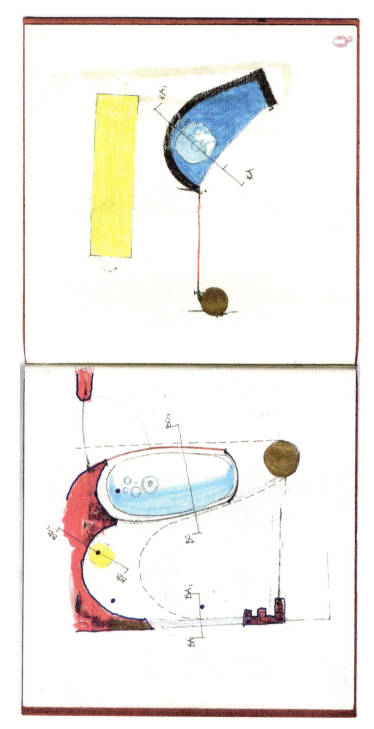

Figure 40 Sketchbook 161, f.16v/17r (25 × 25 cm). August 1993. *The Architect's Dream, House for the Next Millennium* by Marco Frascari. Plan studies for a bathroom. Colored pencils, inks and markers.

Source: © Courtesy of Marco Frascari Estate.

PORTFOLIO: DRAWINGS, MODEL, AND SKETCHBOOKS

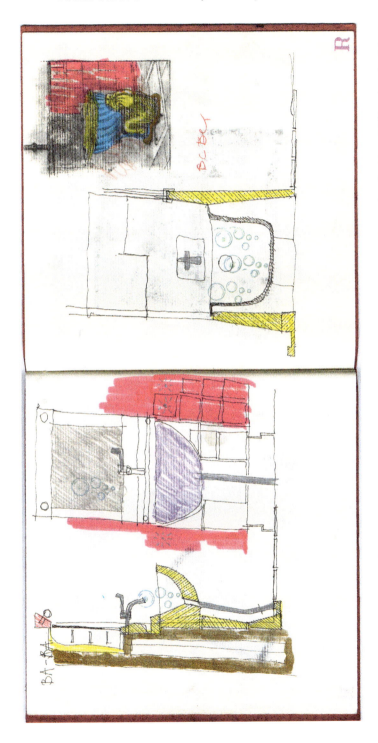

Figure 41 Sketchbook 161, f.17v/18r (25 × 25 cm). August 1993. *The Architect's Dream, House for the Next Millennium* by Marco Frascari. Elevation and section studies for a bathroom. Mixed media. Transfers, colored pencils, inks and markers.

Source: © Courtesy of Marco Frascari Estate.

141

PORTFOLIO: DRAWINGS, MODEL, AND SKETCHBOOKS

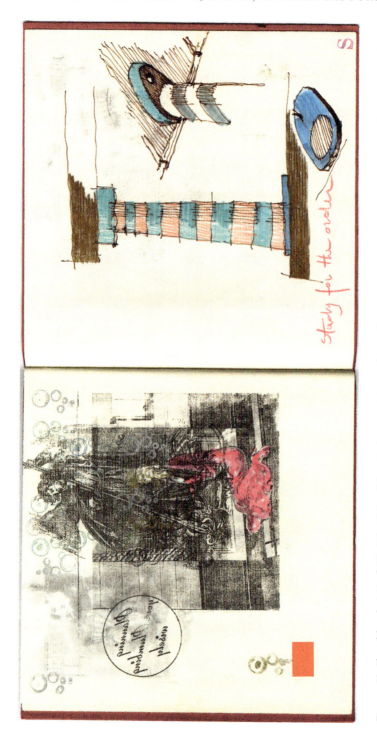

Figure 42 Sketchbook 161, f.18v/19r (25 × 25 cm). August 1993. *The Architect's Dream, House for the Next Millennium* by Marco Frascari. Transfers and studies for the column. Mixed media. Transfers, colored pencils, inks and markers.
Source: © Courtesy of Marco Frascari Estate.

PORTFOLIO: DRAWINGS, MODEL, AND SKETCHBOOKS

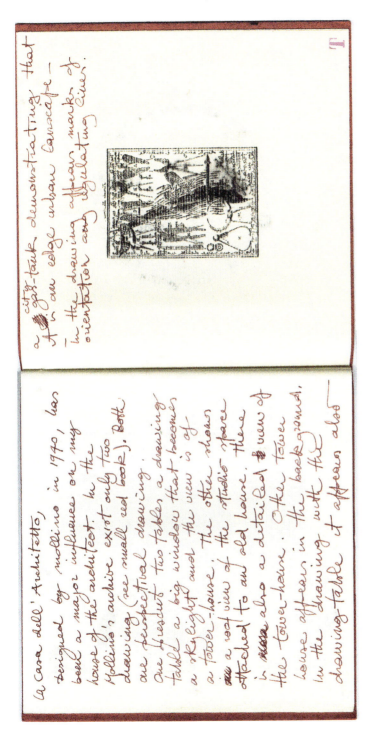

Figure 43 Sketchbook 161, f.19v/20r (25 × 25 cm). August 1993. *The Architect's Dream, House for the Next Millennium* by Marco Frascari. Notes on Carlo Mollino's 1940 drawings for the Architect's House. Handwritten text and transfer.

Source: © Courtesy of Marco Frascari Estate.

PORTFOLIO: DRAWINGS, MODEL, AND SKETCHBOOKS

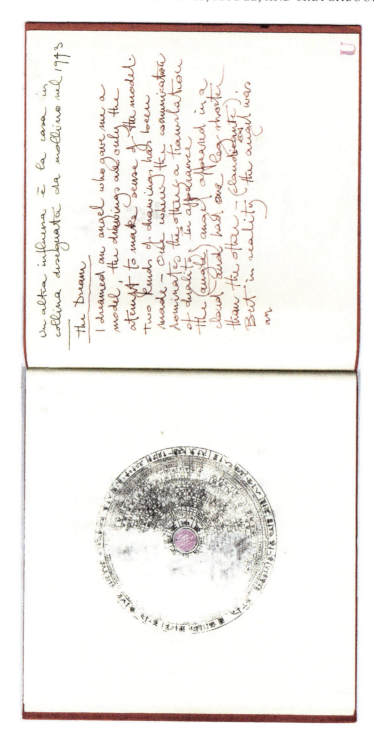

Figure 44 Sketchbook 161, f.20v/21r (25 × 25 cm). August 1993. *The Architect's Dream, House for the Next Millennium* by Marco Frascari. The compass of divination and notes on a dream of the author. Handwritten text, colored ink and transfer.

Source: © Courtesy of Marco Frascari Estate.

PORTFOLIO: DRAWINGS, MODEL, AND SKETCHBOOKS

Figure 45 Sketchbook 161, f.21v/22r (25 × 25 cm). August 1993. *The Architect's Dream, House for the Next Millennium* by Marco Frascari. Two angels holding the model of the house-tower. Crazy cat transfer. Mixed media, transfer, colored pencils, inks and markers.

Source: © Courtesy of Marco Frascari Estate.

PORTFOLIO: DRAWINGS, MODEL, AND SKETCHBOOKS

Figure 46 Sketchbook 160, back and front cover (18 × 18 cm). August–September 9, 1993. *The Architect's Dream, House for the Next Millennium* by Marco Frascari. Hand-written text, mixed media.

Source: © Courtesy of Marco Frascari Estate.

PORTFOLIO: DRAWINGS, MODEL, AND SKETCHBOOKS

Figure 47 Sketchbook 160, f.1v/2r (18 × 18 cm). August–September 9, 1993. *The Architect's Dream, House for the Next Millennium* by Marco Frascari. "I think therefore I dream …" Hand-written text and transfer from *Little Nemo*. Mixed media.

Source: © Courtesy of Marco Frascari Estate.

147

PORTFOLIO: DRAWINGS, MODEL, AND SKETCHBOOKS

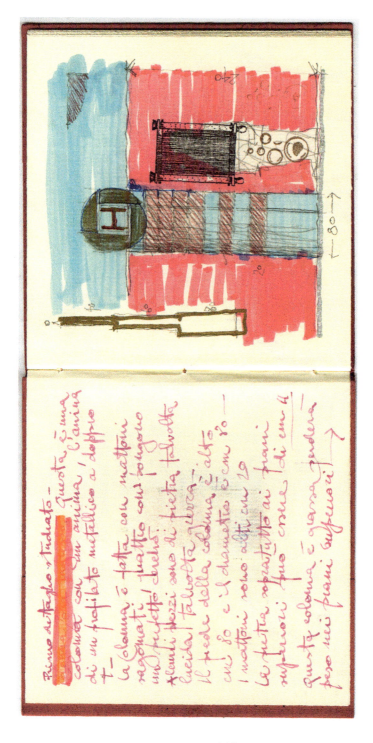

Figure 48 Sketchbook 160, f.2v/3r (18 × 18 cm). August–September 9, 1993. *The Architect's Dream, House for the Next Millennium* by Marco Frascari. Notes and sketches for the first detail for the house-tower: a column with a soul in the entrance area. Handwritten text. Mixed media. Transfers, colored pencils, inks and markers.

Source: © Courtesy of Marco Frascari Estate.

PORTFOLIO: DRAWINGS, MODEL, AND SKETCHBOOKS

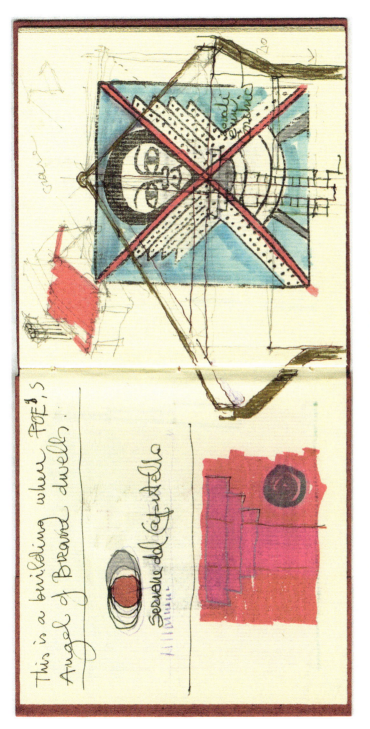

Figure 49 Sketchbook 160, f.3v/4r (18 × 18 cm). August–September 9, 1993. *The Architect's Dream, House for the Next Millennium* by Marco Frascari. "This is a building where Poe's Angel of Bizarre dwells." Section and elevation for a column and other sketches for the roof of the tower-house. Mixed media. Transfers, colored pencils, inks and markers.

Source: © Courtesy of Marco Frascari Estate.

149

PORTFOLIO: DRAWINGS, MODEL, AND SKETCHBOOKS

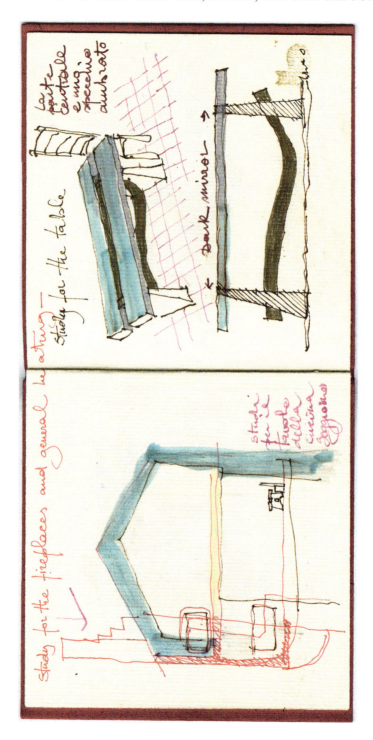

Figure 50 Sketchbook 160, f.4v/5r (18 × 18 cm). August–September 9, 1993. *The Architect's Dream, House for the Next Millennium* by Marco Frascari. Loom. The Origin of Architecture. Transfers and pen.

Source: © Courtesy of Marco Frascari Estate.

150

PORTFOLIO: DRAWINGS, MODEL, AND SKETCHBOOKS

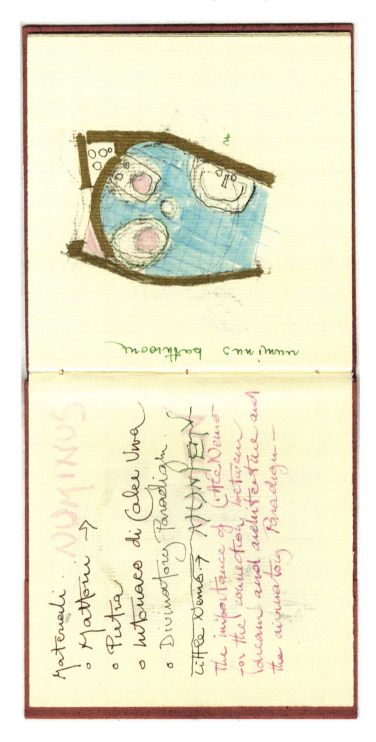

Figure 51 Sketchbook 160, f.5v/6r (18 × 18 cm), August–September 9, 1993. *The Architect's Dream, House for the Next Millennium* by Marco Frascari. Notes on the materials of the tower and the importance of Little Nemo. Plan sketch for a numinous bathroom with a gold poché. Colored pencils, inks and markers.

Source: © Courtesy of Marco Frascari Estate.

PORTFOLIO: DRAWINGS, MODEL, AND SKETCHBOOKS

Figure 52 Sketchbook 160, f.6v/7r (18 × 18 cm). August–September 9, 1993. *The Architect's Dream, House for the Next Millennium* by Marco Frascari. The divination of architecture is a reading and a translation ("La divinazione dell'architettura é una lettura con traduzione"). Transfers and notes.

Source: © Courtesy of Marco Frascari Estate.

152

PORTFOLIO: DRAWINGS, MODEL, AND SKETCHBOOKS

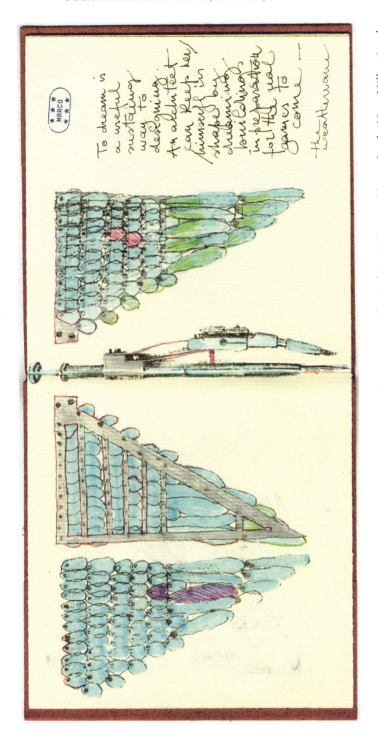

Figure 5.3 Sketchbook 160, f.7v/8r (18 × 18 cm). August–September 9, 1993. *The Architect's Dream, House for the Next Millennium* by Marco Frascari. A compass and a winged triangle. Notes about dreaming. Mixed media. Transfers, colored pencils, inks and markers.

Source: © Courtesy of Marco Frascari Estate.

153

PORTFOLIO: DRAWINGS, MODEL, AND SKETCHBOOKS

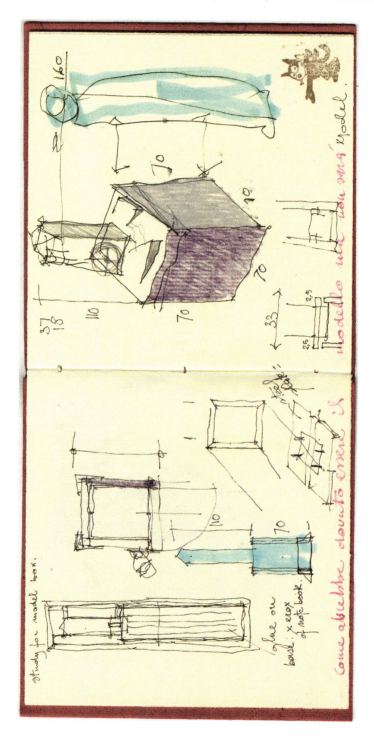

Figure 54 Sketchbook 160, f.8v/9r (18 × 18 cm). August–September 9, 1993. *The Architect's Dream, House for the Next Millennium* by Marco Frascari. Studies for a model box that has not been realized. Mixed media. Transfers, colored pencils, inks and markers.

Source: © Courtesy of Marco Frascari Estate.

154

PORTFOLIO: DRAWINGS, MODEL, AND SKETCHBOOKS

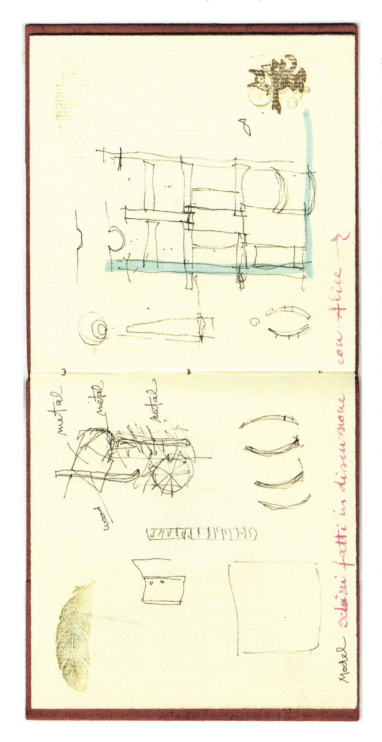

Figure 55 Sketchbook 160, f.9v/10r (18 × 18 cm). August–September 9, 1993. *The Architect's Dream, House for the Next Millennium* by Marco Frascari. Model sketches. Mixed media. Transfers, colored pencils, inks and markers.

Source: © Courtesy of Marco Frascari Estate.

PORTFOLIO: DRAWINGS, MODEL, AND SKETCHBOOKS

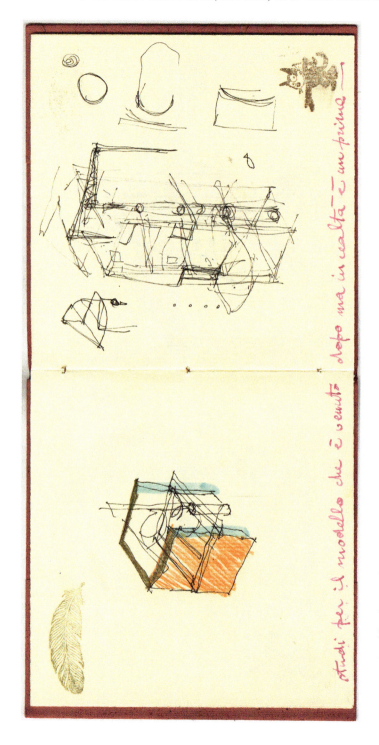

Figure 56 Sketchbook 160, f.10v/11r (18 × 18 cm). August–September 9, 1993. *The Architect's Dream, House for the Next Millennium* by Marco Frascari. Sketches for the model that was made after but was conceived before. Mixed media. Transfers, colored pencils, inks and markers.

Source: © Courtesy of Marco Frascari Estate.

PORTFOLIO: DRAWINGS, MODEL, AND SKETCHBOOKS

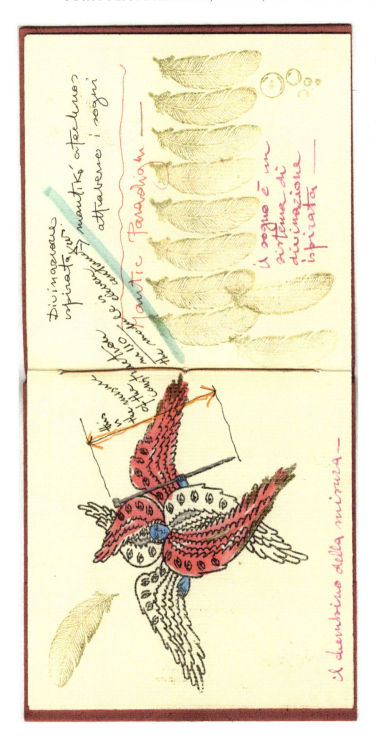

Figure 57 Sketchbook 160, f.11v/12r (18 × 18 cm). August–September 9, 1993. *The Architect's Dream, House for the Next Millennium* by Marco Frascari. The dimensioning cherubim and the module of 11 centimeters. Mantic Paradigm: dreams are a system of inspired divination. Mixed media. Transfers, colored pencils, inks and markers.

Source: © Courtesy of Marco Frascari Estate.

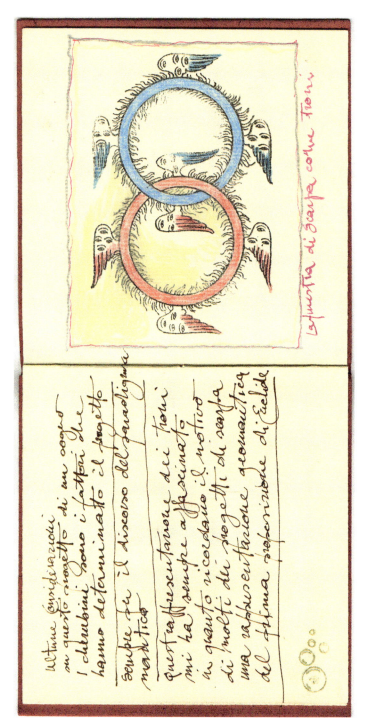

Figure 58 Sketchbook 160, f.12v/13r (18 × 18 cm). August–September 9, 1993. *The Architect's Dream, House for the Next Millennium* by Marco Frascari. Notes and sketch inspired by Scarpa's window design based on the first Euclidean proposition. Mixed media. Transfers, colored pencils, inks and markers.

Source: © Courtesy of Marco Frascari Estate.

PORTFOLIO: DRAWINGS, MODEL, AND SKETCHBOOKS

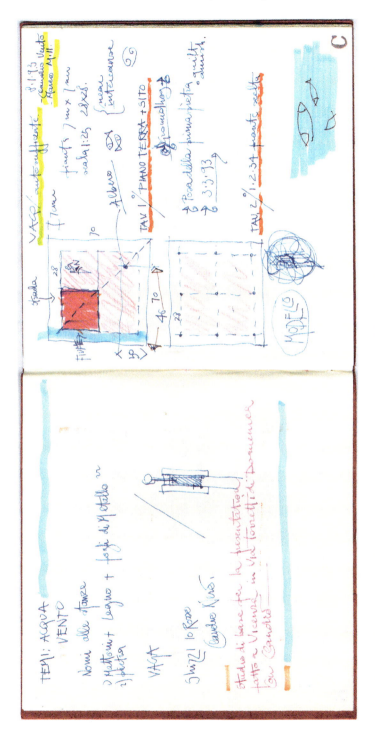

Figure 59 Sketchbook 160, f.13v/14r (18 × 18 cm). August–September 9, 1993. *The Architect's Dream, House for the Next Millennium* by Marco Frascari. Studies for the fireplaces and the kitchen table with a dark mirror. Colored inks and markers.

Source: © Courtesy of Marco Frascari Estate.

PORTFOLIO: DRAWINGS, MODEL, AND SKETCHBOOKS

Figure 60 Sketchbook 160, f.14v/15r (18 × 18 cm). August–September 9, 1993. *The Architect's Dream, House for the Next Millennium* by Marco Frascari. Studies for the room of Morpheus and the room of Metis. Colored pencils, inks and markers.

Source: © Courtesy of Marco Frascari Estate.

PORTFOLIO: DRAWINGS, MODEL, AND SKETCHBOOKS

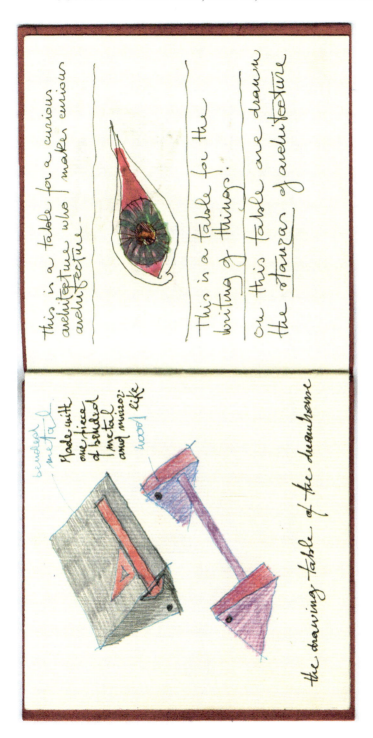

Figure 61 Sketchbook 160, f.15v/16r (18 × 18 cm). August–September 9, 1993. *The Architect's Dream, House for the Next Millennium* by Marco Frascari. Studies for the drafting table of the dream house. Colored pencils, inks and markers.

Source: © Courtesy of Marco Frascari Estate.

161

PORTFOLIO: DRAWINGS, MODEL, AND SKETCHBOOKS

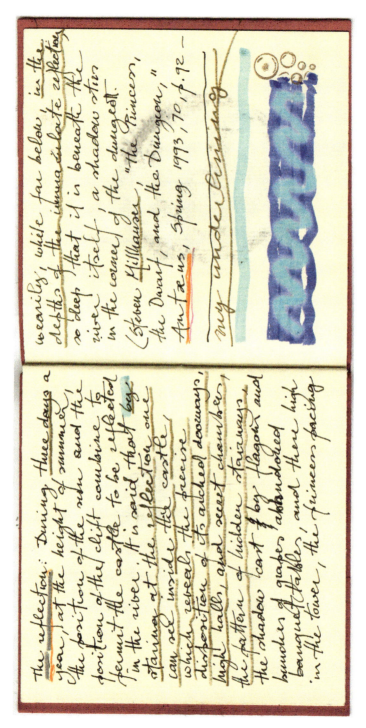

Figure 62 Sketchbook 160, f.16v/17r (18 × 18 cm). August–September 9, 1993. *The Architect's Dream, House for the Next Millennium* by Marco Frascari. The reflection. Notes from Steven Millhauser's novel "The Princess, the Dwarf, and the Dungeon," Antaeus, special fiction issue. Spring 1993, 70, p. 92.

Source: © Courtesy of Marco Frascari Estate.

PORTFOLIO: DRAWINGS, MODEL, AND SKETCHBOOKS

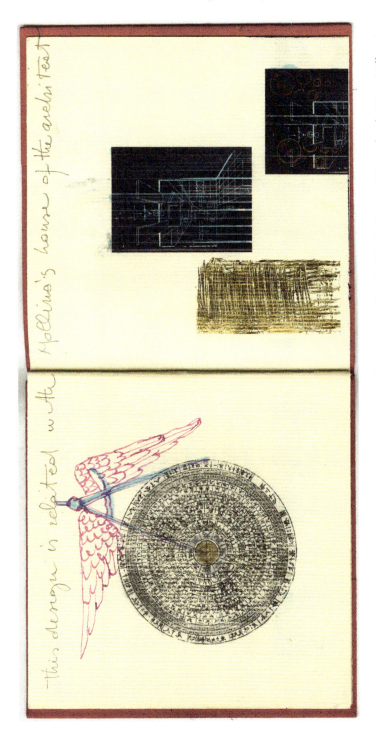

Figure 63 Sketchbook 160, f.17v/18r (18 × 18 cm). August–September 9, 1993. *The Architect's Dream, House for the Next Millennium* by Marco Frascari. "This design is related to Mollino's house of the architect." The compass of divination. Transfer of Mollino's drawing. Mixed media. Transfers, pencil, colored inks and markers.

Source: © Courtesy of Marco Frascari Estate.

163

PORTFOLIO: DRAWINGS, MODEL, AND SKETCHBOOKS

Figure 64 Sketchbook 160, f.18v/19r (18 × 18 cm). August–September 9, 1993. *The Architect's Dream, House for the Next Millennium* by Marco Frascari. Sketch of the dream house on site. The compass of divination and some notes about dreaming as a "game of imagination." Mixed media. Transfers, colored pencils, inks and markers.

Source: © Courtesy of Marco Frascari Estate.

164

PORTFOLIO: DRAWINGS, MODEL, AND SKETCHBOOKS

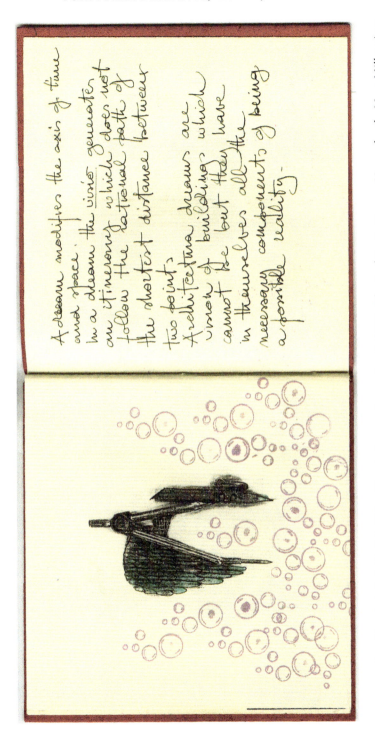

Figure 65 Sketchbook 160, f.19v/20r (18 × 18 cm). August–September 9, 1993. *The Architect's Dream, House for the Next Millennium* by Marco Frascari. Sketch of a winged compass and notes on dreaming. Mixed media. Transfers, colored pencils, inks and markers.

Source: © Courtesy of Marco Frascari Estate.

165

PORTFOLIO: DRAWINGS, MODEL, AND SKETCHBOOKS

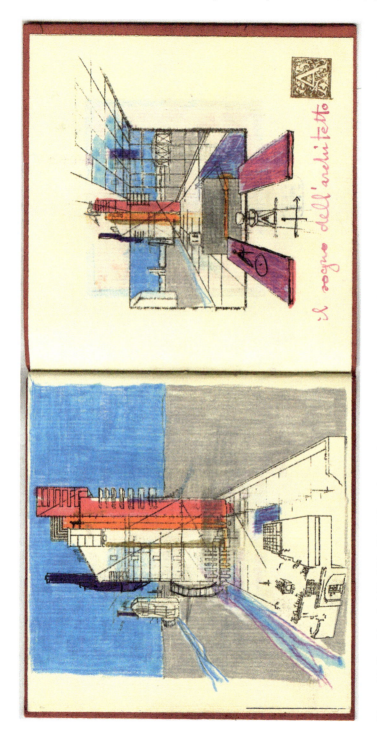

Figure 66 Sketchbook 160, f.20v/21r (18 × 18 cm). August–September 9, 1993. *The Architect's Dream, House for the Next Millennium* by Marco Frascari. The architect's dream: hand-colored transfers of Mollino's two drawings for the architect's house. Mixed media. Transfers, colored pencils, inks and markers.

Source: © Courtesy of Marco Frascari Estate.

PORTFOLIO: DRAWINGS, MODEL, AND SKETCHBOOKS

Figure 67 Sketchbook 160, f.21v/22r (18 × 18 cm). August–September 9, 1993. *The Architect's Dream, House for the Next Millennium* by Marco Frascari. The dream of the angel. Series of winged compasses. Mixed media. Transfers, colored pencils, inks and markers.

Source: © Courtesy of Marco Frascari Estate.

PORTFOLIO: DRAWINGS, MODEL, AND SKETCHBOOKS

Figure 68 Sketchbook 159, back and front cover (25 × 25 cm). May 1994. *Il Terzo Libro dei sogni d'architettura* by Marco Frascari. With a postcard of the 1932 Lonely Metropolitan, Gelatin-silver print and photomontage by Herbert Bayer, on the cover.

Source: © Courtesy of Marco Frascari Estate.

168

PORTFOLIO: DRAWINGS, MODEL, AND SKETCHBOOKS

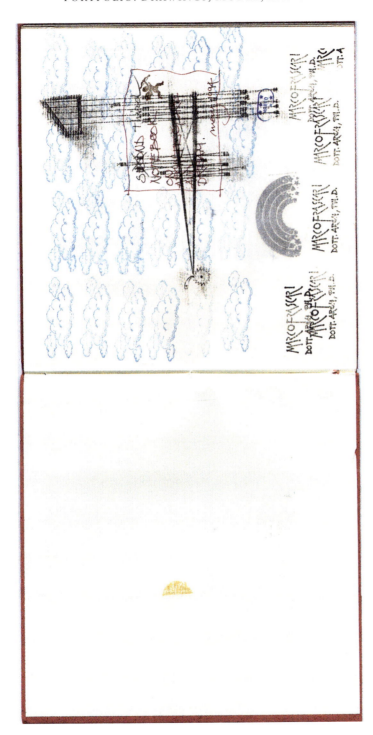

Figure 69 Sketchbook 159, f.1v/2r (25 × 25 cm). May 1994. *Il Terzo Libro dei sogni d'architettura* by Marco Frascari. Transfers of cumulous clouds, Frascari's ex libris and other sketches.

Source: © Courtesy of Marco Frascari Estate.

PORTFOLIO: DRAWINGS, MODEL, AND SKETCHBOOKS

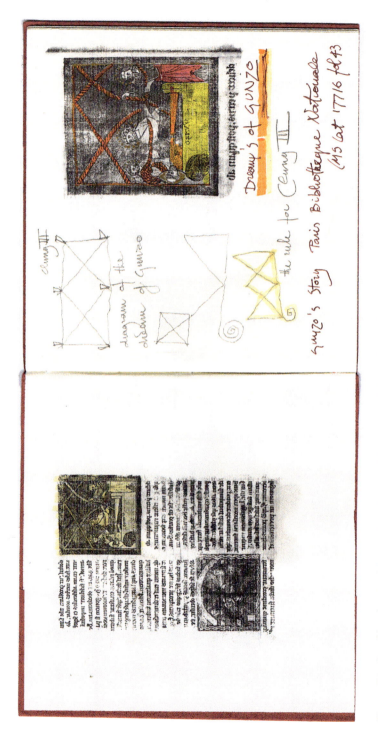

Figure 70 Sketchbook 159, f.2v/3r (25 × 25 cm). May 1994. *Il Terzo Libro dei sogni d'architettura* by Marco Frascari. Gunzo's dream (MS Lat. 17716 f.43, Paris Bibliothèque Nationale de France) and other sketches. Mixed media. Transfers, colored pencils, inks and markers.

Source: © Courtesy of Marco Frascari Estate.

170

PORTFOLIO: DRAWINGS, MODEL, AND SKETCHBOOKS

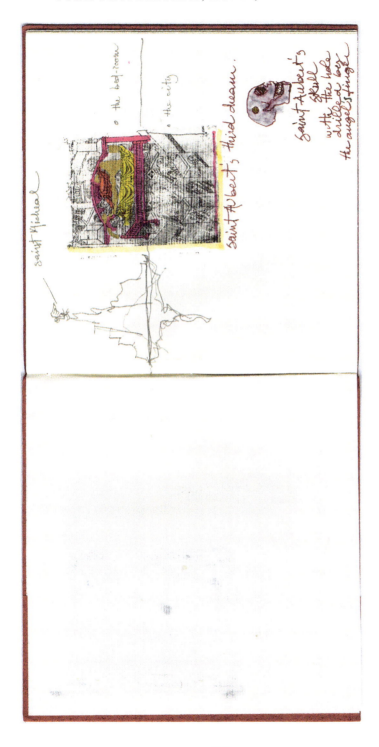

Figure 71 Sketchbook 159, f.3v/4r (25 × 25 cm). May 1994. *Il Terzo Libro dei sogni d'architettura* by Marco Frascari. Saint Aubert's third dream and other sketches. Mixed media. Transfers, colored pencils, inks and markers.

Source: © Courtesy of Marco Frascari Estate.

PORTFOLIO: DRAWINGS, MODEL, AND SKETCHBOOKS

Figure 72 Sketchbook 159, f.4v/5r (25 × 25 cm). May 1994. *Il Terzo Libro dei sogni d'architettura* by Marco Frascari. Magazine clipping of a tattooed hand and black and white clipping of a printout of Thomas Cole's 1840 painting "The Architect's Dream."

Source: © Courtesy of Marco Frascari Estate.

PORTFOLIO: DRAWINGS, MODEL, AND SKETCHBOOKS

Figure 73 Sketchbook 159, f.5v/6r (25 × 25 cm). May 1994. *Il Terzo Libro dei sogni d'architettura* by Marco Frascari. Transfers of Thomas Cole's 1840 painting "The Architect's Dream," which has been colored over with markers.

Source: © Courtesy of Marco Frascari Estate.

173

PORTFOLIO: DRAWINGS, MODEL, AND SKETCHBOOKS

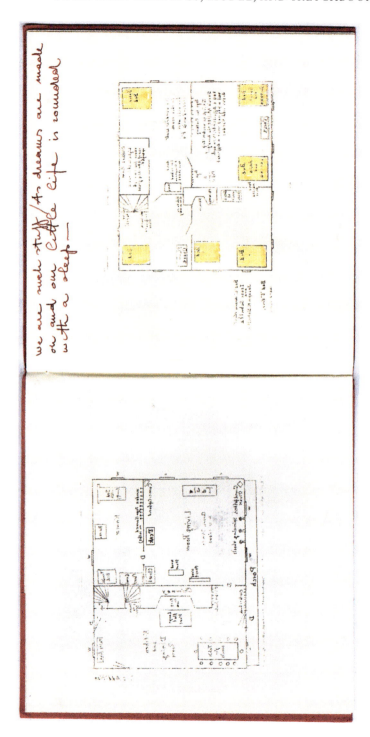

Figure 74 Sketchbook 159, f.6v/7r (25 × 25 cm). May 1994. *Il Terzo Libro dei sogni d'architettura* by Marco Frascari. House plans transfers with a citation from Shakespeare's *The Tempest* (Act 4, Scene 1): "We are such stuff / As dreams are made on and our little life is rounded with a sleep."

Source: © Courtesy of Marco Frascari Estate.

PORTFOLIO: DRAWINGS, MODEL, AND SKETCHBOOKS

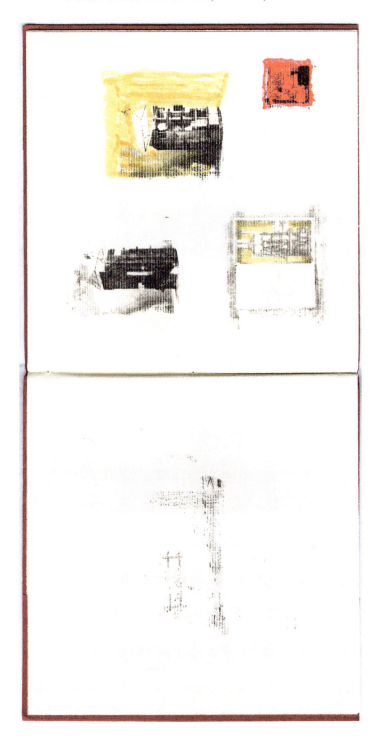

Figure 75 Sketchbook 159, f.7v/8r (25 × 25 cm). May 1994. *Il Terzo Libro dei sogni d'architettura* by Marco Frascari. Hand-colored transfers of photographs of the model of the dream house. Mixed media.

Source: © Courtesy of Marco Frascari Estate.

175

PORTFOLIO: DRAWINGS, MODEL, AND SKETCHBOOKS

Figure 76 Sketchbook 159, f.8v/9r (25 × 25 cm). May 1994. *Il Terzo Libro dei sogni d'architettura* by Marco Frascari. Transfer of a photograph of the model of the dream house.
Source: © Courtesy of Marco Frascari Estate.

PORTFOLIO: DRAWINGS, MODEL, AND SKETCHBOOKS

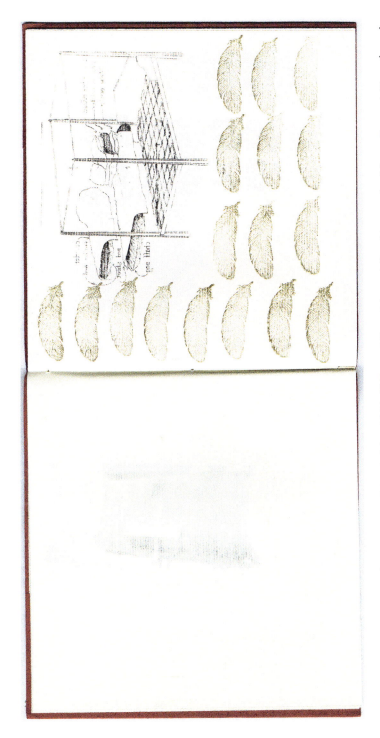

Figure 77 Sketchbook 159, f.9v/10r (25 × 25 cm). May 1994. *Il Terzo Libro dei sogni d'architettura* by Marco Frascari. Transfers of a bed frame, floating mattresses and feathers.

Source: © Courtesy of Marco Frascari Estate.

PORTFOLIO: DRAWINGS, MODEL, AND SKETCHBOOKS

Figure 78 Sketchbook 159, f.10v/11r (25 × 25 cm). May 1994. *Il Terzo Libro dei sogni d'architettura* by Marco Frascari. Transfers of floor patterns and photo of the model of the dream house.

Source: © Courtesy of Marco Frascari Estate.

PORTFOLIO: DRAWINGS, MODEL, AND SKETCHBOOKS

Figure 79 Sketchbook 159, f.11v/12r (25 × 25 cm). May 1994. *Il Terzo Libro dei sogni d'architettura* by Marco Frascari. Hand-colored transfers of patterns.

Source: © Courtesy of Marco Frascari Estate.

PORTFOLIO: DRAWINGS, MODEL, AND SKETCHBOOKS

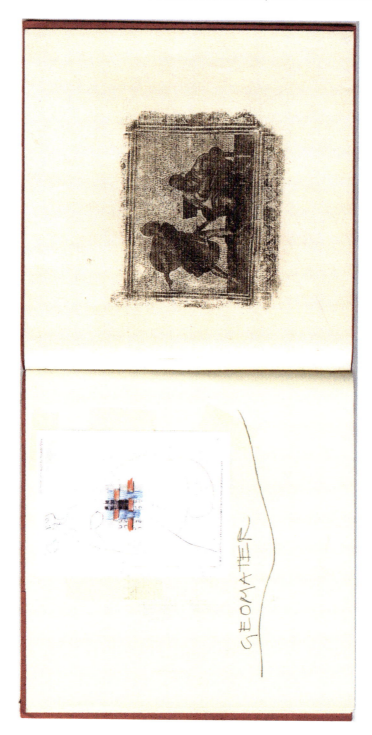

Figure 80 Sketchbook 159, f.12v/13r (25 × 25 cm). May 1994. *Il Terzo Libro dei sogni d'architettura* by Marco Frascari. Geomater. Clipping of a sketch of a pregnant woman and floor patterns by Carlo Scarpa for the main entrance to Palazzo Steri, Palermo. Transfer.

Source: © Courtesy of Marco Frascari Estate.

PORTFOLIO: DRAWINGS, MODEL, AND SKETCHBOOKS

Figure 81 Sketchbook 159, f.13v/14r (25 × 25 cm). May 1994. *Il Terzo Libro dei sogni d'architettura* by Marco Frascari. Transfer of Carl Jung's Bollingen Tower on Lake Zurich in Switzerland (1923–1935).

Source: © Courtesy of Marco Frascari Estate.

POSTSCRIPT
Interview with Claudio Sgarbi

Federica Goffi and Claudio Sgarbi

Oneiric recollections of a design

FG: What are your recollections of the ideas explored in the house-tower project?

CS: The description that was given in the panel for the 1993 Cincinnati Art Museum exhibit explains the basic principles of the design (Figure 0.1 in the Portfolio). The reflections about this project extended well beyond its exhibition and each of us has been designing the "house-tower" over and over again. There were then, and there still remain now, many undesignable concerns. There is absolute asymmetry between what a project shows and pretends to be and that which it inherently evokes but should be unexpressed, removed, discharged or even forgotten. I am not talking about that which a project ignores, excludes, or that which is next to the verge of existence and is discarded, dismissed, marginalized, or neglected—which is indeed, another interesting realm of investigation. Nor am I talking about things that are irrelevant, incoherent, or incongruent in a design. I am talking about those things that are inherent and relevant and yet are meant to remain hidden, in the shadows and then forgotten. These are the things that come to presence, serve a purpose and then fade away. There are moments when I suspect that this is the essence of design.

FG: What do you remember about the beginning of this project?

CS: Because of a note left by Marco (Figure 26 in the Portfolio), I remember a chronological detail, one which would otherwise have been forgotten—that being the birthday of the house-tower. I mention it now so that it can be forgotten again. Our design collaboration began with a family celebration: my son Fabio Elia turned three years old on March 3rd, 1993. This caused a cascade of coincidences. I played with the idea of the down-pouring of

POSTSCRIPT: INTERVIEW WITH CLAUDIO SGARBI

"happen-stances." Together with di-stances, circum-stances, in-stances and sub-stances, it became the leitmotif for the design of the stances/stanzas: the rooms of the tower. One might think that a private family celebration is a marginal and irrelevant occurrence. The role and the relevance of marginalia in design were an aspect that we enjoyed discussing. Fortuities—what a beautiful word! It is in the midst of fortuity that we commit ourselves to reality. I understand that it may seem contrary to the logical process of finding a good reason for something to be. Fortuitous chance, causation, and necessity (Greek Καιρός and Ἀνάγκη; kairos and ananke) are incredible tools to open or unhinge the doors between day-dreams and night-dreams to jump into the flesh of the world. I think that one needs the courage to make coincidences stand out just in order to allow them to be forgotten. We played with the numerals from the birth-date of the house-tower, 3-3-1993. For example, we took 1 and 3 as the end numbers of 1-99-3 to be related with the four sides of the square to form the three walls plus the one column (Figures 7, 8 in the Portfolio). Without daring to compromise oneself with latent coincidences, the space we live in, like a castle of cards, collapses. It might be the ambition of a nihilist or a playful cattish fellow to make it collapse, but what does nourish the ephemeral practice of everyday life? We wanted to see and capture coincidences.

FG: How did you develop the fundamental dimensions of the house-tower?

CS: The decisions we made about the dimensions of the tower were the result of an inspiration (pneumatic sufflation) of concurrences. We combined "our" numerology with the dimensions of the standard sheet of Mylar that Marco chose. We generated a geometric subdivision of the translucent sheet to create a central space to accommodate four horizontal sections at 1:25 scale (Figures 9, 10 in the Portfolio). This would create the opportunity to design four plans of approximately 7 by 7 meters. One of the initial themes for discussion was precisely this dimension—the exterior side of the square plan. How did we settle on a dimension between 6.6 and 7 meters? Almost, about, quasi, more or less … how does one fix the dimensions of a space? A square that is not a square is more square than a square. This theory of approximation was my intercalation throughout the project. The profile of the walls inside shows no direct correlation with the outside profile. The interior inflates and deflates the dimensions of the pneumatic stanza. The outside dimensions go from 6.6 to 7 meters, while the inside goes from 3.3 to 5.5 meters. The variable thickness of the walls is the space where this approximation is explored. The "right" dimensions of the stanza are something that one can explore by inhabiting the space of the walls around the three sides of the house. While moving from room to room, one is invited to continuously re-orient and re-tune oneself, like strumming a score.

FG: What is the role of the "ponderous column" inserted in the façade of the house-tower?

CS: The "fourth wall" required special care. In theatrical space, the fourth wall is the frame of the stage. One sees, or pretends to see, through it, as if the wall was/was not really there. The fully glazed fourth wall in the house-tower was a celebration of its central occlusion: the column. We played with the expression "a beam in one's eye." In our case the expression became "a column in one's eye." The Polyphemic column, the individual column on the south side, was located right of centre, in that place which, in a temple in antis is a void between the two columns on either side of the exterior walls. This for me was the celebration of a trick that was quite meaningful for an architect trained in the Venetian tradition. A central column in a bifora (double lancet window) is not just there to support the mullion, which is what we might tend to assume; rather it is a celebration of the central column itself: the main figure in the ground of the view.

FG: Would you tell me something about the idea of the "stanza," which is something that Marco theorized at length in his text, and seems to have been critical to the project's inception?

CS: The interior side of the approximate square was a fluid volume that we called the "stanza." Stanza in Italian is the most common term used to indicate a room, whereas in English it has a poetic and musical connotation. The relation between the English term "room" and the German "Raum" for "space" is also something that we discussed. A stanza is the essence of approximation: it approximates "all the stanzas" that Marco and I could remember. In the same way the central column was meant to be "all the columns." In order to make something to become "all of that something," one must stratify and overlap meanings in such a way that its definition, the limits of its figure, becomes uncertain and fuzzy. That "something" must shine and tremble, glare and blur right where the lines and its limits appear and become visible. Each line becomes both a cut, a wound, and a sediment. Its manifestation must be an evocation of its latent invisible dimensions. The 660/700 centimeters (the exterior side of the square plan) were shrunk, dilated, and twisted inside to make them coincide with the different stanzas in our imagination: the margins between the inner stanza and the outer stanza became the poché—the rammed earth wall of my verso house-tower. After overlapping many intuitive and fantastic "stanzas," one reaches a point of mnemonic saturation and cannot remember what is what, within the possible limits of the stanza. One is fully confused/fused with those limits and having reached the margins of incompleteness, approximation is gained. One could then provide measurements to be passed on to the builders who will further approximate them, allowing for a measure of play.

POSTSCRIPT: INTERVIEW WITH CLAUDIO SGARBI

FG: Can you tell me about the recto and the verso drawings and how the design progressed through them?

CS: The recto/verso was an idea that we enjoyed discussing because of our interest in ambiguity. The conflagration of the recto/verso condition is one that we were bound to experience. I kept designing an inverted tower that digs down, even after Marco convinced me to design a "tower" that rose up (Figure P1). Next to the tower that celebrates day-dreaming, I imagined the tower of night staring. The tower that digs down would provide the soil to be used to build the rammed earth walls of my upright tower. I envisioned that the tower that digs down would be progressively filled by the goods that become "bads." The archaic *mundus* becomes a "well" of debris (*immundus*). While the recto plans are a sequence of sections going up (Figure 9 in the Portfolio), the verso plans are a sequence of sections going down into the depths of the *mundus/immundus* (Figure 10 in the Portfolio). This was meant to be a place where you create dis-order and accumulate obsolete items that are part of our contemporary life, a digging hole for the archeologist of the next millennium. I also had the intention to build a physical model that was meant to work like an hourglass and flip upside/down and up again. It was inevitable to have many symbolic tower references in mind: from Nuragic and Babel towers to contemporary skyscrapers, the evidence is overwhelmingly symbolic. What happens when a phenomenon like the tower gains an excess of symbolism and everyone ends up seeing into it whatever they like? We need the courage to design for a coexistence of happenstances that drift into one another, contaminating, and healing each other. The Oedipic tower of Sigismondo in *Life is a Dream* (Calderón de la Barca, 1636) was our favorite tease, together with the manipulation offered by Hugo von Hofmannsthal in *The Tower* (1925) and Pier Paolo Pasolini's horizontal tower—in Calderón (1966).

FG: There are some curious details in the drawings, like the ark that you placed on top of your verso design for the house-tower. Can you tell us about some of them?

CS: The verso vertical sections show a sequence of stanzas with various ephemeral activities to celebrate the ubiquity of bodily functions. We began to see this tower not like a free-standing object in the land but as a kind of duct that connected the sky (the atmosphere above) with the depths of the earth (below the fertile layer of superficial soil). This square duct connects that which floats above with that which lies below in a sort of inverted symmetry. It was really a "pipe." Floors, ceilings, furniture, and all the other happenstances were occlusions of the inhabitable pipe, the house-tower itself. The two sides of the pipe were celebrated by each of us in different yet complementary ways. The wind-dial was the guiding spirit for Marco, whereas mine was the aeolian harp. I added a water cistern in the shape of an ark, the hull of which formed the ceiling of the upper stanza: it waits for the deluge on the top of the tower but the water is already inside.

FG: Tell me more about the double-sidedness of the design.

CS: The recto plans concentrate on the design of the bathrooms and the coherence of their pipes. In the verso, one can find portable toilets and movable bathtubs. On the recto, the bathroom is a manifestation of sacredness. On the verso, I wonder about the depth to which the waste falls along with other debris in their alchemical mix. On the recto, the geometry of the bathroom is a demonstration of spherical distortion: its center is everywhere and its circumference is nowhere. The recto vertical sections show a sequence of floors for storing, cooking, and sleeping, which culminate with an angelic weathervane. The verso vertical sections consist of a sequence of stanzas where everything can take place anywhere and culminate with an ark filled with water and an aeolian harp/windmill. The recto and verso explain each other in the midst of difference and change. The difference stands out by means of an occlusion of visibility: the image of the tower on the recto will becloud the image of the tower on the verso, thus blurring our reciprocal gaze.

FG: Do you still think about the ideas that you explored in this project? It seems fresh in your recollections.

CS: This project is alive in my imagination. It is now the stanza of an interior dialogue, where I exchange views with "Others." We began this project through a real dialogue, in the sense that we ventured into every possible, complicated, and surreal discussion. We ventured into the oneiric realm and we dared to wander. We traced graphs, drew images, read books, shared meals, and discussed our ideas with friends, colleagues, our dearest ones, and people met by chance. I decided to keep notebooks and to record all our thoughts. The nocturnal wanderings seemed impossible to decipher. One of my dreams was a dream where I dreamt that I was writing down my dreams. I have always had a problem trying to remember my dreams. I decided to fool my lazy dream-memory. I kept a notebook and a pen next to my bed with the intention of waking up from my dreams to write them down. The dreams came as rich as I expected and I woke up and wrote my notes. In the morning I discovered that my notebook was bare, blank, empty. My imagination forbade me to violate the volatile essence of my dreams. The dreams had to fade away and be forgotten. The dream protected itself from the threat of being unveiled. It refused to disclose its immediacy and made a fool of me. It was as if the dream anticipated my intentions. My dream claimed and defended its space of oblivion. This oblivion, and its necessity for forgetfulness, are the most convincing truth of the art of making. All the involuntary disclosures of the drawings now surpass in importance the voluntary ones.

FG: You worked on your respective projects at a considerable distance from each other. How did you work this out?

CS: Marco and I agreed and disagreed, made fools of our different positions and even switched roles. We decided that we were going to continue our designs from two different sides of the Atlantic Ocean, and we were going to draw on two different sheets of the same size of paper, which became the recto and the verso, to be re-joined at a later time. Two different sheets of paper were therefore meant to travel through considerable distances, both literally and phenomenally. There were times when we worked independently and pursued different ideas. We were far away indeed and yet the distance was contracted by the transparent quality of the Mylar sheet. To look through from afar (*tra-guardare*) was our way of thinking about imagination and distance. Two sections in plan and two in elevation is what we decided to draft. The house-tower is "The Tower" where we encountered one another, through simulation, dissimulation, and the suspension of disbelief. This project is a series of sections through all our reflections. It is a downpouring of possible infinites, an epiphany of tropes. An excess of thoughts, gifts, concerns, and goods, like those that are offered in a potlatch. Too much and not enough yet. This idea of a possible dissipation of thoughts, concerns, intentions, passions, and errors—through a full commitment and the courage to take responsibility—has given ground to my dearest principles that are the geometry of turmoil and the stenosis of being. I still try to practice them but the ideal friend who knows how to think and draw and build is always appearing and vanishing like in a dream.

FG: As a last question, can I ask you how does one enter and exit the dream house?

CS: According to a very ancient Greek tradition, one enters the realm of dream, or better yet, the dream invites one in, across two doors. Two is a convenient number to start with. The dream seems to invite us into "its" realm. Indeed, the dream passes through us, takes hold of us by overcoming our resistance. It transfixes us. The so-called "external senses" (an expression that is indeed a non-sense)—the sights, the sounds, the tastes, the smells, the tactile awareness—are both repressed and amplified in an immense interior universe. The dream is a kind of interiority with most vulnerable limits. The façade of the dream house never existed. No doubt, you can dream that you are dreaming, or you can believe that you are not dreaming while you dream, and so on. You can put any possible deception into an abyss if this is of comfort to you. The numinous doors of the dream are without hinges to ensure that they will open and close imperceptibly, that they will slide untracked and non-counterweighted. How many precautions are taken just to fool around deceptively!? One of the doors has a degree of transparency, while the other has a degree of opaqueness. Because of a linguistic pun, one is led to believe that one was made of horn and the other was made of ivory. We never delved far enough into the design of these two doors and we never decided which one would open or close. Which would be the door to the recto and which one to the verso? Upon what would they open or close? The project is incomplete. It is the incompleteness of a design that we longed for, and which we elected to be our everlasting task.

Figure P1 Above and Below Ink and watercolors on paper by Claudio Sgarbi (ca. 9 × 14 cm).

Source: © Courtesy of Claudio Sgarbi.

BIBLIOGRAPHY

All of the authors' names in bold identify texts listed by Marco Frascari in the original bibliography of the book; all other texts have been added by the editor of this publication.

Ackerman, Diane. (1990) *A Natural History of the Senses.* New York: Vintage Books.
Agamben, Giorgio. (1993) *Stanzas.* Minneapolis, MN: University of Minnesota Press.
Agamben, Giorgio. (2009) *What Is an Apparatus?* Stanford, CA: Stanford University Press.
Aichen, Otl. (1994) *Analogous and Digital.* Berlin: Ernst & Sohn.
Alberti, Leon Battista. (1966a) *De Re Aedificatoria.* Trans. Orlandi, Giovanni. Milano: Il Polifilo.
Alberti, Leon Battista. (1966b) *On Painting.* Trans. Spencer, John. New Haven, CT: Yale University Press.
Alberti, Leon Battista. (1973) *Opere Volgari.* Edited by Grayson, Cecil. Roma: Laterza.
Alberti, Leon Battista. (1997) *On the Art of Building in Ten Books.* Trans. Rykwert, Joseph, Leach, Neil and Tavernor, Robert. Cambridge, MA: MIT Press.
Andersen, Kirsti. (1992) *Brook Taylor's Work on Linear Perspective: A Study of Taylor's Role in the History of Perspective Geometry, Including Facsimiles of Taylor's Two Books on Perspective.* New York: Springer.
Anderson, Stanford. (1995) Public Institutions: Louis I. Khan's Reading of Volume Zero. *JAE* 49–1, 10–21.
Aristotle. (1965) *De Anima.* Trans. Hicks, R. D. New York: Arno Press.
Aristotle. (2003) *Physics II 3 and Metaphysics V 2.* Trans. Höffe, Otfried. Albany, NY: SUNY Press.
Artemidorus, Daldianus. (1975) *The Interpretation of Dreams.* Trans. White, Robert. Park Ridge, NJ: Noyes Press.
Auer, Gerhard. (1995) Living Wetter: On Consumption of Water in the Townhouse. *Daedalus* 55: 38–55.
Bachelard, Gaston. (1971) *The Poetics of Reverie: Childhood, Language and the Cosmos.* Trans. Russell, Daniel. Boston: Beacon Press.

Bachelard, Gaston. (1983) *Water and Dreams: An Essay on the Imagination of Matter*. Trans. Farrell, Edith. Dallas, TX: The Pegasus Foundation.
Bachelard, Gaston. (1994) *The Poetics of Space*. Trans. Jolas, Maria. Boston: Beacon Press.
Bakhtin, Mikhail. (1984) *Rabelais and His World*. Trans. Iswolsky, Hélène. Bloomington, IN: Indiana University Press.
Banes, Sally. (2007) *Before, Between and Beyond: Three Decades of Dance Writing*. Madison, WI: The University of Wisconsin Press.
Barasch, Moshe. (1993) *Icons: Studies in the History of an Idea*. New York: New York University Press.
Barbieri, Giuseppe. (1983) *Andrea Palladio e la Cultura Veneta del Rinascimento*. Roma: Il Veltro Editrice.
Barnes, Carl F., Jr. (2009) *The Portfolio of Villard de Honnecourt*. Farnham: Ashgate.
Bartram, Angela, El-Bizri, Nader and Gittens, Douglas. (2014) *Recto Verso: Redefining the Sketchbook*. Farnham: Ashgate.
Bauman, Andrea. (1994) How to get your dream house! *McCall's* 122: 144–147.
Belardi, Paolo. (2014) *Why Architects Still Draw*. Trans. Nowak, Z. Cambridge, MA: MIT Press.
Benjamin, Walter. (1968) The Task of the Translator. In *Illuminations*. Trans. Zohn, Harry. New York: Harcourt, Brace & World.
Benjamin, Walter. (1977) *Walter Benjamin, Gesammelte Schriften*, Vol. 2. Edited by Schweppenhäuser, Hermann and Tiedemann, Rolf. Frankfurt: Suhrkamp.
Benjamin, Walter. (2003) *Selected Writings, 1938–1940*, Vol. 4. Trans. Jephcott, Edmund, edited by Eiland, Howard and Jennings, Michael W. Cambridge, MA: The Belknap Press of Harvard University Press.
Bernardi Perini, Giorgio and Marangoni Claudio. (eds.) (1993) Il Parnaso e la Zucca. In *Teofilo Folengo nel Quinto Centenario (1491–1991)*. Firenze: L.S. Olschki.
Blanc, Charles. (1870) *Grammaire des Arts du Dessin: Architecture, Sculpture, Peinture*. Paris: Jules Renouard.
Bleeker, C. J. (ed.) (1968) Guilt or Pollution and Rites of Purification. In *Proceedings of the XI International Congress of the International Association for the History of Religions*, Sept. 1965, Vol. II. Leiden: Brill.
Bono, James. (1984) Medical Spirits and the Medieval Language of Life. *Traditio* 40: 91–130.
Borges, Jorge Luis. (1964a) *Labyrinths: Selected Stories and Other Writings*. Edited by Yates, Donald A. and Irby, James E. New York: New Directions.
Borges, Jorge Luis. (1964b) Pierre Menard, Author of the Quixote. In *Collected Fictions*. Trans. Hurley, Andrew. London: The Penguin Press.
Bosco, Nynfa. (1959) *La Filosofia Pragmatica di Charles Sanders Peirce*. Torini: Edizioni di Filosofia.
Bosnak, Robert. (1993) *A Little Course in Dreams*. Boston: Shambala.
Boyle, Sheryl and Frascari, Marco. (2009) Architectural Amnesia and Architectural Smell. *AI, Architecture & Ideas* 9: 36–47.
Braham, William and Frascari, Marco. (1994) On the Mantic Paradigm in Architecture: The Projective Evocation of Future Edifices. In *ACSA Proceedings of the National Meeting*. Montreal.

Braham, William and Frascari Marco. (1995a) The Curious Architect or the Curiosity of Critical Practice. In *83rd ACSA Proceedings*. Washington, DC: Association of Collegiate Schools of Architecture Press.

Braham, William and Frascari, Marco. (1995b) The Geomater of Architecture. *Paradosso* 8: 16–27.

Brann, Eva (1991) *The World of the Imagination: Sum and Substance*. Lanham, MD: Rowman & Littlefield.

Bregman, Jay. (1982) *Synesius of Cyrene*. Berkeley, CA: University of California Press.

Brino, Giovanni. (1987) *Carlo Mollino: Architecture as Autobiography: Architecture, Furniture, Interior Design, 1928–1973*. New York: Rizzoli.

Brunn, Ole. (2011) *Fengshui in China: Geomantic Divination between State Orthodoxy and Popular Religion*. Honolulu: University of Hawaii Press.

Bruno, Giordano. (1955) *La Cena de le Ceneri*. Edited by Aquilecchia, Giovanni. Torino: Einaudi.

Bruno, Giordano. (1986) *De Magia: De Vinculis in Genere*. Pordenone: Edizioni Biblioteca dell'Immagine.

Bruno, Giordano. (1995 [1584]) *The Ash Wednesday Supper*. Trans. Gosselin Edward A. and Lerner, Lawrence. S. Toronto: University of Toronto Press.

Bryant, William Cullen. (1848) *A Funeral Oration, Occasioned by the Death of Thomas Cole, Delivered Before the National Academy of Design*. New York: Appleton & Company.

Buck-Morss, Susan. (1995) The City as Dreamworld and Catastrophe. *October* 73: 3–26.

Burks, Arthur. (1946) Peirce's Theory of Abduction. *Philosophy of Science* 13, 4: 301–306.

Burns Gamard, Elizabeth. (2000) *Kurt Schwitters Merzbau: The Cathedral of Erotic Misery*. Princeton, NJ: Princeton Architectural Press.

Burroughs, William. (1995) *My Education: A Book of Dreams*. New York: Viking Press.

Burton, Ernest de Witt. (1918) *Spirit, Soul and Flesh: The Usage of Pneuma, Psyche and Sarx in Greek Writings and Translated Works from the Earliest Period to 225 AD; and of their Equivalents ... in the Hebrew Old Testament*. Chicago: University of Chicago Press.

Bychkov, Viktor. (1993) *The Aesthetic Face of Being: Art in the Theology of Pavel Florensky*. New York: St Vladimir's Seminary Press.

Caillois, Roger. (1963) *The Dream Adventure*. New York: Orion Press.

Cardano, Girolamo. (1585) *Somniorum Synesiorum Omnis Generis Insomnia Explicantes*. Libra IIII. Basileae: Henripetri.

Cardano, Girolamo. (1967) *Opera Omnia*. V. Reprint of the 1662 Lugundi Edition. New York: Johnson Reprint Corporation.

Cardano, Girolamo. (1989) *Sul Sonno e sul Sognare*. I. Trans. Montiglio, Silvia and Grieco, Agnese. Venice: Marsilio.

Cardano, Girolamo. (1993) *Sogni*. II, III, IIII. Trans. Montiglio, Silvia and Grieco, Agnese. Venice: Marsilio.

Carême, Marie-Antonin and Fayot, Charles Frédéric. (1842) *Le Pâtissier pittoresque*. Paris: Renouard.

Carmagnola, Fulvio. (1998) *Parentesi Perdute. Crisi della Forma e Ricerca del Senso nell'Arte Contemporanea*. Milano: Guerini.
Carty, Carolyn. (1988) The Role of Gunzo's Dream in the Building of Cluny III. *Gesta* XXVII: 113–123.
Casey, Edward. (1993) *Getting Back into Place: Toward a Renewed Understanding of the Place-World*. Bloomington, IN: Indiana University Press.
Cavallari-Murat, Augusto. (October 1966) Alcuni Contributi di Simone Stratico alla Storia del 'De Re Aedificatoria' dell'Alberti. *Atti e Rassegna Tecnica della Società Ingegneri e Architetti in Torino* 20: 335–349.
Chenu, Marie-Dominique. (1957) Spiritus. Le Vocabulaire de l'Âme au XIIe Siècle. *Revue des Sciences Philosophiques et Théologiques* 41: 209–232.
Chiesa, Mario. (1993) *Il Parnaso e la Zucca. Teofilo Folengo nel Quinto Centenario (1491-1991)*. Firenze: L.S. Olschki.
Cicero, Marcus Tullius. (1975) *De Divinatione; De Fato; Timaeus*. Leipzig: Teubner.
Colapietro, Vincent. (1988) Dreams: Such Stuff as Meanings Are Made On. *Versus* 49: 65–79.
Colapietro, Vincent. (1989) *Peirce's Approach to Self: A Semiotic Perspective on Human Subjectivity*. Albany, NY: State University of New York Press.
Collins, Peter. (1998) *Changing Ideals in Modern Architecture, 1750–1950*. Montreal: McGill-Queen's University Press.
Colonna, Francesco. (1499) *Hypnerotomachia Poliphili*. Venezia: Aldus Manutius.
Colonna, Francesco. (1950) *The Dream of Poliphilo*. Trans. Hottinger, Mary. Bollingen Series XXV. New York: Pantheon Books.
Colonna, Francesco. (1973) *Hypnerotomachia, the Strife of Love in a Dream* (1592). Trans. Dallington, Robert. New York: Scholars Facsimiles & Reprints.
Copeland, Rita. (1991) *Rhetoric, Hermeneutics and Translation in the Middle Ages: Academic Traditions and Vernacular Texts*. New York: Cambridge University Press.
Corbin, Henry. (1976) *Mundus Imaginalis or the Imaginary and the Imaginal*. Ipswich: Golgonooza Press.
Corboz, André. (1985) *Canaletto: Una Venezia Immaginaria*. Milano: Alfieri Electa.
Cornaro, Alvise. (2014) *Writings on the Sober Life: The Art and Grace of Living Long*. Trans. Fudemoto, Hiroko. Toronto: University of Toronto Press.
Corona-Martinez, Alfonso. (2003) *The Architectural Project*. College Station, TX: Texas A&M University Press.
Couliano, Ioan Petru. (1987) *Eros and Magic in the Renaissance*. Chicago: The University of Chicago Press.
Croce, Benedetto. (1902) *Estetica come Scienza dell'Espressione e Linguistica Generale*. Milano: Sandron.
Croce, Benedetto. (1995) *Aesthetic as Science of Expression and General Linguistic*. Trans. Ainslie, Douglas. New Brunswick, NJ: Transaction Publishers.
Curtis, William. (1986) *Le Corbusier: Ideas and Forms*. London: Phaidon.
Dal Co, Francesco and Mazzariol, Giuseppe. (1986) *Carlo Scarpa: The Complete Works*. Milan: Electa.
Dällenbach, Lucien. (1989) *The Mirror in the Text*. Translated by Whiteley, Jeremy and Hughes, Emma. Chicago: University of Chicago Press.
Daumal, Rene. (1992) *Mount Analogue: A Novel of Symbolically Authentic Non-Euclidean Adventures in Mountain Climbing*. Boston: Shambala.

BIBLIOGRAPHY

de Certeau, Michel. (1988) *The Practice of Everyday Life.* Trans. Rendall S. F. Berkeley, CA: University of California Press.

Drury, Annmarie. (2015) *Translation as Transformation in Victorian Poetry.* Cambridge: Cambridge University Press.

Durand, Jean-Nicolas-Louis. (1805) *Précis des Leçons d'Architecture Données à l'Ecole Politéchnique.* Paris: Chez l'Auteur et Bernard.

Dürer, Albrecht. (1977) *The Painter's Manual: A Manual of Measurement of Lines, Areas, and Solids by Means of Compass and Ruler Assembled by Albrecht Dürer for the Use of All Lovers of Art with Appropriate Illustrations Arranged to Be Printed in the Year MDXXV. Underweysung Der Messung, mit dem Zirckel und Richtscheyt, in Linien, Ebenen und Gantzen Corporen.* Trans. Strauss, Walter. L. New York: Abaris Books.

Eco, Umberto. (1989a) *Sugli Specchi e altri Saggi.* Milano: Bompiani.

Eco, Umberto. (1989b) *Open Work.* Trans. Cancogni, Anna. Cambridge, MA: Harvard University Press.

Edwards, Betty. (1979) *Drawing on the Right Side of the Brain.* New York: Penguin Putnam.

Emmons, Paul. (2005) Size Matters: Virtual Scale and Bodily Imagination in Architectural Drawing. *ARQ* 9, 3–4: 227–235.

Emmons, Paul. (2007) Drawing Sites: Site Drawings. In *Tools of the Imagination: Drawing Tools and Technologies from the Eighteenth Century to the Present.* Edited by Piedmont-Palladino, Susan. New York: Princeton Architectural Press.

Emmons, Paul and Frascari, Marco. (2006) Making Visible the Invisible: Signs of Air in Architectural Treatises. In *Aeolian Winds and the Spirit in Renaissance Architecture.* Edited by Kenda, Barbara. London: Routledge.

Evans, Robin. (1995) *The Projective Cast: Architecture and its Three Geometries.* Cambridge, MA: MIT Press

Evans, Robin. (1997) *Translations from Drawing to Building and Other Essays.* Cambridge, MA: MIT Press.

Fabbrichesi Leo, Rossella. (1986) *Sulle Tracce del Segno. Semiotica, Faneroscopia e Cosmologia nel Pensiero di Charles S. Peirce.* Firenze: La Nuova Italia.

Feberayend, Paul. (1993) *Against Method.* London: Verso.

Filarete, Antonio Averulino. (ca. 1461–1664) *Trattato di Architettura.* MS. Codex Magliabechianus (M), II, I, 140. Firenze: Biblioteca Nazionale Centrale.

Filarete, Antonio Averulino. (1965) *Treatise on Architecture.* Trans. Spencer, John. R. New Haven, CT: Yale University Press.

Filarete, Antonio Averulino. (1972) *Trattato di Architettura.* Edited by Finoli Anna M. and Grassi Liliana. Milano: Il Polifilo.

Florenskij, Pavel. (1977) *Le Porte Regali: Saggio sull'Icona.* Edited by Zolla, E. Milano: Adelphi.

Florenskij, Pavel. (1983) *La Prospettiva Rovesciata ed Altri Scritti.* Roma: Casa del Libro Editrice.

Florensky, Pavel. (1976) On the Icon. *Eastern Churches Review* VIII: 11–37.

Florensky, Pavel. (1996) *Iconostasis.* Trans. Sheehan, D. and Andrejev, O. New York: St. Vladimir's Seminar Press.

Florensky, Pavel. (2002) *Beyond Vision: Essays on the Perception of Art.* London: Reaktion Books.

Focchi, Marco. (1981) Sonno/Sogno. In *Enciclopedia Einaudi*. XIII: 227–243. Torino: Einaudi.
Folena, Gianfranco. (1991) *Volgarizzare e Tradurre*. Torino: Einaudi.
Folengo, Teofilo. (1517) *Merlini Cocai Poetae Mantuani Liber Macaronices Libri XVII*. Venice: Paganini.
Folengo, Teofilo. (1882) *Le Opere Maccheroniche di Merlin Cocai*. Mantova: Editrice Mondovi.
Folengo, Teofilo. (1911) *Le Maccheronee*. Trans. Luzio, Alessandro. Bari: Laterza.
Folengo, Teofilo. (2006) *Baldus*. Edited by Chiesa, M. Torino: UTET.
Frascari, Marco. (1981) The Tell-The-Tale Detail. *VIA* 7: 23–37.
Frascari, Marco. (Spring 1985) A 'Measure' in Architecture. A Medical-Architectural Theory by Simone Stratico Architetto Veneto. *RES* 9: 79–90.
Frascari, Marco. (1986) Semiotica ab Edendo, Taste in Architecture. *Journal of Architectural Education* 40.1: 2–7.
Frascari, Marco (1987a) Tolerance or Play: Conventional Criticism or Critical Conventionalism in Light of the Italian Retreat from the Modern Movement. *Midgard* 1.1: 7–10.
Frascari, Marco. (October 1987b) The Body and Architecture in the Drawings of Carlo Scarpa. *RES* 14: 123–142.
Frascari, Marco. (1988a) Maidens 'Theory' and 'Practice' at the Sides of Lady Architecture. *Assemblage* 7: 14–27.
Frascari, Marco. (1988b) The Drafting Knife and Pen. In *Implementing Architecture*. Edited by Miller, Rob. Atlanta, GA: Nexus Press.
Frascari, Marco. (1989) Ichnography: The Topical Enigma of Architectural Plans. *Terrazzo* 3 Fall.
Frascari, Marco. (November 1990) A New Angel/Angle in Architectural Research: The Ideas of Demonstration. *Journal of Architectural Education* 44: 11–19.
Frascari, Marco. (1991) *Monsters of Architecture: Anthropomorphism in Architectural Theory*. Savage, MD: Rowman & Littlefield Publishers.
Frascari, Marco. (1995) *Una Pillola per Sognare*. Milano: Editrice Progetti.
Frascari, Marco. (1997) The Pneumatic Bathroom. In *Plumbing: Sounding Modern Architecture*. Edited by Lahiji, Nadir and Friedman Daniel S. New York: Princeton Architecture Press.
Frascari, Marco. (1998) The Silent Architect and the Unutterable Nature of Architecture. In *The Culture of Silence. Architecture's Fifth Dimension*. Edited by Quantrill, Malcolm and Webb, Bruce. College Station, TX: Texas A&M University Press.
Frascari, Marco. (1999) The Mirror Theatre of Vincenzo Scamozzi. In *Paper Palaces*. Edited by Hart V. and Hicks P. New Haven, CT: Yale University Press.
Frascari, Marco. (2003) Architects, Never Eat your Maccheroni Without the Proper Sauce. *Nordisk Arkitekturforskning* 2: 41–55.
Frascari, Marco. (2004) Semiotica ab Edendo. Taste in Architecture. In *Eating Architecture*. Edited by Horwitz, Jamie and Singley, Paulette. Cambridge, MA: MIT Press.
Frascari, Marco. (2007a) Models and Drawings – The Invisible Nature of Architecture. In *From Models to Drawings: Imagination and Representation in Architecture*. Edited by Frascari, Marco, Hale, Jonathan and Starkey, Bradley. London: Routledge.

Frascari, Marco. (2007b) A Reflection on Paper and its Virtues. In *From Models to Drawings. Imagination and Representation in Architecture*. Edited by Frascari, Marco, Hale, Jonathan and Starkey, Bradley. London: Routledge.

Frascari, Marco. (2007c) Horizons at the Drafting Table: Filarete and Steinberg. In *Chora: Intervals in the Philosophy of Architecture* 5: 179–200. Edited by Pérez-Gómez, Alberto and Parcell, Stephen. Montréal: McGill-Queen's University Press.

Frascari, Marco. (2008a) *Honestamente Bella. Alvise Cornaro's Temperate View of Lady Architecture and her Maids, Phronesis, and Sophosine.* Available at: www.arch.mcgill.ca/theory/conference/papers/Frascari_Cornaro.pdf (accessed February 7, 2016).

Frascari, Marco. (2008b). Elegant Curiosity. *Log* 12: 69–79.

Frascari, Marco. (2009) Lines as Architectural Thinking. *Architectural Theory Review* 14.3: 200–212.

Frascari, Marco. (2010) Splendor and Miseries of Architectural Construction Drawings. *Interstices* 11: 107–113.

Frascari, Marco. (2011) *Eleven Exercises in the Art of Architectural Drawings: Slow Food for the Architect's Imagination.* London: Routledge.

Frascari, Marco. (2012) The *Beata Architectura*: Places for Thinking. In *The Cultural Role of Architecture*. Edited by Emmons, Paul, Hendrix, John, and Lomholt, Jane. London: Routledge.

Frascari, Marco. (2015) The Ambiguity of Non-Finito Architecture: The Deceiving of Time. *Perspecta (Amnesia): The Yale Architectural Journal* 10: 104–107.

Freud, Sigmund. (1978) *The Interpretation of Dreams.* Trans. Brill, A. A. New York: Random House.

Friedman, Daniel. (1993) *The Architect's Dream: Houses for the Next Millennium.* Cincinnati, OH: The Contemporary Arts Center.

Gabetti, Roberto and Irace Fulvio. (1989) *Carlo Mollino, 1905–1973.* Milano: Electa.

Gandolfo, Francesco. (1978) *Il Dolce Tempo: Mistica, Ermetismo e Sogno nel Cinquecento.* Roma: Bulzoni.

Gentile, Giovanni. (1920) Il Torto e il Diritto delle Traduzioni. In *Frammenti di Estetica e Letteratura.* Lanciano: Carabba.

Gentile, Giovanni. (1994) *L'Estetica di Giovanni Gentile: Esistenza ed Inesistenza dell'Arte.* Palermo: L'Epos.

Goldin, Marco. (1999) *Clerici. Opere 1928-1992.* Conegliano: Linea d'Ombra Libri.

Gombrich, Ernst. (2000) *Art and Illusion: A Study in the Psychology of Pictorial Representation.* Princeton, NJ: Princeton University Press.

Gordon, Donald James. (1949) Poet and Architect: The Intellectual Setting of the Quarrel between Ben Jonson and Inigo Jones. *Journal of the Warburg and Courtauld Institutes* XII: 152–178.

Gregory, Tullio. (1955) *Anima Mundi: La Filosofia di Guglielmo di Conches e la Scuola di Chartres.* Firenze: Sansoni.

Griffin, Randall C. (Summer 1993) The Untrammeled Vision: Thomas Cole and the Dream of the Artist. *Art Journal* 52.2: 66–73.

Grunebaum, Gustav E. von and Caillois, Roger. (eds.) (1966) *The Dream and Human Societies.* Berkeley, CA: University of California Press.

Hacker, Peter M. S. and Schulte, Joachim. (2009) *Philosophy of Psychology: A Fragment*. Oxford: Wiley-Blackwell.
Hedges, Susan. (2012) On Frascari's Notion of Construal. Doctoral dissertation. Auckland: The University of Auckland.
Hendrix, John. S. (2011) Leon Battista Alberti and the Concept of Lineament. School of Architecture, Art, and Historic Preservation Faculty Publications. *Paper 30*. Available at: http://docs.rwu.edu/saahp_fp/30
Heraclitus. (1987) *Fragments*. Trans. Robinson, T. M. Toronto: University of Toronto Press.
Husserl, Edmund. (1989) *Origin of Geometry*. Lincoln, NE: University of Nebraska Press.
Illich, Ivan. (1988) *ABC The Alphabetization of the Popular Mind*. San Francisco: North Point Press.
Illich, Ivan. (1998) The Scopic Past and the Ethics of the Gaze: A Plea for the Ocular Study of Ocular Perception. Available at: www.davidtinapple.com/illich/1998_scopic_past.PDF (accessed April 10, 2016).
Ingold, Tim. (2007a) Materials against Materiality. *Archeological Dialogues* 14.1: 1–16.
Ingold, Tim. (2007b) *Lines: A Brief History*. London: Routledge.
Isidore of Seville. (2006) *The Etymologies of Isidore of Seville*. Trans. Barney, Stephen, Lewis W. J., Beach J. A., and Berghof, Oliver. Cambridge: Cambridge University Press.
Jakobson, Roman. (1959) On Linguistic Aspects of Translation. In *On Translation*. Edited by Brower, Reuben A. Cambridge, MA: Harvard University Press.
Jarzombek, Mark. (1989) *On Leon Battista Alberti: His Literary and Aesthetic Theories*. Cambridge, MA: MIT Press.
Joyce, James. (1976) *Finnegans Wake*. New York: The Viking Press.
Jung, Carl G. (1961) *Memories, Dreams, Reflections*. New York: Pantheon Books.
Kahn, Louis I. (1962) *The Notebooks and Drawings of Louis I. Kahn*. Edited by Wurman, Richard S. and Feldman Eugene. Philadelphia, PA: Falcon Press.
Kahn, Louis I. (1986) *What Will Be Has Always Been: The Words of Louis I. Kahn*. Edited by Wurman, Richard S. New York: Access & Rizzoli.
Kenda, Barbara. (2006) *Aeolian Winds and the Spirit in Renaissance Architecture*. London: Routledge.
Kessling, C. R. (1992) The ὄχημα-πνευμα of the Neoplatonists and the *De Insomniis* of Synesius of Cyrene. *American Journal of Philology* 43: 319–330.
Klein, Robert. (1975) *La Forma e l'Intelligibile. Scritti sul Rinascimento e l'Arte Moderna*. Trans. Federici, R. Torino: Einaudi.
Klein, Robert. (1979) *Form and Meaning: Essays on the Renaissance and Modern Art*. Trans. Jay, M. and Wieseltier, L. New York: The Viking Press.
Kohr, Leopold. (1976) *The City of Man*. Puerto Rico: Editorial Universitaria, Universidad de Puerto Rico.
Kubler, George. (2008) *The Shape of Time: Remarks on the History of Things*. New Haven, CT: Yale University Press.
Kunze, Donald. (1994) Architecture as Site of Reception, Part I: Cuisine, Frontality and the Infra-Thin. In *Chora: Intervals in the Philosophy of Architecture* 1: 83–108. Edited by Pérez-Gómez, Alberto and Parcell, Stephen. Montréal: McGill-Queen's University Press.

Kunze, Donald. (1996) Architecture as Site of Reception, Part II: Sea-Food and Vampires. In *Chora: Intervals in the Philosophy of Architecture* 2: 109–135. Edited by Pérez-Gómez, Alberto and Parcell, Stephen. Montréal: McGill-Queen's University Press.
Lacombrade, Christian. (1951) *Synésios de Cyrène, Hellène et Chrétien*. Paris: Les Belles Lettres.
Lang, Susan. (1965) *De lineamentis*: Leon Battista Alberti's Use of a Technical Term. *Journal of the Warburg and Courtauld Institutes* 28: 335.
Lanternari, Vittorio. (1981) Sogno-Visione. In *Enciclopedia Einaudi* XIII: 94–126. Torino: Einaudi.
Lanza, Diego and Longo, Ottone. (1989) *Il Meraviglioso e il Verosimile: Tra Antichità e Medioevo*. Firenze: Leo S. Olschki.
Lear, John. (1965) *Kepler's Dream: with the Full Text and Notes of Somnium, Sive Astronomia Lunaris Joannis Kepleri*. Trans. Frueh Kirkwood, Patricia. Berkeley, CA: University of California Press.
Le Corbusier. (1995) *Le Corbusier, Painter and Architect*. Aalborg: Nordjyllands Kunstmuseum.
Le Corbusier. (2013) *Le Corbusier's Secret Laboratory: From Painting to Architecture*. Edited by Cohen, Jean-Louis and Ahrenberg, Staffan. Ostfildern: Hatje Cantz.
Lefaivre, Liane. (1997) *Leon Battista Alberti's Hypnerotomachia Poliphili: Re-Cognizing the Architectural Body in the Early Italian Renaissance*. Cambridge, MA: MIT Press.
Le Goff, Jacques. (1988) *The Medieval Imagination*. Chicago: The University of Chicago Press.
Le Guerer, Annick. (1992) *Scent: The Mysterious and Essential Powers of Smell*. Trans. Miller, Richard. New York: Turtle Bay Books.
Lepschy, Giulio C. (1981) Traduzione. In *Enciclopedia Einaudi* 14: 446–459. Torino: Einaudi.
Lindberg, David C. (2007) *The Beginnings of Western Science: The European Scientific Tradition in Philosophical, Religious and Institutional Context, Prehistory to A.D. 1450*. Chicago: The University of Chicago Press.
Lobell, John. (1985) *Between Silence and Light: Spirit in the Architecture of Louis I. Kahn*. Boston: Shambala.
Los, Sergio, Pastor, Valeriano and Tubini, Umberto. (2011) *Arrigo Rudi: Architettura, Restauro e Allestimento*. Venezia: Marsilio.
Macrobius. (1990) *Commentary on the Dream of Scipio by Macrobius*. Trans. Stahl, W. H. New York: Columbia University Press.
Maldonado, Tomàs. (1974) *Avanguardia e Razionalità*. Torino: Einaudi.
Malinowski, Bronislaw. (1948) *Magic, Science and Religion*. Boston: Beacon Press.
Mancini, Girolamo. (1911) *Vita di Leon Battista Alberti*. Firenze: Carnesecchi & Figli.
Mancini, Girolamo. (1967) *Vita di Leon Battista Alberti*. Roma: Bardi Editore.
Manetti, Antonio. (1970) *The Life of Brunelleschi*. University Park, PA: Pennsylvania State University Press.
Manetti, Antonio. (1991) *The Fat Woodworker*. Trans. Martone, Robert. L. and Martone, Valeria. New York: Italica Press.

Manetti, Antonio. (1992) *Vita di Filippo Brunelleschi*. Edited by Perrone, Carlachiara. Roma: Salerno Editrice.
Mantura, Bruno and Millesimi, Ines. (1990) *Fabrizio Clerici*. Roma: De Luca Edizioni d'Arte.
Maritain, Jacques. (1937) Sign and Symbol. *Journal of the Warburg Institute* I: 1–11.
Massironi, Manfredo. (1982) *Vedere con il Disegno. Aspetti Tecnici, Cognitivi, Comunicativi*. Padova: Muzzio.
McCay, Winsor. (1959) *The Complete Little Nemo in Slumberland*. Edited by Marschall, Richard. Hong Kong: Remco Worldservice Books.
Merleau-Ponty, Maurice. (2012) *Phenomenology of Perception*. Trans. Landes, D. London: Routledge.
Michaud, Philippe-Alain. (2004) *Aby Warburg and the Image in Motion*. New York: Zone Books.
Millhauser, Stephen. (1993) *Little Kingdoms: Three Novellas*. New York: Simon & Schuster.
Millhauser, Stephen. (Spring 1993) The Princess, The Dwarf and the Dungeon. *Antaeus* 70: 92.
Millon, Henry A. (1994) *The Renaissance from Brunelleschi to Michelangelo: The Representation of Architecture*. New York: Rizzoli International.
Minkowski, Helmut. (1983) Turris Babel. Mille Anni di Rappresentazioni. *Rassegna* 16: 8–89.
Mollino, Carlo. (October 1933) Vita di Oberon. III. Lo Studio di Oberon. *Casabella* 70: 44.
Mollino, Carlo, Brukhardt, François and Eveno, Claude. (1992) *L'Étrange Univers de l'Architecte Carlo Mollino. Exposition, October 1989–January 1990*. Paris: Editions du Centre Pompidou.
Montani, Pietro. (1981) Riproduzione/Riproducibilità. In *Enciclopedia Einaudi* 12: 112–131. Torino: Einaudi.
Montano, Giovan Battista. (1624) *Scielta di Varii Tempietti Antichi*. Edited by Soria, Giovan B. Roma.
Monteil, Pierre. (1964) *Beau et Laid en Latin: Etude de Vocabulaire*. Paris: Klincksieck.
Mukarovsky, Jan. (1977) *Structure, Sign and Function: Selected Essays*. Trans. Burbank, John and Steiner, Peter. New Haven, CT: Yale University Press.
Mumford, Eric. (2000) *The CIAM Discourse on Urbanism, 1928–60*. Cambridge, MA: MIT Press.
Nietzsche, Friedrich. (1974) *The Gay Science*. Trans. Kaufmann, Walter. New York: Random House.
Nishimoto, Shinji *et al.* (October 2011) Reconstructing Visual Experiences from Brain Activity Evoked by Natural Movies. *Current Biology* 22: 1641–1646.
North, Helen F. (1979) *From Myth to Icon: Reflections on Greek Ethical Doctrine in Literature and Art*. Ithaca, NY: Cornell University Press.
Novalis (von Hardenberg, G. P. F. F.) (1901) *Sämtliche Werke Ergänzungsband*. Leipzig: Diederichs.
Novalis (von Hardenberg, G. P. F. F.) (1977) *Novalis Schriften. Die Werke Friedrich von Hardenbergs*. Vol. III. Edited by Kluckhohn, P. and Samuel, R. *et al.* Stuttgart: Kohlhammer.

Novalis (von Hardenberg, G. P. F. F.) (1993) *Opera Filosofica. Studi Scientifico-Naturali di Freiberg. Frammenti di Fisica.* Vol. II. Edited by Moretti, G. and Desideri, F. Torino: Einaudi.
Novalis (von Hardenberg, G. P. F. F.) (1997) *Philosophical Writings.* Trans. Mahoni Stoljar, M. Albany, NY: State University of New York Press.
Novalis (von Hardenberg, G. P. F. F.) (2007) *Notes for a Romantic Encyclopaedia. Das Allgemeine Brouillon.* Trans. Wood, D. W. Albany, NY: State University of New York Press.
Olson, David. (1994) *The World on Paper: The Conceptual and Cognitive Implications of Writing and Reading.* Cambridge: Cambridge University press.
Onians, John. (2008) *Neuroarthistory: From Aristotle and Pliny to Baxandall and Zeki.* New Haven, CT: Yale University Press.
Osler, Margaret J. (1991) *Atoms, Pneuma, and Tranquility: Epicurean and Stoic Themes in European Thought.* Cambridge: Cambridge University Press.
Otto, Rudolf. (1950) *The Idea of the Holy.* Trans. Harvey, J. W. Oxford: Oxford University Press.
Palladio, Andrea. (1570) *I Quattro Libri di Architettura.* Venezia: Domenico de Franceschi.
Palladio, Andrea. (1997) *Four Books on Architecture.* Trans. Tavernor, Robert and Schofield, Richard. Cambridge, MA: MIT Press.
Parry, D. M. (Spring 1994) Burial of the Dead and the Immortality of the Soul: The Principles of Humanity and the 'Limits of Human Reason.' Paper presented at the Vico Seminar, Folger Library, Washington, DC.
Pascal, Blaise. (2009) *Thoughts, Letters and Minor Works.* New York: Cosimo.
Pattuelli, M. Cristina. (2011) The Warburg Library: Morphology of a Library as a Laboratory of the Mind. Paper presented at *19th Annual Conference of the Society for the History of Authorship, Reading and Publishing* (SHARP Proceedings). Washington, DC.
Pausanias. (1913) *Pausanias's Description of Greece.* Vol. 1. Trans. Frazer, G. London: Macmillan and Company.
Peirce, Charles Sanders. (1923) *Chance, Love, and Logic: Philosophical Essays.* Edited by Cohen, Morris. R. New York: Harcourt, Brace and Company.
Peirce, Charles Sanders. (1931–1958, CP) *Collected Papers of Charles Sanders Peirce,* 8 vols. Edited by Hartshorne, Charles and Weiss, Paul. Cambridge, MA: Harvard University Press.
Peirce, Charles Sanders. (1966) *Charles S. Peirce: Selected Writings. Values in a Universe of Chance.* Edited by Wiener, Philip. New York: Dover Press.
Peirce, Charles Sanders. (1982) *Writings of Charles S. Peirce: A Chronological Edition.* (MS 614). Bloomington, IN: Indiana University Press.
Perec, George. (1974) *Espèces d'Espaces.* Paris: Editions Galilée.
Perec, George. (1989) *Infra-ordinaire.* Paris: Editions du Seuil.
Perec, George. (1997) *Species of Spaces and Other Pieces.* London: Penguin Books.
Pérez-Gómez, Alberto. (1983) *Architecture and the Crisis of Modern Science.* Cambridge, MA: MIT Press.
Pérez-Gómez, Alberto. (1992) *Polyphilo or the Dark Forest Revisited.* Cambridge, MA: MIT Press.
Pérez-Gómez, Alberto. (2008) *Built upon Love: Architectural Longing after Ethics and Aesthetics.* Cambridge, MA: MIT Press.

Pérez-Gómez, Alberto. (2016) *Attunement: Architectural Meaning After the Crisis of Modern Science*. Cambridge, MA: MIT Press.

Pérez-Gómez, Alberto and Pelletier, L. (1997) *Architectural Representation and the Perspective Hinge*. Cambridge, MA: MIT Press.

Pfefferkorn, Kristin. (1988) *Novalis: A Romantic's Theory of Language and Poetry*. New Haven, CT: Yale University Press.

Piaget, Jean. (1962) *Play, Dreams and Imitation in Childhood*. Trans. Gattegno Caleb and Francis M. Hodgson. New York: W. W. Norton & Company.

Pietropoli, Guido. (1983) L'Invitation au Voyage. *Quaderns d'Arquitectura y Urbanisme* 158: 90–97.

Plato. (1892) *The Dialogues of Plato*. Vol. I. Trans. Jowett, B. Oxford: Oxford University Press.

Plato. (1975) *Phaedo*. Trans. Gallop, D. Oxford: Clarendon Press.

Poe, Edgar Allen. (1843) The Tell-Tale Heart. *Boston Pioneer* 1: 29–31.

Pomian, Krzysztof. (1987) *Collectionneurs, Amateurs et Curieux, Paris, Venise: XVIe–XVIIIe siècle*. Paris: Gallimard.

Price, Simon R. F. (1986) The Future of Dreams: From Freud to Artemidorus. *Past and Present* 113: 3–37.

Quek, Raymond. (2007) Drawing Adam's Navel: The Problem of *Disegno* as Creative Tension Between the Visible and the Knowledgeable. In *From Models to Drawings*. Edited by Frascari, Marco, Hale, Jonathan and Starkey, Bradley. Farnham: Ashgate.

Revonsuo, Antti. (2009) *Inner Presence: Consciousness as a Biological Phenomenon*. Cambridge, MA: MIT Press.

Revonsuo, Antti. (2010) The Reinterpretation of Dreams: An Evolutionary Hypothesis on the Function of Dreaming. *Behavioral and Brain Sciences* 23: 877–901.

Ridgway, Sam. (2015) *Architectural Projects of Marco Frascari: The Pleasure of a Demonstration*. Farnham: Ashgate.

Rivers, Tony, Cruickshank, Dan, Darley Gillian and Pawley, Martin. (1992) *The Name of the Room: A History of the British House and Home*. London: BBC Books.

Roberts, Don. (1973) *The Existential Graphs of Charles Sanders Peirce*. The Hague: Mouton.

Romano, Elisa. (1987) *La Capanna e il Tempio: Vitruvio o dell'Architettura*. Palermo: Palumbo.

Romanyshyn, Robert D. (1989) *Technology as Symptom and Dream*. London: Routledge.

Ruzzante (Beolco, A.) (1565 [1525]) *Dialogo Facetissimo et Ridiculosissimo*. Venezia: Appresso Giovanni Bonadio.

Rykwert, Joseph. (1982) *The Necessity of Artifice: Ideas in Architecture*. New York: Rizzoli.

Rykwert, Joseph. (1984) On the Oral Transmission of Architectural Theory. *AA Files* 6: 14–27.

Rykwert, Joseph. (1998a) *The Dancing Column: On Order in Architecture*. Cambridge, MA: MIT Press.

Rykwert, Joseph. (1998b) *The First Moderns: The Architects of the Eighteenth Century*. Cambridge, MA: MIT Press.

Rykwert, Joseph. (Autumn 1998) Translation and/or Representation. *RES: Anthropology and Aesthetics* 34: 64–70.
Sabbadini, R. Maccheroni, Tradurre. *Rendiconti dell'Istituto Lombardo* II, XLIX: 43–80.
Sabbatucci, Dario. (1989) *Divinazione e Cosmologia*. Milano: Il Saggiatore, Mondadori.
Said, Edward. (1975) *Beginnings: Intention and Method*. New York: Columbia University Press.
Sartoris, Alberto. (1984) *Metafisica della Architettura*. Trans. Geltmaker, Ty and Ghirardo, Diane. New York: Pamphlet Architecture.
Sartoris, Alberto. (1986) *L'Actualité du Rationalisme*. Paris: Bibliothèque des Arts.
Scheer, David Ross. (2014) *The Death of Drawing: Architecture in the Age of Simulation*. London: Routledge.
Scheerbart, Paul and Taut, Bruno. (1972) *Glass Architecture and Alpine Architecture*. Trans. Palmes, James and Palmer, Shirley. Edited by Sharp, Dennis. New York: Praeger.
Sebeok, Thomas. (1975) *The Tell-Tale Sign: A Survey of Semiotics*. Lisse, the Netherlands: Peter de Ridder Press.
Sebeok, Thomas A. (1984) *Carnival!* New York: Mouton.
Seppilli, Anita. (1977) *Sacralità dell'Acqua e Sacrilegio dei Ponti*. Palermo: Sellerio.
Seznec, Jean. (1961) *The Survival of the Pagan Gods: The Mythological Tradition and Its Place in Renaissance Humanism and Art*. Trans. Sessions, Barbara F. Princeton, NJ: Princeton University Press.
Shakespeare, William. (1892) *The Tempest*. Edited by Furness, Horace. London: Lippincott Company.
Shumaker, Wayne. (1972) *The Occult Sciences in the Renaissance: A Study in Intellectual Patterns*. Berkeley, CA: University of California Press.
Sitte, Camillo. (1980) *L'Arte di Costruire le Città: L'Urbanistica Secondo i Suoi Fondamenti Artistici*. Milano: Jaca Book.
Sitte, Camillo. (2013) *The Art of Building Cities: City Building According to Its Artistic Fundamentals*. Trans. Stewart, C. Eastford, CT: Martino Fine Books.
Snell, Bruno. (1953) *The Discovery of the Mind: The Greek Origins of European Thought*. Oxford: Blackwell.
Spiller, Neil. (2013) Architectural Drawing Grasping for the Fifth Dimension. *AD* 5: 14–19.
Stahl, William H. (1990) *Commentary on the Dream of Scipio by Macrobius*. New York: Columbia University Press.
States, Bert O. (1988) *The Rhetoric of Dreams*. Ithaca, NY: Cornell University Press.
Stewart, Alan. (Spring 1995) The Early Modern Closet Discovered. *Representations* 50: 76–100.
Summerson, John and Jencks, Charles. (1987) Tate and Clore: *Vitruvius Ridens* or Laughter at the Clore. *The Architectural Review* 181, 1084: 38–50.
Surette, Leon. (1993) *The Birth of Modernism: Ezra Pound, T.S. Eliot, W.B. Yeats, and the Occult*. Montreal: McGill-Queen's University Press.
Synesius. (MDCXXXIII) *De imsomniis liber, Opera quae extant Omnia*. Lutetia Parisiorum.
Synesius. (2014) *On Prophecy, Dreams and Human Imagination (De Insomniis)*. Trans. Russell, Donald and Others. Tübingen: Mohr Siebeck.

Tafuri, Manfredo. (1966) *L'Architettura del Manierismo nel Cinquecento Europeo*. Roma: Officina Edizioni.

Tafuri, Manfredo. (1990) *The Sphere and the Labyrinth: Avant-Gardes and Architecture from Piranesi to the 1970ies*. Trans. d'Acierno, Pellegrino and Connolly, Robert. Cambridge, MA: MIT Press.

Tatarkiewicz, Wladyslaw. (1976) *Analysis of Happiness*. New York: Springer.

Taut, Bruno. (1919) *Alpine Architektur*. Hagen: Folkwang Verlag Publishing.

Treib, Marc. (2008) *Drawing/Thinking: Confronting an Electronic Age*. London: Routledge.

Troisi, Sergio. (2007) *Fabrizio Clerici: Opere 1937–1992*. Palermo: Sellerio.

Trumbull, H. Clay. (1896) *The Threshold Covenant or the Beginning of Religious Rites*. New York: Charles Scribner's Sons.

Tupitsyn, Margarita. (1999) *El Lissitzky: Beyond the Abstract Cabinet: Photography, Design, Collaboration*. New Haven, CT: Yale University Press.

Vandevelde, Pol. (2005) *The Task of the Interpreter: Text, Meaning and Negotiation*. Pittsburgh, PA: University of Pittsburgh Press.

Verene, Donald P. (1981) *Vico's Science of Imagination*. Ithaca, NY: Cornell University Press.

Vesely, Dalibor. (2004) *Architecture in the Age of Divided Representation: The Question of Creativity in the Shadow of Production*. Cambridge, MA: MIT Press.

Vico, Giambattista. (1744) *Principi di Scienza Nuova, d'Intorno alla Comune Natura delle Nazioni*. Naples.

Vico, Giambattista. (1953) Il Metodo degli Studi del Tempo Nostro: Prolusione Tenuta alla Gioventù Studiosa il 18 Ottobre 1708 in Occasione della Solenne Inaugurazione della Regia Universtà del Regno di Napoli, indi Accresiuta. In *Opere di Gian Battista Vico* 43: 169–243. Trans. Nicolini, F. Milano: Ricciardi.

Vico, Giambattista. (1984) *The New Science of Giambattista Vico*. Trans. Goddard Bergin, Thomas and Fisch, Max H. Ithaca, NY: Cornell University Press.

Vico, Giambattista. (1988) *On the Most Ancient Wisdom of the Italians*. Trans. Palmer, Lucia. M. Ithaca, NY: Cornell University Press.

Vigarello, Georges. (1985) *Le Propre et le Sale: L'Hygiène du Corps depuis le Moyen Age*. Paris: Éditions du Seuil.

Vigarello, Georges. (2008) *Concepts of Cleanliness: Changing Attitudes in France since the Middle Ages*. Cambridge: Cambridge University Press.

Vitruvio, M. P. (1997) *Vitruvio: De Architectura*. Edited by Gross, Pierre. Trans. Corso, Antonio and Romano, Elisa. Torino: Einaudi.

Vitruvius, M. P. (1931) *On Architecture [De Architectura]*. Edited from the Harleian Manuscript 2767. Trans. Granger, Frank. Cambridge, MA: Harvard University Press.

Welton, J. Michael. (2015) *Drawing from Practice: Architects and the Meaning of Freehand*. London: Routledge.

Whittington, Karl. (2013) *Body-Worlds: Opicinus de Canistris and the Medieval Cartographic Imagination*. Turnhout: Pontifical Institute of Medieval Studies.

Wilkie, Jacqueline S. (Summer 1986) Submerged Sensuality: Technology and the Perception of Bathing. *Journal of Social History* 19, 4: 649–664.

Windt, Jennifer. (2015) *Dreaming: A Conceptual Framework for Philosophy of Mind and Empirical Research*. Cambridge, MA: MIT Press.

BIBLIOGRAPHY

Wittgenstein, Ludwig. (1953) *Philosophical Investigations*. Trans. Anscombe, G. E. M. Oxford: Blackwell.

Wollheim, Richard. (1980) Seeing as, Seeing is and Pictorial Representation. In *Art and its Objects*. Edited by Wollheim, R. Cambridge: Cambridge University Press.

Wulf, Christopher and Borsari, Andrea. (2007) *Le Idee dell'Antropologia*. Vol. 2. Milano: Mondadori.

Yates, Frances. (1964) *Giordano Bruno and the Hermetic Tradition*. London: Routledge.

Zajonic, Arthur. (1993) *Catching the Light: The Entwined History of Light and Mind*. New York: Bantam Books.

Zeki, Semir. (1999) *Inner Vision: An Exploration of Art and the Brain*. Oxford: Oxford University Press.

Zeki, Semir (2009) *Splendors and Miseries of the Human Brain: Love, Creativity and the Quest for Human Happiness*. Oxford: Wiley-Blackwell.

Zuccari, Federico. (1961) *L'Idea de Pittori, Scultori et Architetti* (Torino 1607). In *Scritti d'Arte di Federico Zuccari*. Edited by Heikamp, Detlef. Firenze: Olschki.

Zuss, Mark. (2012) *The Practice of Theoretical Curiosity*. New York: Springer.

INDEX

aesthesis: aesthetic contemplation 42; anti-aesthetic 101; *loci aesthetici* 48
aesthetic 101; anti-aesthetic 101; hyper-aesthetic 101
Agamben, G. 11, 21, 23, 92, 93
Alberti, L. B. 23, 27, 36, 43, 49, 68, 76, 93, 95–6, 99; *concinnitas* 27; *costruzione legittima* 33, 50, 54–64, 71, 76–9, 91; *De Re Aedificatoria* 27, 49; legitimate perspective 63, 76; *see also* dream-like status
alchemy 1, 36; alchemic tradition 68; alchemical twins 29, 36; *Aurora Consurgens* 36
Alexandrine Period 68
allegory 37
alterity 74
ambiguity 14, 58, 62, 70, 185
Amish 79, 81; quilt 79
anagogy 16, 24
analogy 24, 26, 27, 45, 49, 56, 64, 72, 95; mimesis 57–64, 68–9, 95; analogical thinking 45, 95; food 2, 6, 24, 26, 36, 80, 99; *see also* gastronomy 27
Andronicus of Cyrra 86
Anthropomorphism: anthropomorphic form 95; *see also* architectural anthropomorphism 1

Antiphon 45
antiquity 31, 45, 68
appearance 19, 60, 79
architect: *as* augur 98; designer 30, 62, 65, 83, 85, 101; design-build professional 57; mad architect 55, 61; magus 54, 56, 61; role of the 54, 59, 64, 87; professional architect 101; wise architect 61; *see also* cunning
architecture: anthropomorphism 1; architectural imagination 1–2, 10–16, 21, 23, 31, 46–8, 54, 71, 77, 94–5; construction and construing 26, 54, 61, 75, 79, 87; contemporary 1, 8, 9, 14, 62, 65, 85–6, 93; discipline 10, 13, 27, 30, 52, 68, 92, 96; dream architecture 42, 45; Greek 67, 71; Medieval 46, 66; profession 57, 60, 62–4, 68, 73–4, 83–4, 101; Renaissance 16; representation 1–2, 6–14, 28, 58, 60, 65, 70, 75, 94, 98–9; therapeutic 45, 74–5, 84, 89; as virtuous art 86; *see also* dream, imagination, practice, representation and theory
Aristotle 11, 19, 24, 36; *De Anima* 71
Artemidorus of Daldis 36, 45; oneiric categories 45

INDEX

Artusi, P. 36
aura 85, 86
author: authoritative documents 62; authority 46, 57–8, 62; sole author 62

Bachelard, G. VI, 10, 22, 24; infraordinary 47–8, 53
bathroom 87–9, 91; *De Luxe* 87, 92; rest room 84; Spartan design 87; Trenton Potteries Company 88; *see also* hygiene and pneuma
beatific life 26–9, 74, 86, 88–91; *see also* Vita Beata
behavior 83
Benjamin, W. 72; *Illuminations* 62
Beolco, A. (Ruzzante) 29, 37; *see also* Vita Beata
Bergson, H. 63
boredom 86
Borges, J. L. 72; *Pierre Menard, autor del Quijote* 66
Brillat-Savarin, J. A. 36
Brunelleschi, F. 21, 77–9, 91; baptistery tablet 76–9; dome of the Florentine cathedral 77; *see also* Manetti and perspective
Bruno, G. 11, 46, 92, 102; *spiritus fantasticus* 54, 88; *De Magia* 93; *La Cena delle Ceneri* 87
building: art of building (well) 68, 74, 86; material 68; miasmic building 90; *see also* artifact, construction, edifice and numinous
building contractor 60
Byzantine icon 77; *see also* icon

CAD (Computer Aided Design) 58–9
Canaletto: *Capricci* 44
Cardano, G. 31, 36, 37
Carême, M.A. 36; *pièces montées* 27
casting: act of 38, 52

back-casting 38
figures 61
forecasting 38, 49, 81, 83
multi-directional 38
catoptromancy 56, 71, 77
chimera 38
civic: space 69, 85; stanza 84–5
client 38, 42–4, 57, 60, 64, 73–4, 82, 93; user 83, 86, 101
Clerici, F.: *Colloquio* 34
Cognition: cognitive assimilation 26; cognitive function 39, 40, 91; cognitive imagination 39–40; cognitive representations 98–9
Cole, T. 53–4, 180–1; *The Architect's Dream* 53
collage 2; body parts 95
Colonial America: Palladian columns 68
Colonna, F. 73; *Hypnerotomachia Poliphili* 46–7
of Conces, W. 26
consciousness 9, 32, 35, 96; imaginative 39; *see also* perception
construction 29, 63; building 67, 77, 79, 86; management 63; numinous 75–6; *see also* construction drawing, facture and structure
contractor 57, 60
conversion 28, 63, 69; transformation 26, 32, 41, 53, 65, 68–9, 88
cooking: as a metaphor 27; *see also* craft and gastronomy 27
copy 35, 42
Corbin, H.: *intermondo* 3, 39; *mundus imaginalis* 3, 8, 39, 43, 49, 53, 77, 90–1; *see also* imaginal
Corbusier, Le 46, 50
Cornaro, A. 11, 21, 36, 37; *see also* Vita Beata

205

INDEX

cosmopoiesis 1, 10–11
cosmos: κόσμος 88; *mundus* 87–8, 100
craft 64, 93; craftsperson 79, 92; gourmet craft 26
creativity 74, 89
Croce, B. 66–7
cunning 31; architect 77–9; intelligence 52, 66

dance 56
daylight 55, 88
deduction 20, 86
demonstration XIX, 28, 32; architectural 74, 84; drafting 23; dream 50, 95; *see also* monstrous demonstration
descriptio 60
design 74–6, 79, 83; *see also* therapeutic design
details XIX, 1, 16, 19, 25, 89, 91, 96; architectural detailing 48, 57, 71
divination 3, 21, 37, 50, 56, 75, 77; architectural 97; as imaginative form of reading and writing 98; by memory 40, 45; graphic 60–1, 65, 97; philosophical 45; urban 85; *see also* catoptromancy, graphic divination and mirror
drafting 13, 23, 52, 97; drafting machine 54, 58; drafting table 6, 16, 74
draftsman 58–59; eye of the 33–4
drawing: action 52; construction drawing 3, 5–6, 24, 67–71; design drawing XXI, 2–3, 21, 24, 40, 50, 58, 60–2, 65; inverted perspective 49, 54; legal documents 57, 59, 62–3; orthographia 15; plan 40, 44, 46, 48; predictive 29; presentation drawing 57, 60, 91; production drawing 62; reading of 10–20, 23, 58, 98, 160; recto/verso XXI, 2–3, 6, 14, 97–9; rendering 39, 41, 60; section 25, 39–40, 46, 57, 87, 91, 99; sketch 73, 91; survey drawing 40, 44, 49, 70, 99; *see also* facture, graphic divination, graphic prognostication, interpretation, mantic projection, representation, tools and Zuccari, F.
Dream House: *Dream House for the Next Millennium* 73; house-tower 3, 6, 21, 41, 73, 76, 79–81, 86, 87, 90, 91, 95, 97–100
dream 8–14, 28–30, 83–4, 101; allegoric 31; architectural 31, 38–47, 74, 92, 95, 101; Brunelleschi's joke 78; causal inverse time 32, 97; daydream 1, 26, 76, 84; double dream 3, 47, 73; dream-like status (Latin *sopor*) 96; dreamless condition 58; Gunzo's dream 48; hypnagogic dream 29; hypnopompic dream 32; illusion 41; images 25, 47; light of the dream 54; mirror dream 78; non verbal structures 28; non virtual-reality 41; as prosperous vision 101; psychological 29–30, 50; realm of 34, 61; reverie 26, 29, 54, 84; slumber 29; solidified 32; theorematic 31; as therapeutic tool 45, 74–5, 84; *see also* casting, dreamscape, dreamtime, imaginal, mantic, tectonic activity; translation of dreams
Durand 46
Dürer, A. 33–4, 64
dwelling 60, 65, 74; art of 42; spaces 25, 85, 88, 89–90

edifice: therapeutic edifice 75, 84, 89

education: architectural 10, 15, 19, 30, 48, 64, 75
eidetic process 60, 98
eidola 31; *eidolon* 71, 97
emblem 75, 91
embodiment 48, 56
empirical 24, 33, 36; non-empirical 28
emulation 68
Enlightenment period 62
Existenz 59–61; *Existenzminimum* 59, 87, 93
experiential knowledge 26

fable 38, 102
fabric 79, 96, 101
facture 10–11, 13–16; *see also* construction drawing and cosmopoiesis
fantasy 40, 47, 96; *see also* imagining
feng shui 3, 21, 86, 92; *ch'I* (life giving energy) 86
fictitious 65; imaginary 57
Filarete (Antonio Averulino) 11, 29, 46, 93; *Treatise on Architecture* 32, 77
Florensky, P.: inverse perspective *(Obratnaya Perspektiva)* 32–3
Folengo, T. (Merlinus Cocaius) 27, 36, 87; *Baldus* VI, 36
Freud, S. 29–30, 46

Galen of Pergamum 26, 36
Gastronomy: French 27
gaze 8, 14, 33, 77; *see also* Wollheim, R. (seeing in)
Gentile, G. 66–7
geomater 91, 94; *see also* geometry and Joyce, J.
geometry 19, 23, 33, 47, 49, 91; body 56; metaphysical 77, 79; *see also* geomater and mantic
Ghiberti, L. 78

graphic representation 40–1, 46, 60, 84, 87, 98; divination 97; forecasting 49, 81; mark 71; prognostication 49, 98; recording 59; standards manual 87; *see also* Joyce, J. and Peirce, C. S. (Existential Graphs)
Greenaway, P.: *The Draughtsman's Contract* 59

happiness 9, 86–7; virtuous happiness 29, 91; *see also* Vita Beata
Heraclitus: *idios kosmos* 6, 62; *koinos kosmos* 6
Hermes 67
Hero of Alexandria: *spiriti flati* 86; *see also* pneumatic machine
hesitation 96
hierophany 74, 81, 88
Hippocrates of Kos 36
Holy House of Loreto 69; *see also* Loreto Houses
Human: body 92; condition 6, 59, 90, 96, 102; cosmogony 88; dwelling 65, 88; existence 29, 87, 91; habitation 44; mind 30, 38; representation 56, 71, 96; scale figures 56, 71; thinking 28, 48; vision 34; *see also* beatific existence and *Vita Beata*
hygiene 87, 92; clean 92–3; *mondo/immondo* 88; sanitize air 90
Hypnos 96

icon 15, 25, 28, 39, 49, 53, 95–8; as magic 35, 52; Byzantine 77; iconology 10; use of gold *(lumeggiature)* 32; verbal and visual 25; *see also* light of the dream 32
iconostasis 32, 37; Orthodox churches 32; pneumatic 90; window of the architect 56

207

INDEX

Illich, I. 2, 69, 72
image: architectural image 28, 62, 75; *bild* 52–4; civilization of the 28; conjuring images 57; construction 34, 45, 48–9, 52, 58, 96, 98–9, 101; conversion of the 63; mental 26, 35; oneiric 28, 32; topical 53, 94; visual 28, 33; *see also* mirror images and phenomenology of images
imaginal 42, 54; dream 40; imaginative universal 57; realm 32–5, 40, 56–7, 71–9; wall enclosing the 32
imaginary 39, 57, 63; space 32; reality 98
imagination 26, 30–1, 35, 40, 44, 47, 57–9, 74–5, 91, 96; architectural 10–20, 46, 48, 71, 77–8, 94; discipline of 30, 52–4; *Imaginatio* 30; theory of 1–9; transcendental 96; visual 39; *see also* cognition (cognitive imagination), imaginal, imaging, Corbin, H. *(mundus imaginalis)*, phantasy and sign 39
imaging 22, 35, 58
imitation 40. 62–5, 69
induction 86, 20
Industrial Revolution 88
innovation 68
instrument 28, 47, 55, 58, 63, 76, 81, 86, 99; *see also* tools
intangible 38, 40, 46, 58, 94
interpretation 16, 19, 23, 45, 98; etymological 27; of dreams 46, 60; interpretive scheme 62, 70; *see also* phenomenology and *sollertia*
intuition 29; intellectual 40, 91; pseudo-artistic 57
invention: architectural 65, 92
irrational 28, 98; *see also* non-rational;
Isidore of Seville 26, 36

Jacob: Biblical dream 48–9
Jones, I. 11, 27, 56
Jonson, Ben 56; *Neptune's Triumph for the Return of Albion* 27
Joyce, J.: Geomater 91, 94; graphplot 94

Kahn, L. I. 87; wonder 65
knowledge 47, 63, 65, 68, 74, 95; analogical 39–40; encyclopedic 68; experiential 26; imaginative 39; tacit 23; *see also* cognitive assimilation and cognitive awareness

labyrinth 47, 75, 95; Theseus 75
leisure 84
light: daylight 55, 88–9, 97; inner 26; internal and external 33; *lume naturale* 35, 54, 99; rays 59
likeness 33, 40, 58, 60, 97–8; *see also* Wollheim, R. (seeing as)
line 16, 19, 23, 26, 28, 34, 70, 91, 99
Loreto houses 58

macaronic 26–8; architecture XIX; art (*ars macaronica*) 27, 36, 87; language 36, 43, 47; thinking 86, 90, 96; sapience 96; *see also* Teofilo, F.
machine: drawing machine 34, 58–9; perspective machine 33, 64; pneumatic machine 85–6, 88–9; *see also* drafting machine
Macrobius, A. T. 45, 50
macrocosm 42, 89; *see also* microcosm
magic 1, 8, 26, 35, 38–40, 49, 52–64, 71, 72, 74, 81, 93; conversion 63; grimoire 10, 22, 72; conjuring 57; mimesis 57, 62–4, 68–9; translation 64; primitive magic 39; *see also* icons as magic representation and sign

208

INDEX

maieutic 61
making 2, 10, 14, 16, 19, 58, 62–3, 77, 79, 84, 187; *see also* facture
Manetti, T. 77; *The Life of Filippo Brunelleschi* 76; *The Fat Woodworker* 78
mantic 57, 76; architectural procedures 95; dream 53; images 99; geometry 94; projection 98
map: cosmopoietic 10–14; *mappa mundi* 95
mask 34
material 40; construction 54; imagination 10, 22; lines 16; materiality 14, 19, 23; non-semiotic materials 98; symbolic materials 98
McCay, W. 25; *Little Nemo in Slumberland* 6, 35, 47, 50
memory 14, 45, 86, 90; collective memory 75; ontogenetic memory 40; phylogenetic memory 40
mente locale 47
metamorphosis 69
metaphor 16, 19, 27, 40, 47, 62, 69, 77, 94; corporeal metaphor 56; *metaphoro* 68; *see also* gastronomy
mezzanine 84–5
microcosm 42, 89, 92; *see also* macrocosm
Middle Ages 16, 69, 92
mimesis 57–8, 64, 95; codified 60; *see also* analogy (mimesis) and magic (mimesis)
mirror 3, 15, 19, 21, 34, 56, 71, 76, 79, 81; ceiling *(stucco lucido)* 91; dreams 78; images 40, 49, 77–8
model 71, 77–8, 97
Modern Movement 59, 65
Mollino, C. 56; *Architect's House* 3, 54, 71; *Life of Oberon* 55, 71; photographic reflection 56

monster 93, 95–6; of architecture XVIII–XIX, 75–6; as imaginative concept 96; monstrous demonstration 96; monstrous evidence 28; monstrous semiosis 28; *see also* macaronic speculation
mundane 85, 88, 101
mythopoetic 95

Neoplatonic School of Chartres 26
Neurology 1, 12
Nietzsche, F. 95
non-rational 65, 76, 84–6, 101; approach to design 98
Novalis (Georg Friedrich Philipp von Hardenberg) 25–6, 97; *Allgemeine Brouillon* 26; *Heinrich von Ofterdingen* 97; *Scientific-Natural Studies of Freiberg* 26
numinous 81, 84, 93; building 74–5, 80, 102; door 188; places 84–5, 88–91; *see also* stanza

oneiric realm 61

Palladio, A. 43–4, 46, 50, 58, 67–9, 84, 92; Basilica di Vicenza 44; Chiericati Palace 44; *Four Books on Architecture* 43; Palazzo della Ragione 69; Palladian Architecture 43; Palladian Villa 85, 89; San Pietro di Castello 67
Paradeigma 68
Pascal, B.: *Pensées* 79
Peirce, C. S.: abduction 16, 23, 86; Existential Graphs 35; musement 30, 41–2, 87
perception 6, 30, 39, 59, 75, 81, 96; imaginative 49; phenomenology of 62; sensory 9, 28, 40, 70, 95
Perec, G.: infraordinary 47–8, 53

perspective 59; *costruzione legittima* 33, 50, 54–6, 63–4, 71, 76–9, 91; inverted 49, 54, 71; mistakes 33; portable machine *(lucinda)* 33–4; *see also* drawing machine
phantasy 30
phenomenology: of images 35; of perception 62; of representation 60; phenomenological reading 28; primary phenomena 40; visible and invisible 89
Plato 11, 61; *Phaedrus* 71
play 1, 41, 74, 92; musement 102
pneuma 93; *phantastikon pneuma* 31, 88; pneumatic building 75; pneumatic iconostasis 90–1; pneumatic light 26; pneumatic machine 85–9; pneumatology 80; *spiritus phantasticus* 31, 80
polarity 65, 72; dualistic choices 83
practice XIX, 1, 29, 36–7, 56, 62, 64, 97; critical practice 57–8; *see also* theory
psychology 92
Pythagoras 45; *see also* sleep

rational 28, 30–1, 40, 52, 65, 83–5, 101; *see also* irrational, leisure and non-rational
reading 49, 58, 60–1; of drawings 10–20; misreading 9; pragmatic 98; *see also* interpretation
real 35, 38–40, 52, 59, 65, 81, 91; illusions 41; physical reality 101; visible sphere of the 32
reality 46–8, 53
reason 28; human reasoning 34
Renaissance: Italian 33; *see also* Alberti, L. B. and Palladio, A.
replica 69; Disney's Epcot Center in Florida 66; Parthenon in Nashville 66

representation 38, 44, 98–9; analog 85; architectural XVIII, 1–9, 65, 70, 94; descriptive 60; digital 85; graphic 40, 60, 98; mechanical 58; prescriptive 60; subjunctive mode of 97; *see also* cognition (cognitive representation)
resemblance 57; legal 57, 59, 62
Roman architecture 68
Rossi, A.: Monumento alla Resistenza 67; Monumento a Sandro Pertini 67
Rudi, A. XVIII, 87, 92
Rykwert, J. 2, 93; oral tradition in architecture 70

sacred 74, 88; odor of memory 90; signs 76; spaces 83–5
scale 88, 183; figures 71
Scamozzi, V.: Villa Duodo 66
Scarpa, C. XVIII, 21, 53, 73–4, 76, 88–93, 98; Fondazione Angelo Masieri 88; Villa Ottolenghi 89, 93
School of Salerno 26
science 12, 37, 67, 86, 100; Early Modern 15; scientific thinking 28
sémiophores 61
semiotic 12, 21, 34, 37, 39, 60; semantic relationship 95; semiosis 28, 60, 98; *see also* sign
Seneca 68; transmute 66–9; *see also* transmutation
senses 9, 24, 39, 61, 65, 91; sense perception 40, 91; sensory phenomenon 101; visual perception 70; *see also* sight, smell, synesthesia and taste
sight 33–4; *see also* gaze, likeness and Wollheim, R. (seeing as)
sign 38, 49, 63, 76; conventional sign 39; invisible signifiers 61; magic sign 38–9; natural sign 39; pragmatic reading of 98; semiotic

210

INDEX

fallacy 60, 98; signifier and signified 61, 76, 98; visible sign 61; *see also* Semiotic
Sitte, C.: *The Art of Constructing Cities* 85
sleep 31, 45, 47, 78; controlled sleep 45; *sopor* 29, 96
smell 83–8, 92, 95; aroma for physical and mental sanity 90; odor and odorless 90; scented spirit 89
Soane, J. 11, 21, 46, 50
sollertia 77
space 32, 40–1, 49, 54–5, 58, 83, 91, 97, 98; *see also* time (spatial synchronicity and diachronicity)
spirit: *spiritus* 85–8, 92; *see also* Bruno, G. (*spiritus fantasticus*)
spoil 69; architecture 79
stanza 84–5, 89, 91–3, 101–2; *see also* urban stanzas
storytelling XIX, 8, 10, 14, 41
style 13, 54, 62
sublime 96
subliminal 96
substitution 71
symbol 78, 88, 98; symbolic form 88
Synesius of Cyrene 30, 36–7; *De imsomniis* 31; *phantastikon pneuma* 31, 88; *see also* pneuma
synesthesia 1

tactic 10, 20, 76, 80–1, 95
tangible 38, 40, 58, 89, 94, 99; *see also* intangible
tarot deck 75; House of God 49, 75; The Tower 75
taste 27, 95, 96
Taut, B. 46, 50, 102
Techne 67–8
tectonic activity 38, 42
Teofilo, F. 36, 87; *see also* macaronic

thaumaturgic 57, 74, 101; building 75
theory XIX, 1, 10–6; chiasm of theory and practice 97; constructive theories 52; of imagination 8–9; principle-based theories 52
threshold 3, 8, 32, 53–4, 77, 80, 96
time: diachronicity 40; dreamtime 32; fear of death and 38; spatial synchronicity and diachronicity 40; suspension of 96; temporal effect 97; *see also* dream and space
tool: analogical 81; angelic compass 3, 81; divider 77; drawing as 98; drawing as magic tool 39; dream as tool 47, 95
Tower of Babel 75, 102
Tower of the Winds 86; *see also* weathervane 81, 86, 91, 99
trace 14, 23
trade 53, 62, 67–9
transcendent 74, 88, 96
transfiguration 41, 49, 56
transformation 26, 32, 41, 53, 65, 68–9, 88; conversion 28, 63, 69
translation 28, 32, 38, 41, 56, 60–71, 76; backtelling 62; of dreams; foretelling 62, 84; mirroring metaphors of 62; repetitive 63; *see also* magic conversion
transmogrify 43
transmutation 28, 56, 68, 71, 76; *mutare* 68
trope 101

urban 79; designer 83; divination 97; environment 47, 83; space 83–6; stanzas 84; *see also* numinous urban space
utilitarian function 61, 79

211

value 61; moral 16; noetic 40, 91; subjective 56, 84; symbolic 79; verisimilitude 57, 59, 65, 98; constructible verisimilitudes 98
Vico, G. 11–13, 23, 75, 100; *New Science* 23, 90, 92
Victorian England 85
virtue 26, 29, 60, 73, 77, 91; *see also* architecture as virtuous art
vision: external and internal vision 63; late night vision 53
Vita Beata 9, 29, 37, 74, 84, 87, 91, 94; *eudaimonia* 29, 37; *see also* beatific life, Cornaro, A., happiness and virtue
Vitruvius 11, 46, 48, 68, 86, 92; Basilica in Fano 43; Corinthian capital 67

weathervane 81, 86, 99; compass weathervane 91
White House in Washington DC 85
Windows: DOS 81
Wittgenstein, L. 56; rabbit-duck illusion 70
Wittkower, R. 76
Wollheim, R.: seeing as 57, 60, 71, 98; seeing in 60, 71, 98–9

Janus: temple of 80
Jung, C. 29–30, 81; *Memories. Dreams. Reflections* 74; tower in Bollingen 74, 181

Zhuang, Zhou: *Nan Hua Zhen Jing* 53
Zuccari, F.: *disegno interno* and *disegno esterno* 99; *L'Idea de Pittori, Scultori et Architetti* 99